Contents

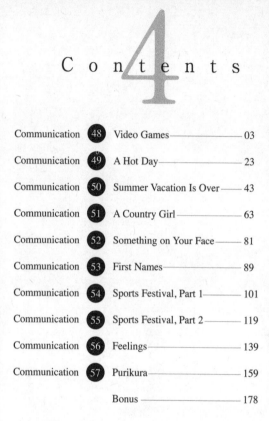

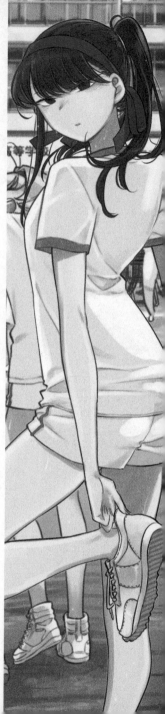

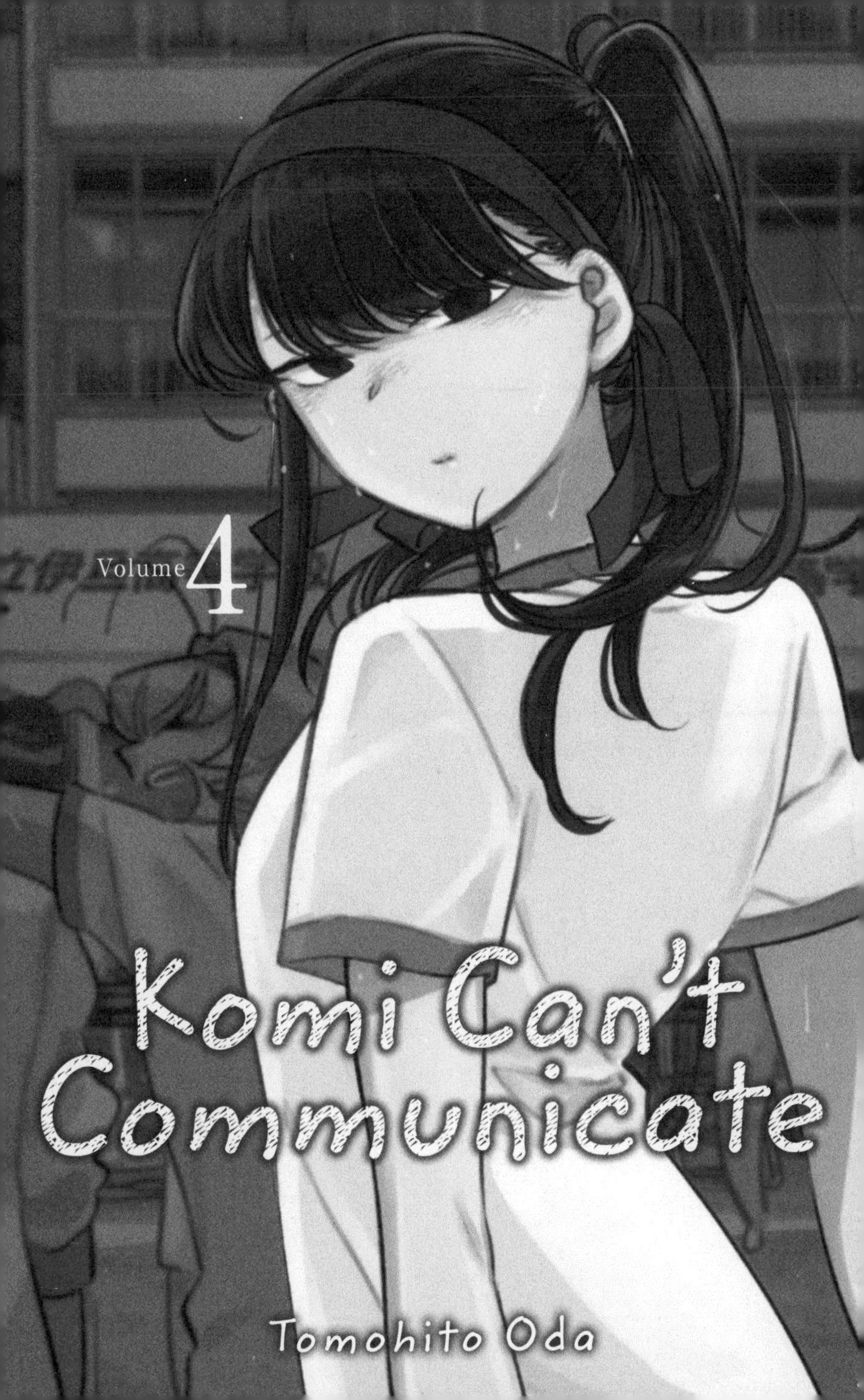
Volume 4
Komi Can't Communicate
Tomohito Oda

Komi Can't Communicate

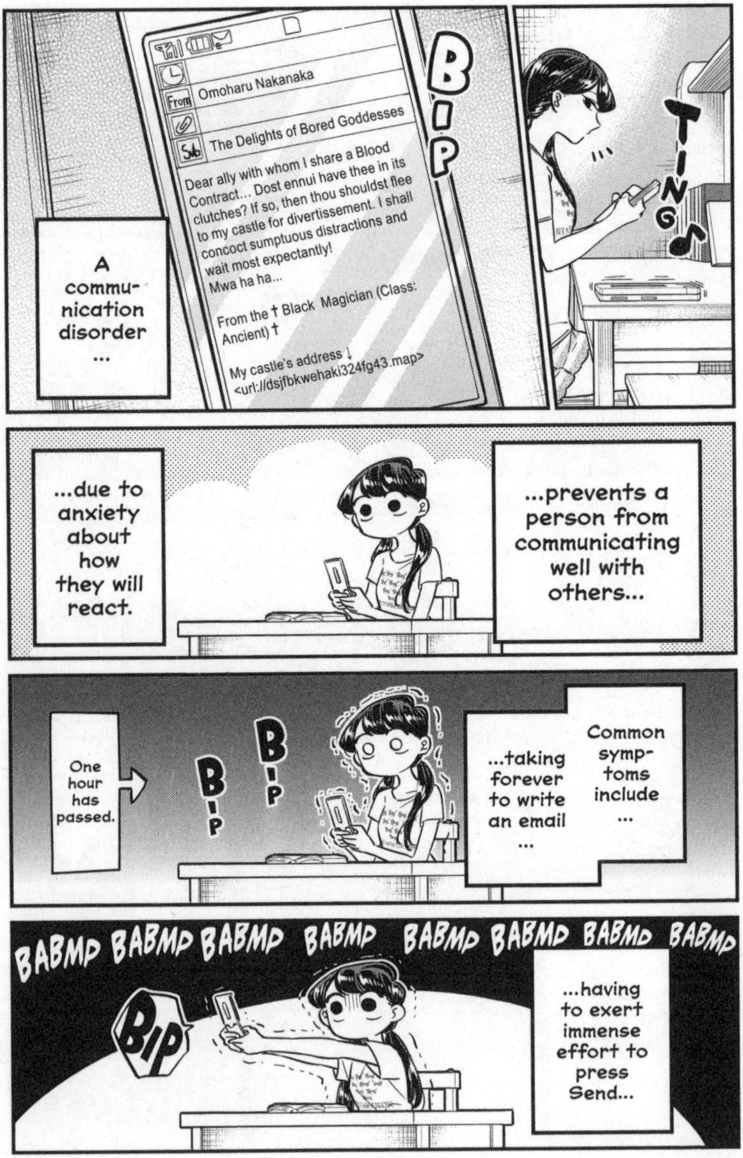
TING♪
BIP
Omoharu Nakanaka
The Delights of Bored Goddesses
Dear ally with whom I share a Blood Contract... Dost ennui have thee in its clutches? If so, then thou shouldst flee to my castle for divertissement. I shall concoct sumptuous distractions and wait most expectantly!
Mwa ha ha...
From the † Black Magician (Class: Ancient) †
My castle's address ↓
<url://dsjfbkwehaki324fg43.map>
A communication disorder ...
...prevents a person from communicating well with others...
...due to anxiety about how they will react.
Common symptoms include ...
...taking forever to write an email ...
BIP
BIP
One hour has passed.
BABMP BABMP BABMP BABMP BABMP BABMP BABMP BABMP
...having to exert immense effort to press Send...
BIP

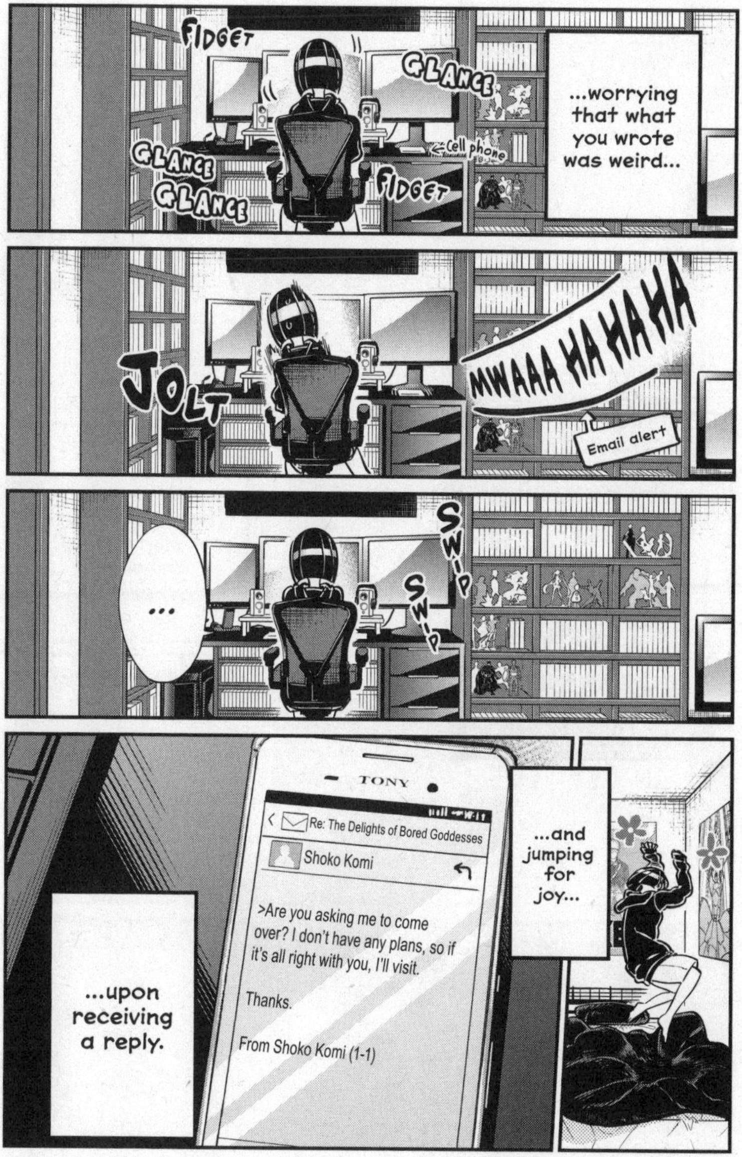
...worrying that what you wrote was weird...
GLANCE
FIDGET
Cell phone
FIDGET
GLANCE
GLANCE
MWAAA HA HA HA
Email alert
JOLT
SWIP
SWIP
...
...and jumping for joy...
TONY
Re: The Delights of Bored Goddesses
Shoko Komi
>Are you asking me to come over? I don't have any plans, so if it's all right with you, I'll visit.
Thanks.
From Shoko Komi (1-1)
...upon receiving a reply.

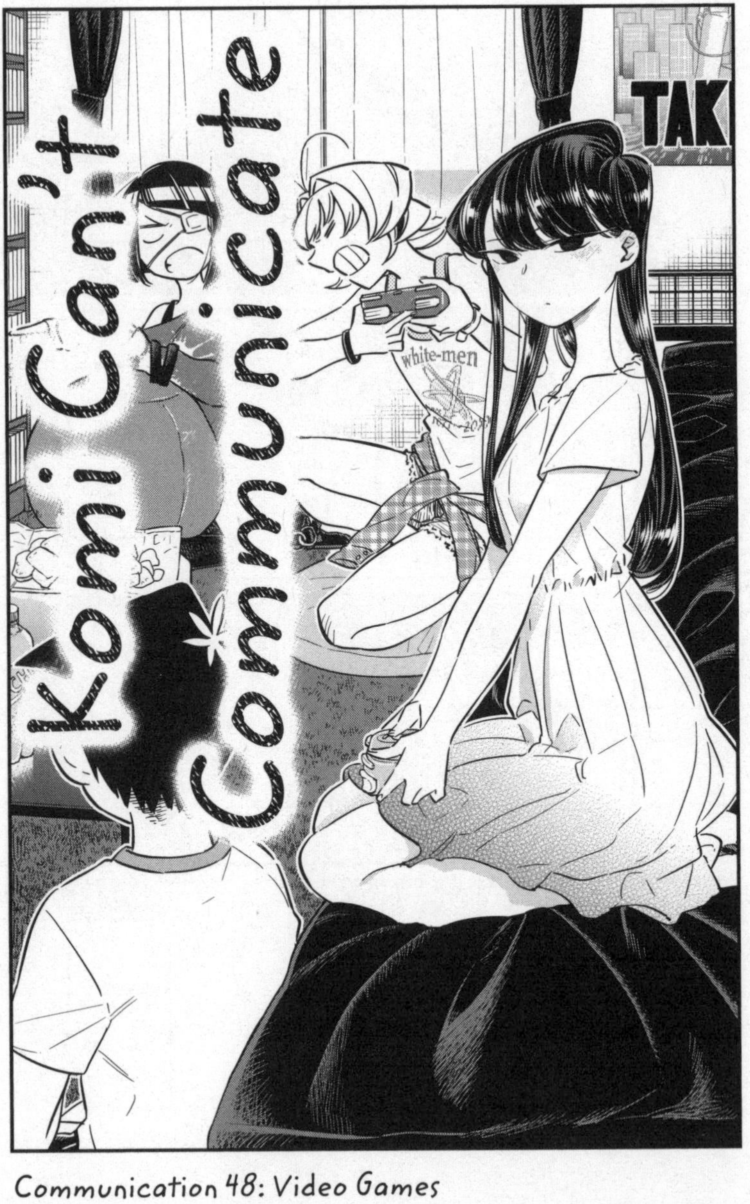
TAK
Komi Can't Communicate
white-men

Communication 48: Video Games

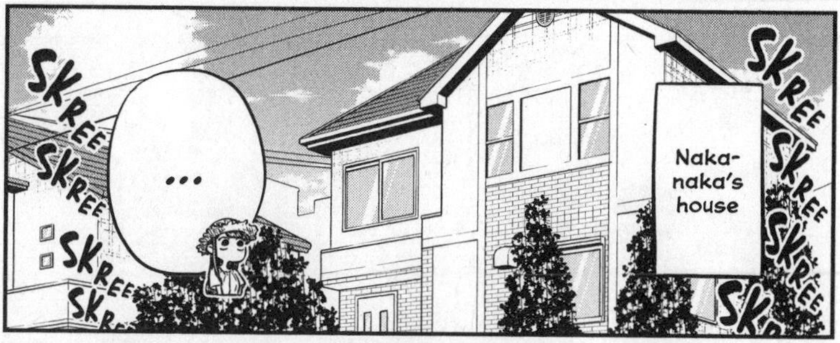
SKREE SKREE SKREE SK
Naka-naka's house
...
SKREE SKREE SKREE SK
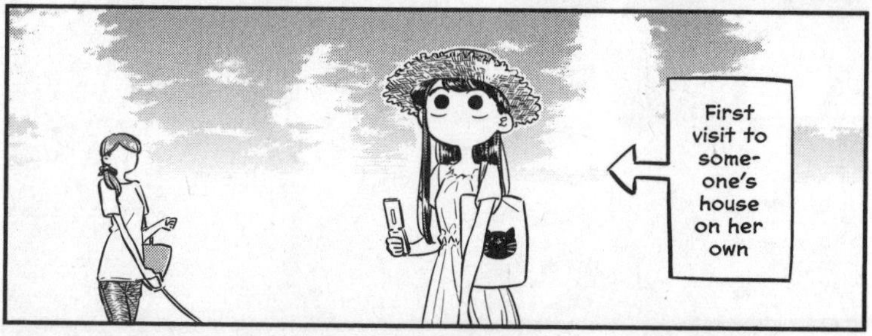
First visit to some-one's house on her own
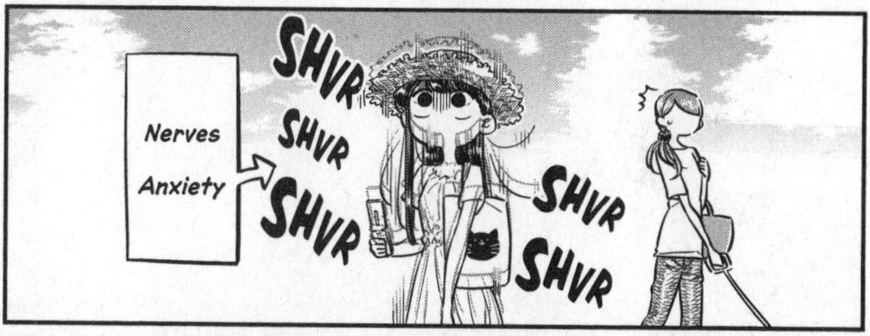
SHVR SHVR
SHVR SHVR SHVR
Nerves Anxiety
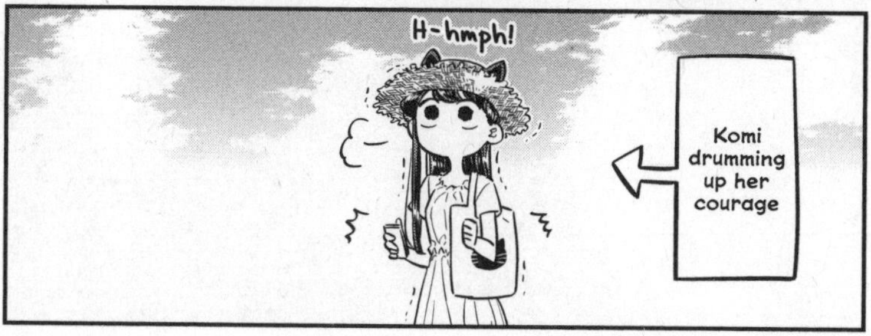
Komi drumming up her courage
H-hmph!

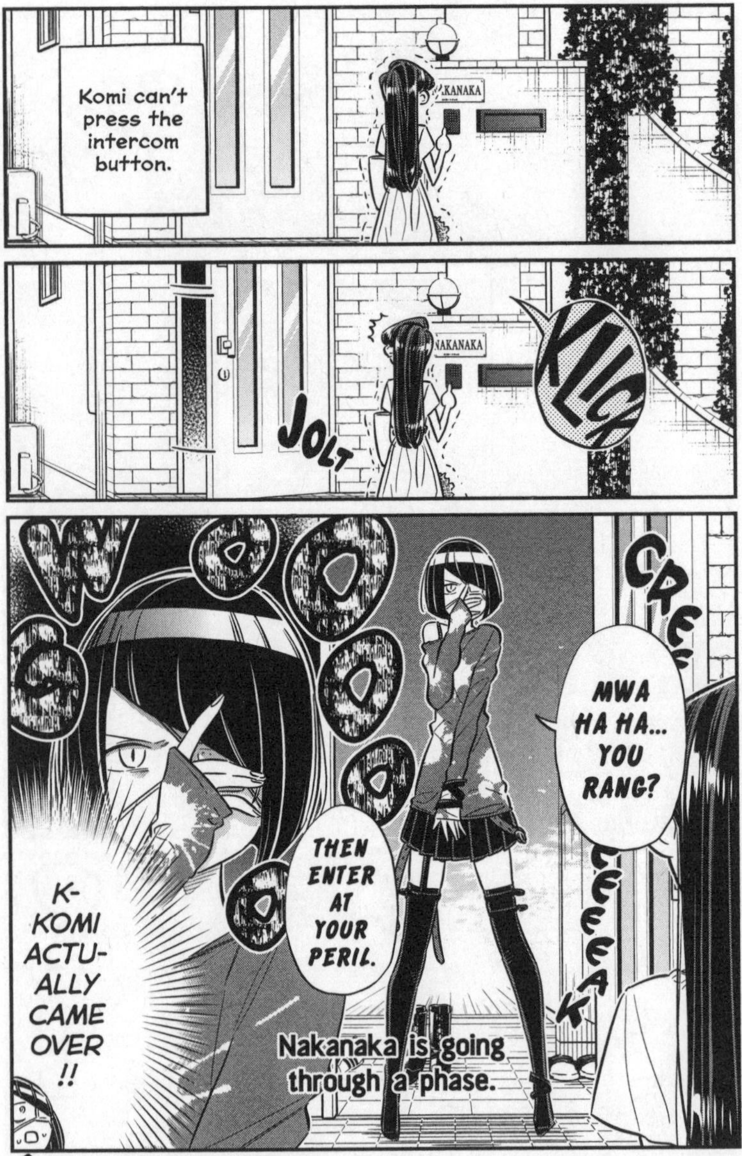
Komi can't press the intercom button.
NAKANAKA
KLICK
NAKANAKA
JOLT
CREE
EEEEAK
MWA HA HA... YOU RANG?
THEN ENTER AT YOUR PERIL.
Nakanaka is going through a phase.
K-KOMI ACTUALLY CAME OVER!!

↰ Waited at the door forever

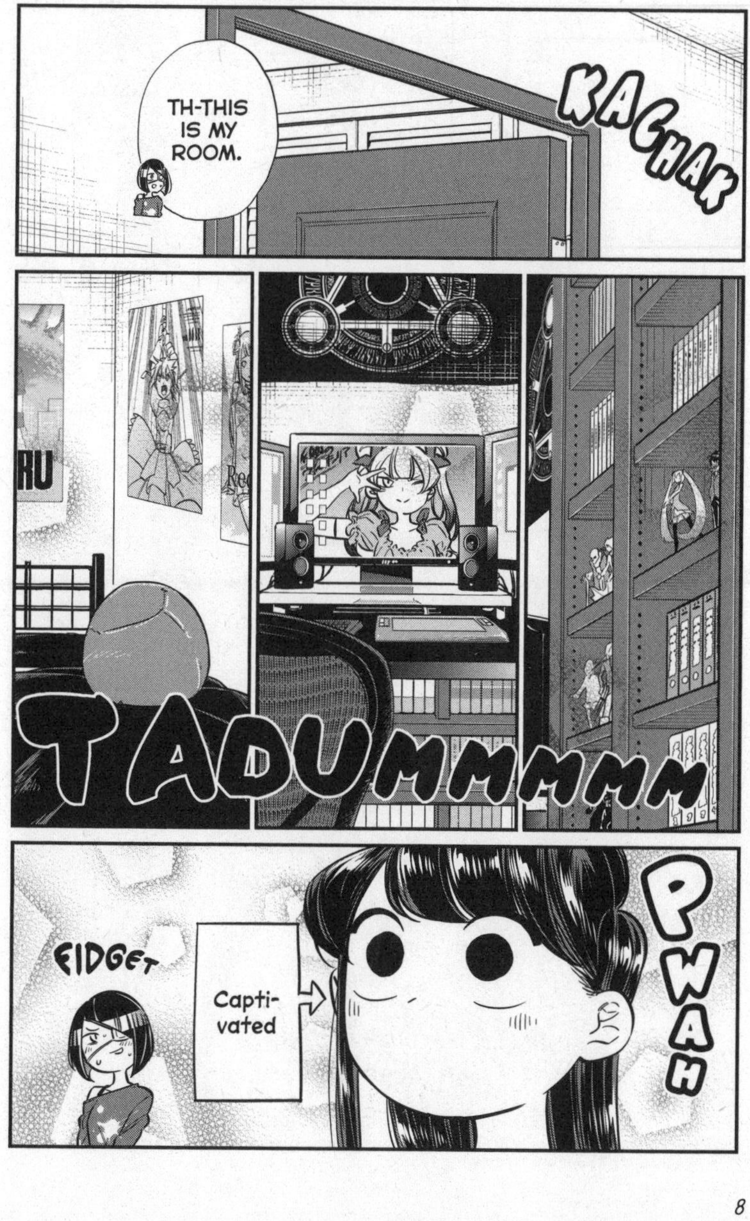
KACHAK
TH-THIS IS MY ROOM.
TADUMMMMMM
PWAH
Capti-vated
FIDGET

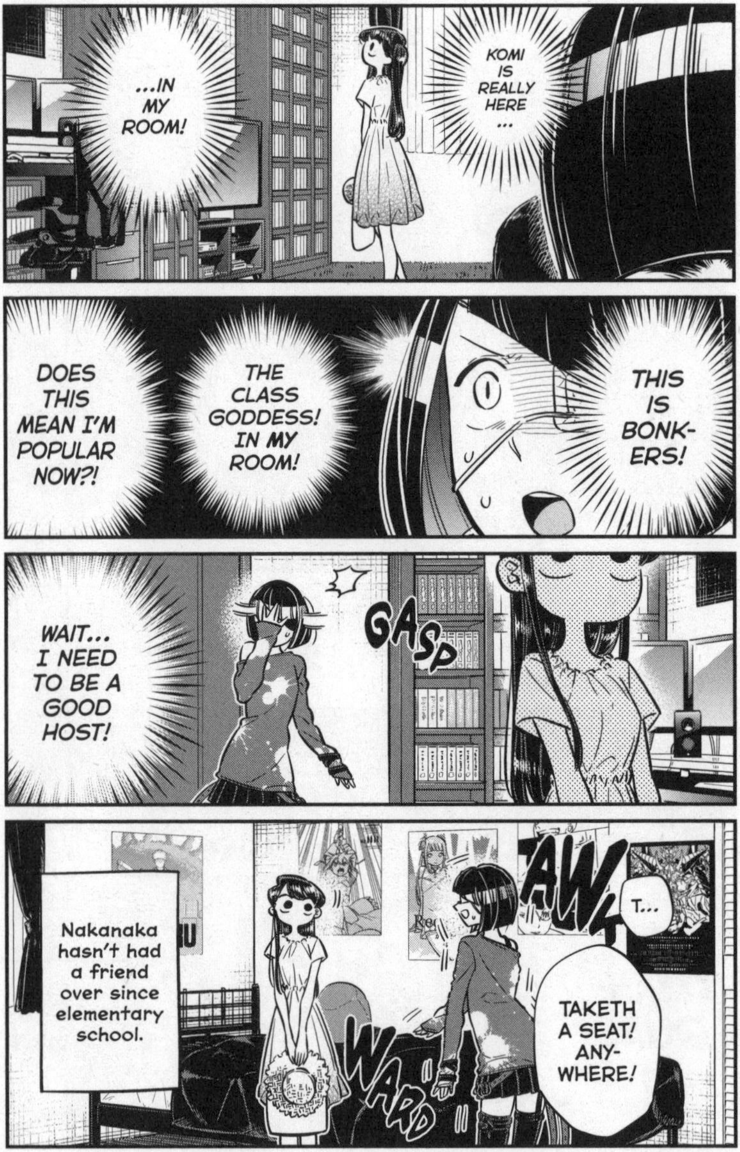
KOMI IS REALLY HERE...
...IN MY ROOM!
THIS IS BONKERS!
THE CLASS GODDESS! IN MY ROOM!
DOES THIS MEAN I'M POPULAR NOW?!
GASP
WAIT... I NEED TO BE A GOOD HOST!
AWK
T...
TAKETH A SEAT! ANY-WHERE!
WARD
Nakanaka hasn't had a friend over since elementary school.

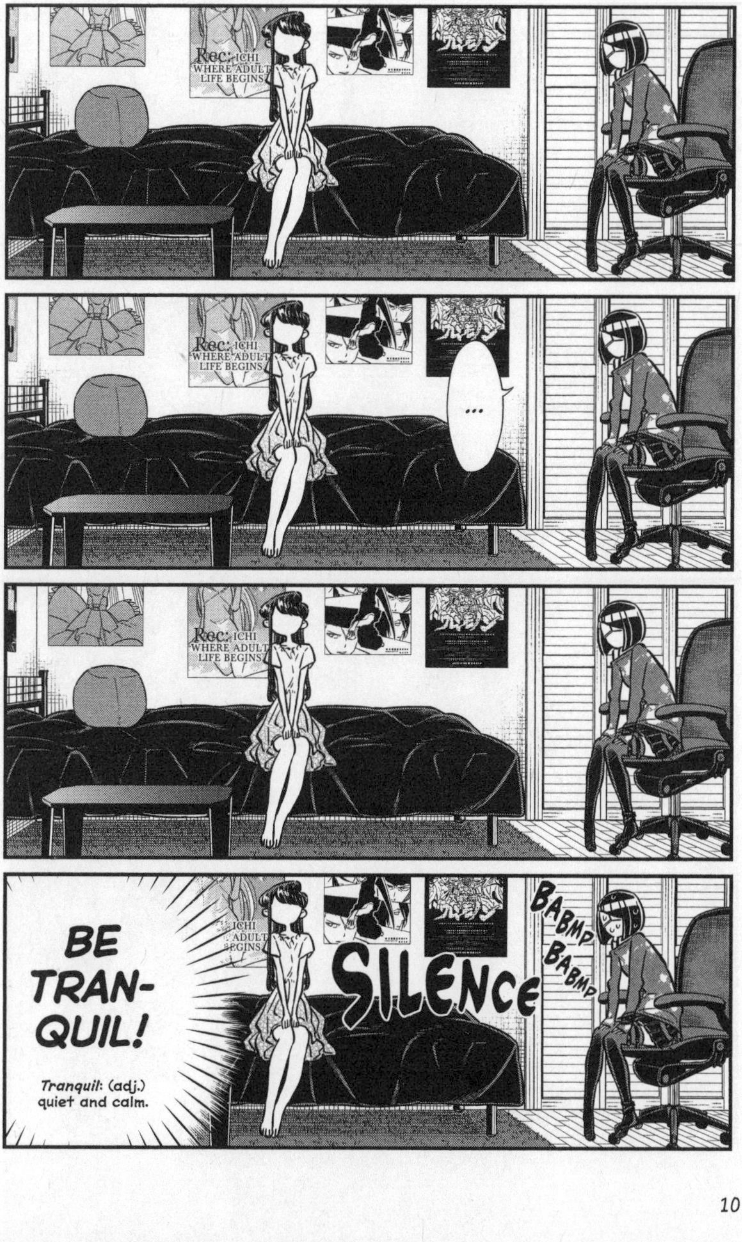
Rec: ICHI WHERE ADULT LIFE BEGINS
Rec: ICHI WHERE ADULT LIFE BEGINS
...
Rec: ICHI WHERE ADULT LIFE BEGINS
BABMP BABMP
SILENCE
ICHI ADULT BEGINS
BE TRAN-QUIL!
Tranquil: (adj.) quiet and calm.

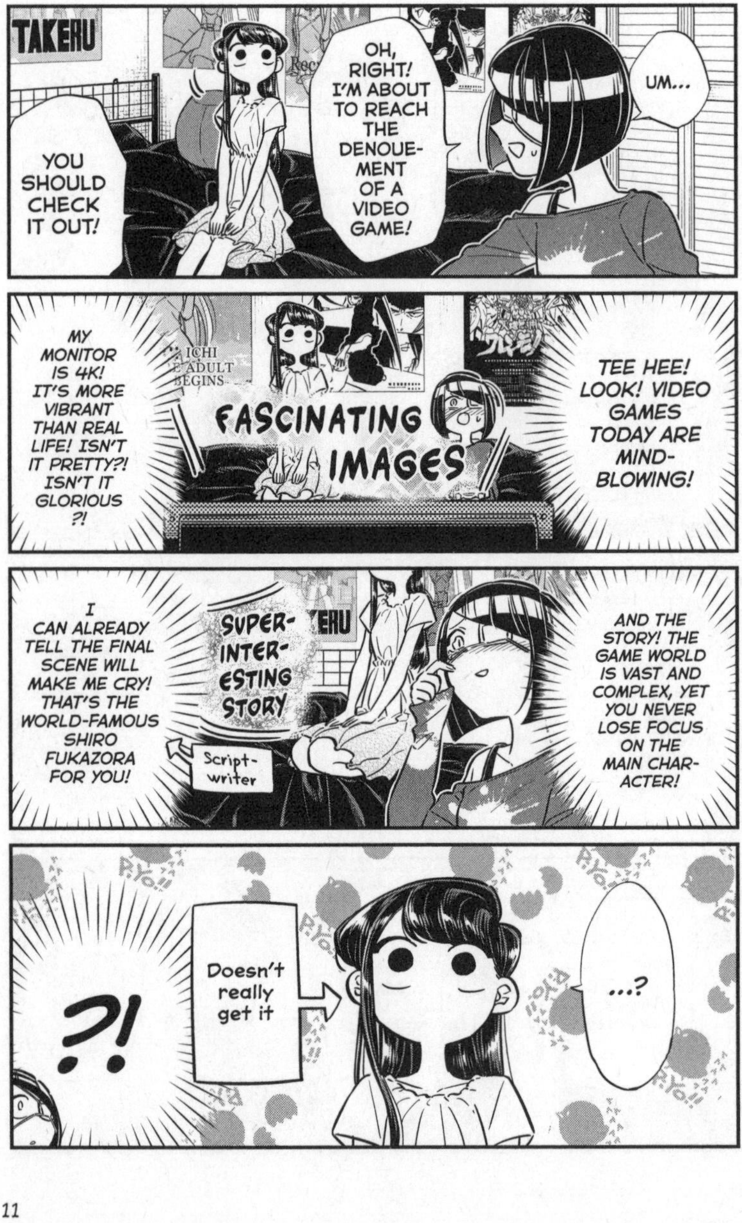
TAKERU
UM...
OH, RIGHT! I'M ABOUT TO REACH THE DENOUEMENT OF A VIDEO GAME!
YOU SHOULD CHECK IT OUT!
TEE HEE! LOOK! VIDEO GAMES TODAY ARE MIND-BLOWING!
FASCINATING IMAGES
MY MONITOR IS 4K! IT'S MORE VIBRANT THAN REAL LIFE! ISN'T IT PRETTY?! ISN'T IT GLORIOUS?!
AND THE STORY! THE GAME WORLD IS VAST AND COMPLEX, YET YOU NEVER LOSE FOCUS ON THE MAIN CHARACTER!
SUPER-INTERESTING STORY
Script-writer
I CAN ALREADY TELL THE FINAL SCENE WILL MAKE ME CRY! THAT'S THE WORLD-FAMOUS SHIRO FUKAZORA FOR YOU!
...?
Doesn't really get it
?!

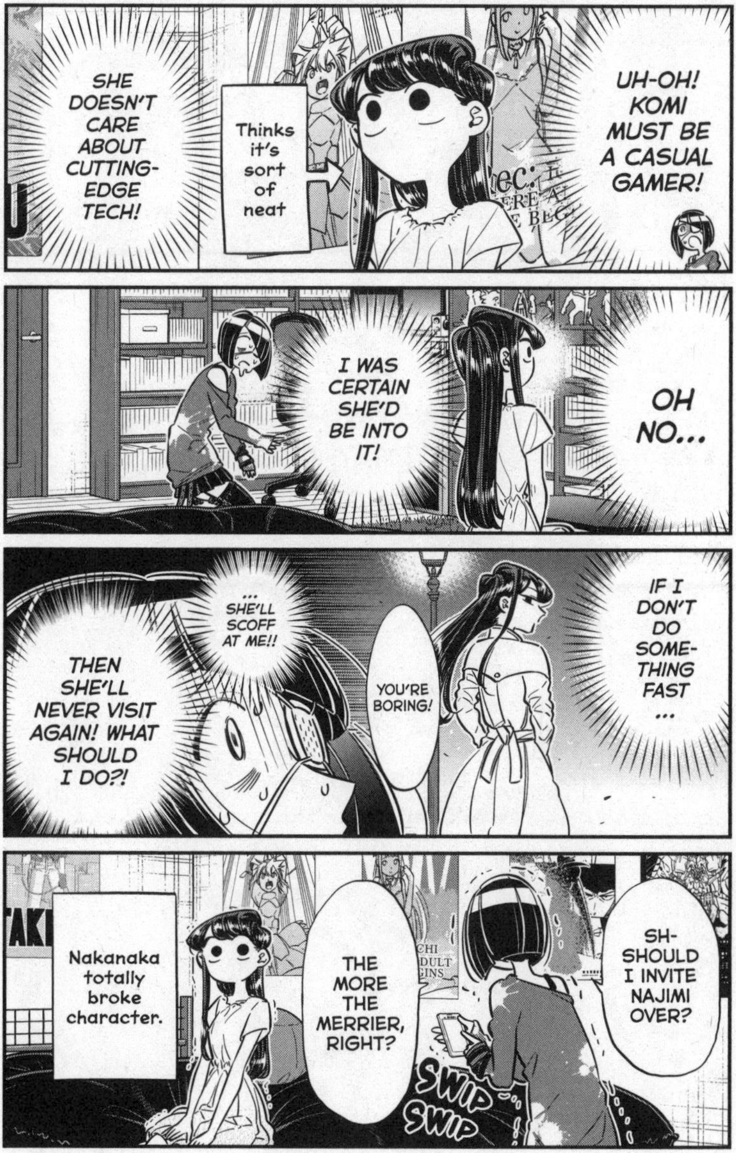
UH-OH! KOMI MUST BE A CASUAL GAMER!
Thinks it's sort of neat
SHE DOESN'T CARE ABOUT CUTTING-EDGE TECH!
OH NO...
I WAS CERTAIN SHE'D BE INTO IT!
IF I DON'T DO SOMETHING FAST ...
YOU'RE BORING!
... SHE'LL SCOFF AT ME!!
THEN SHE'LL NEVER VISIT AGAIN! WHAT SHOULD I DO?!
SH-SHOULD I INVITE NAJIMI OVER?
THE MORE THE MERRIER, RIGHT?
SWIP SWIP
Nakanaka totally broke character.

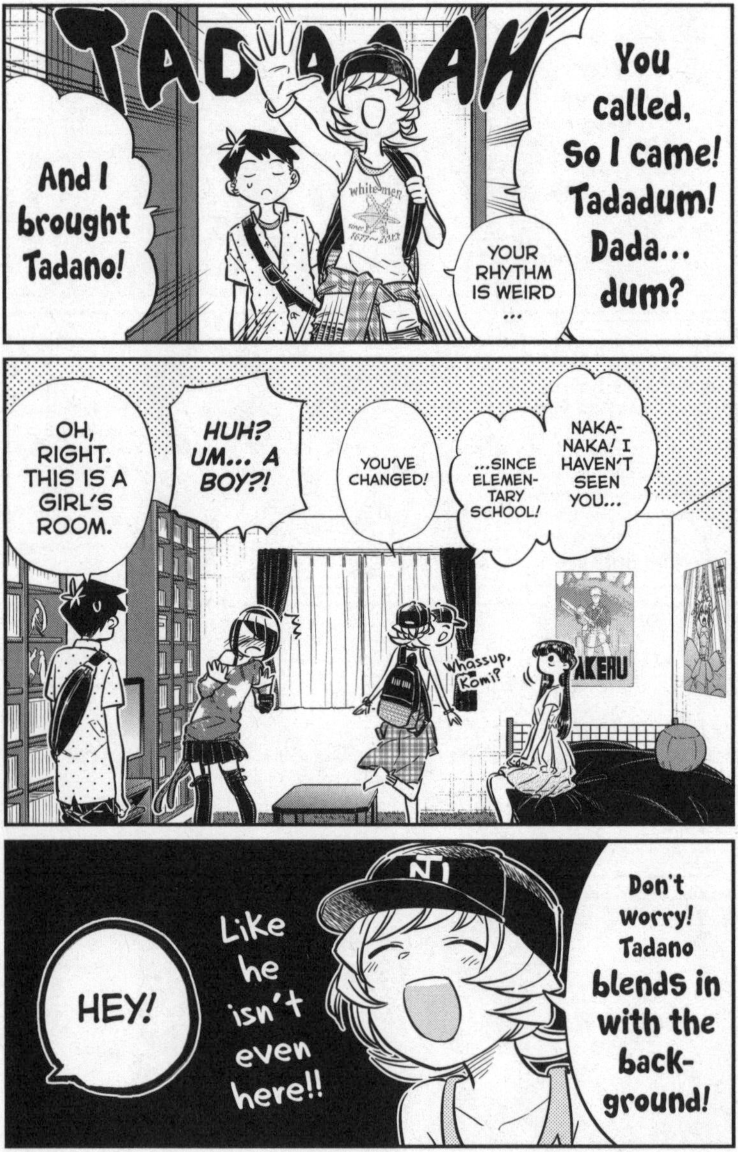
You called, So I came! Tadadum! Dada... dum?
TADAAAH
YOUR RHYTHM IS WEIRD ...
And I brought Tadano!
NAKA-NAKA! I HAVEN'T SEEN YOU...
...SINCE ELEMENTARY SCHOOL!
YOU'VE CHANGED!
Whassup, Komi?
HUH? UM... A BOY?!
OH, RIGHT. THIS IS A GIRL'S ROOM.
Don't worry! Tadano blends in with the back-ground!
Like he isn't even here!!
HEY!

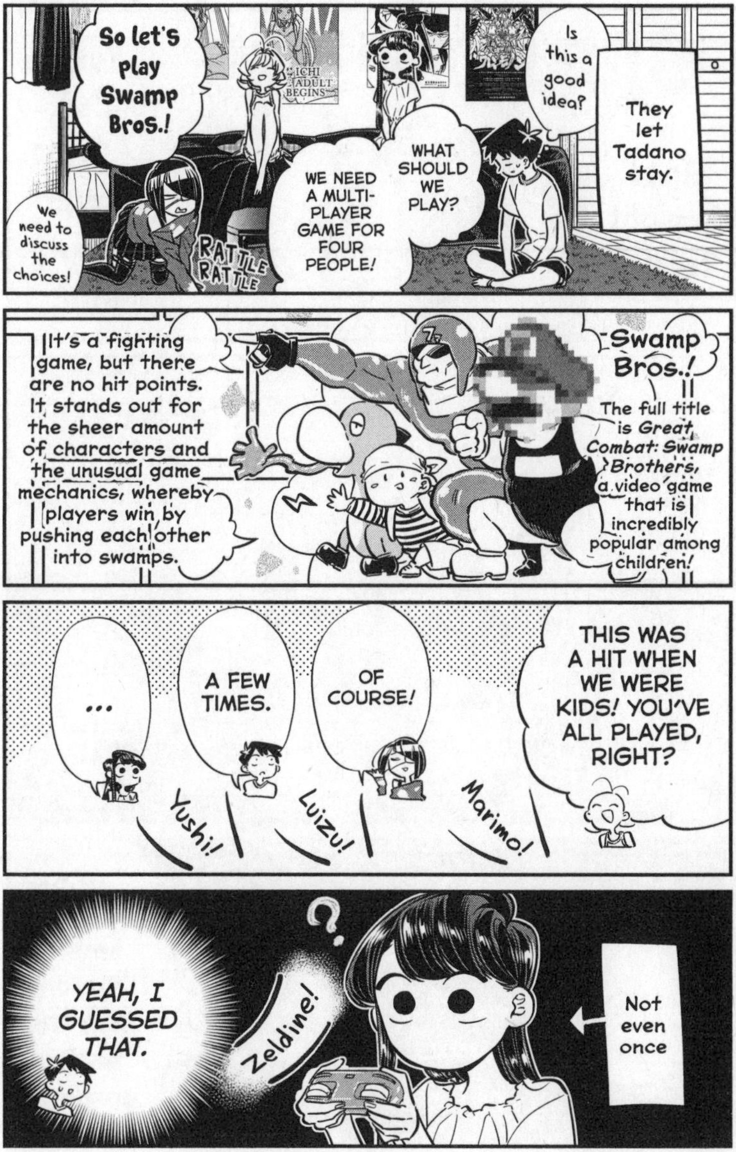
They let Tadano stay.
Is this a good idea?
WHAT SHOULD WE PLAY?
WE NEED A MULTI-PLAYER GAME FOR FOUR PEOPLE!
ICHI ADULT BEGINS
So let's play Swamp Bros.!
RATTLE RATTLE
We need to discuss the choices!
Swamp Bros.!
The full title is *Great Combat: Swamp Brothers*, a video game that is incredibly popular among children!
It's a fighting game, but there are no hit points. It stands out for the sheer amount of characters and the unusual game mechanics, whereby players win by pushing each other into swamps.
THIS WAS A HIT WHEN WE WERE KIDS! YOU'VE ALL PLAYED, RIGHT?
Marimo!
OF COURSE!
Luizu!
A FEW TIMES.
Yushi!
...
Not even once
Zeldine!
YEAH, I GUESSED THAT.

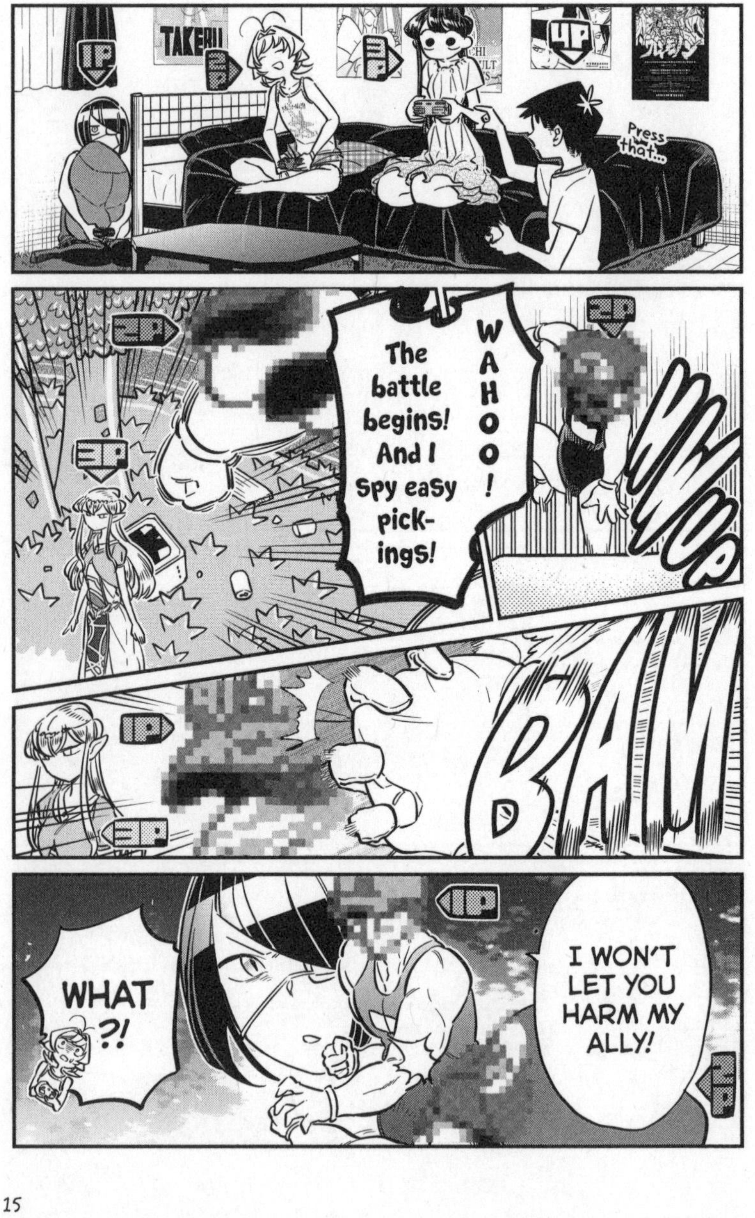
Press that...
WAHOO!
The battle begins! And I spy easy pickings!
BAM
I WON'T LET YOU HARM MY ALLY!
WHAT ?!

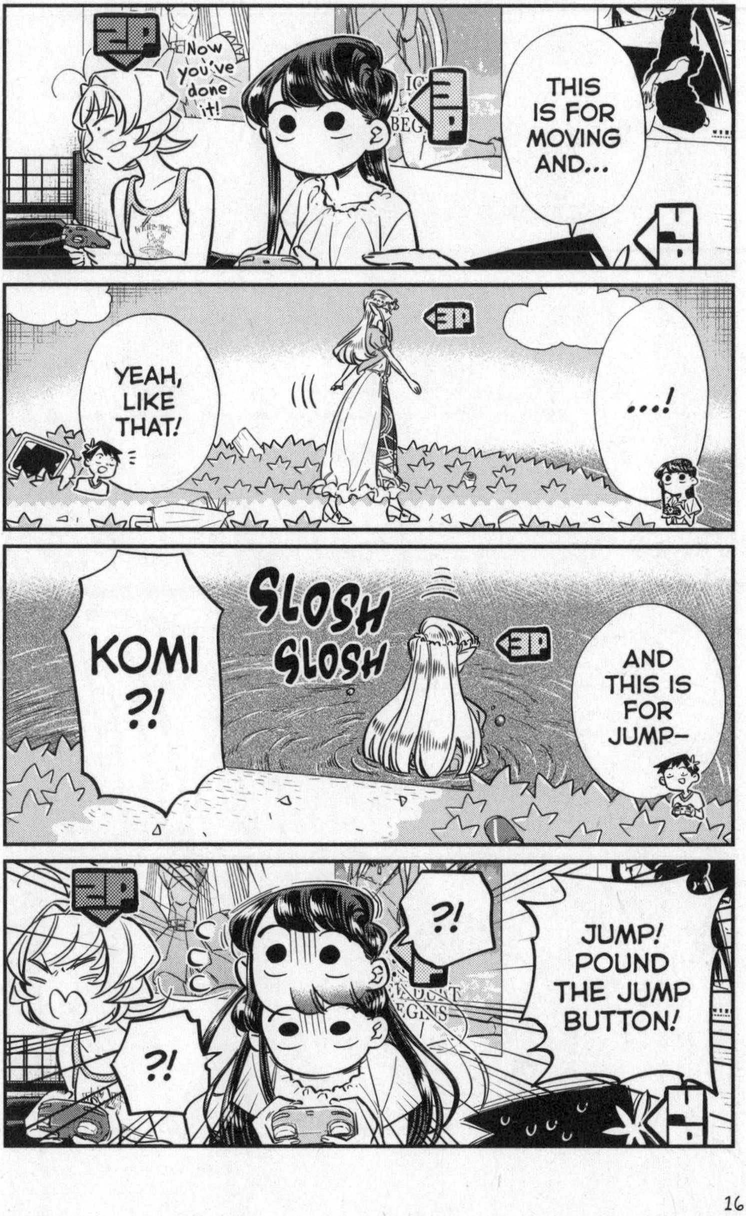
THIS IS FOR MOVING AND...
Now you've done it!
...!
YEAH, LIKE THAT!
AND THIS IS FOR JUMP–
SLOSH SLOSH
KOMI ?!
JUMP! POUND THE JUMP BUTTON!
?!
?!

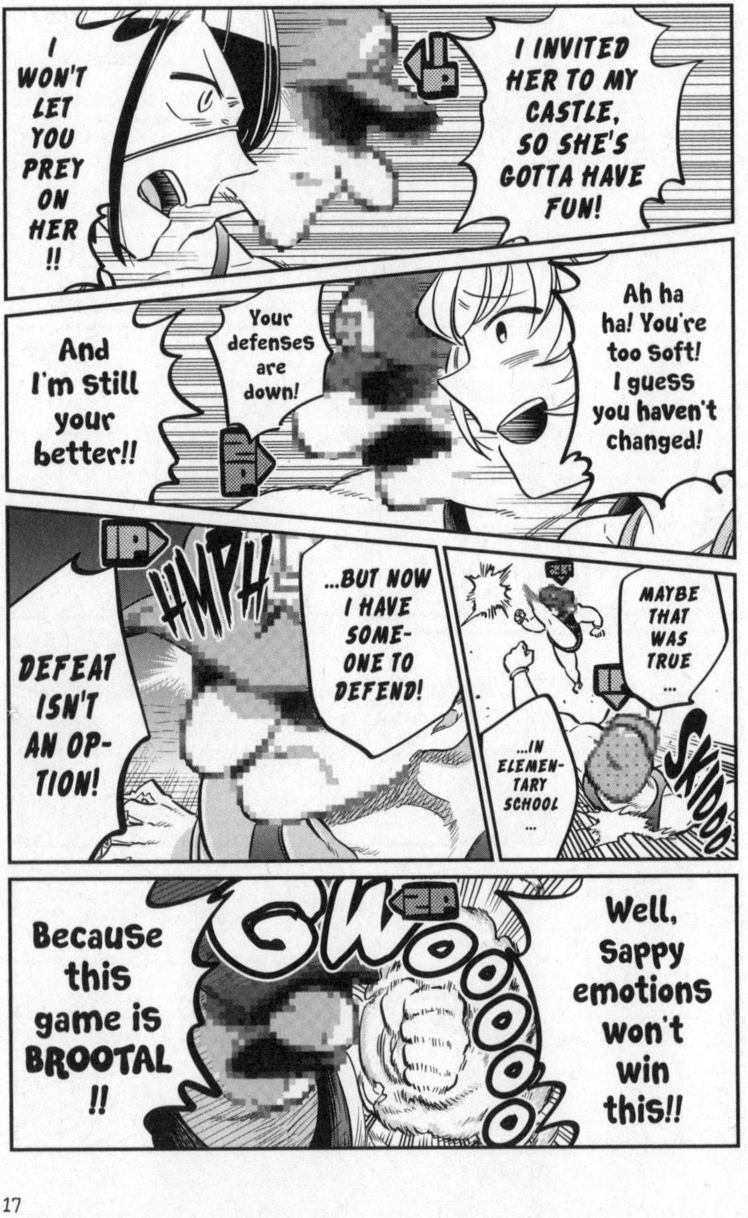
I INVITED HER TO MY CASTLE, SO SHE'S GOTTA HAVE FUN!
I WON'T LET YOU PREY ON HER!!
Ah ha ha! You're too soft! I guess you haven't changed!
Your defenses are down!
And I'm still your better!!
MAYBE THAT WAS TRUE...
SKIDOO
...IN ELEMENTARY SCHOOL...
HMPH
...BUT NOW I HAVE SOMEONE TO DEFEND!
DEFEAT ISN'T AN OPTION!
Well, Sappy emotions won't win this!!
GWOOOOOOO
Because this game is BROOTAL!!

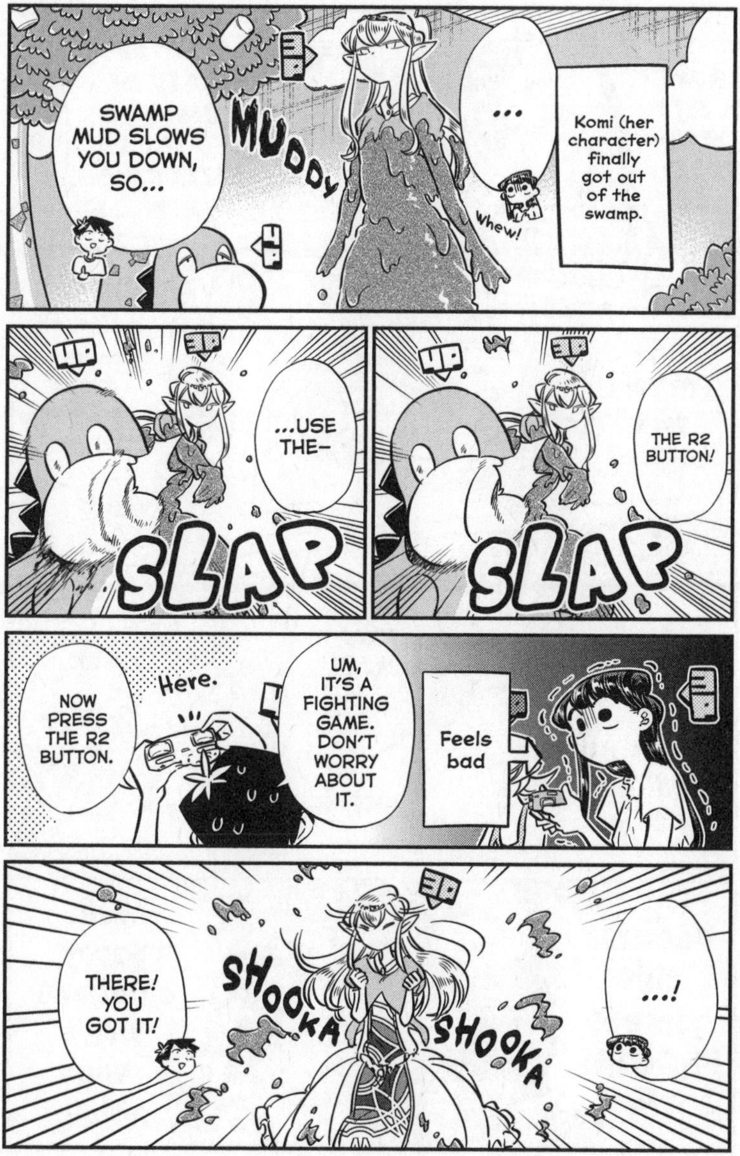
Komi (her character) finally got out of the swamp.
...
Whew!
3P
MUDDY
SWAMP MUD SLOWS YOU DOWN, SO...
4P
THE R2 BUTTON!
3P
4P
SLAP
...USE THE–
3P
4P
SLAP
3P
Feels bad
UM, IT'S A FIGHTING GAME. DON'T WORRY ABOUT IT.
Here.
NOW PRESS THE R2 BUTTON.
...!
3P
SHOOKA SHOOKA
THERE! YOU GOT IT!

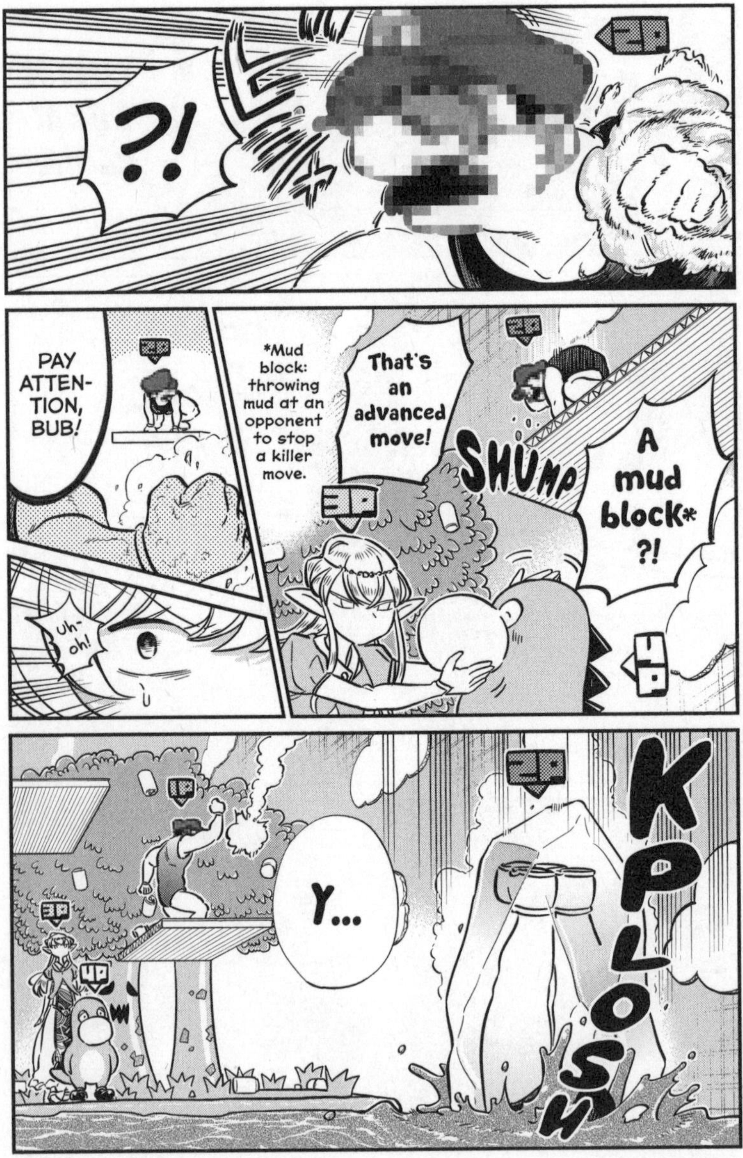
?!
A mud block* ?!
That's an advanced move!
*Mud block: throwing mud at an opponent to stop a killer move.
SHUMP
PAY ATTENTION, BUB!
Uh-oh!
KPLOSH
Y...

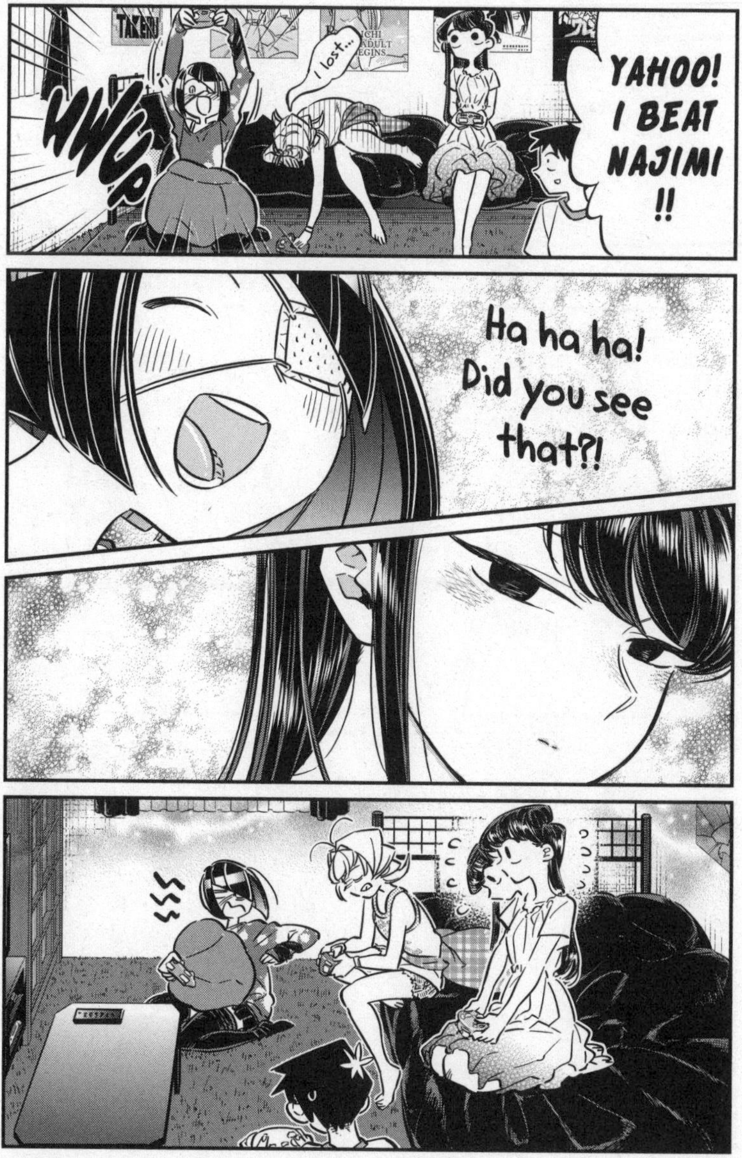
YAHOO! I BEAT NAJIMI !!
I lost...
WWUP
Ha ha ha! Did you see that?!

Communication 48 — The End

Princess Zeldine

She's a quiet tomboy. She disguised herself so she could join the battle, but everyone soon discovered her true identity.

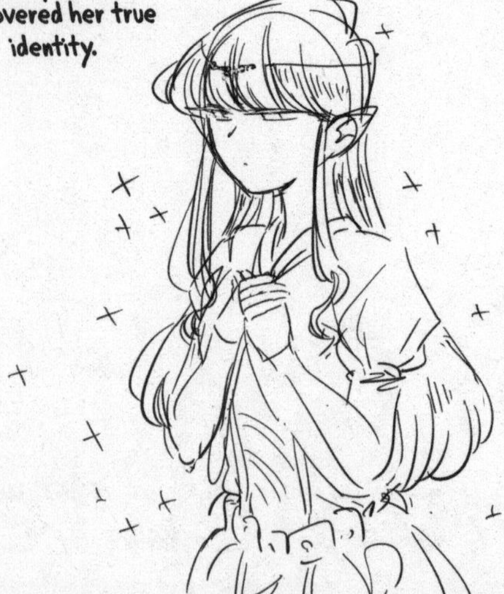

Komi Can't
Communicate

Komi Can't Communicate

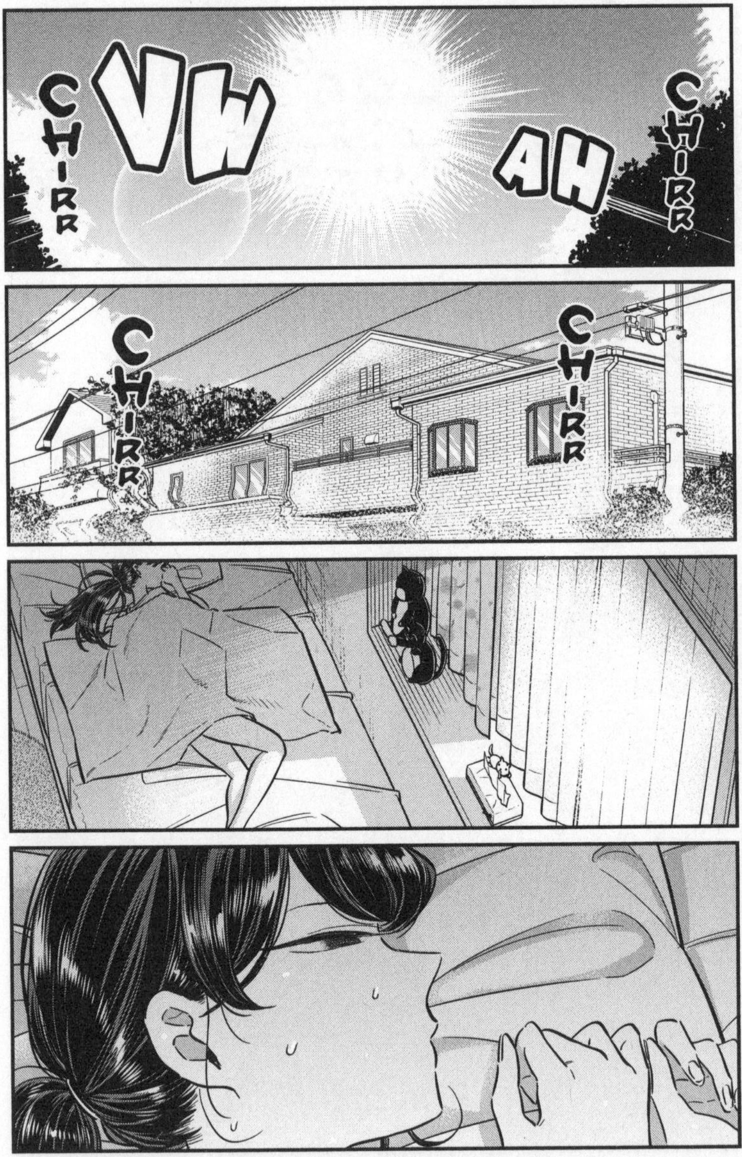
CHIRR
AH
VW
CHIRR
CHIRR
CHIRR

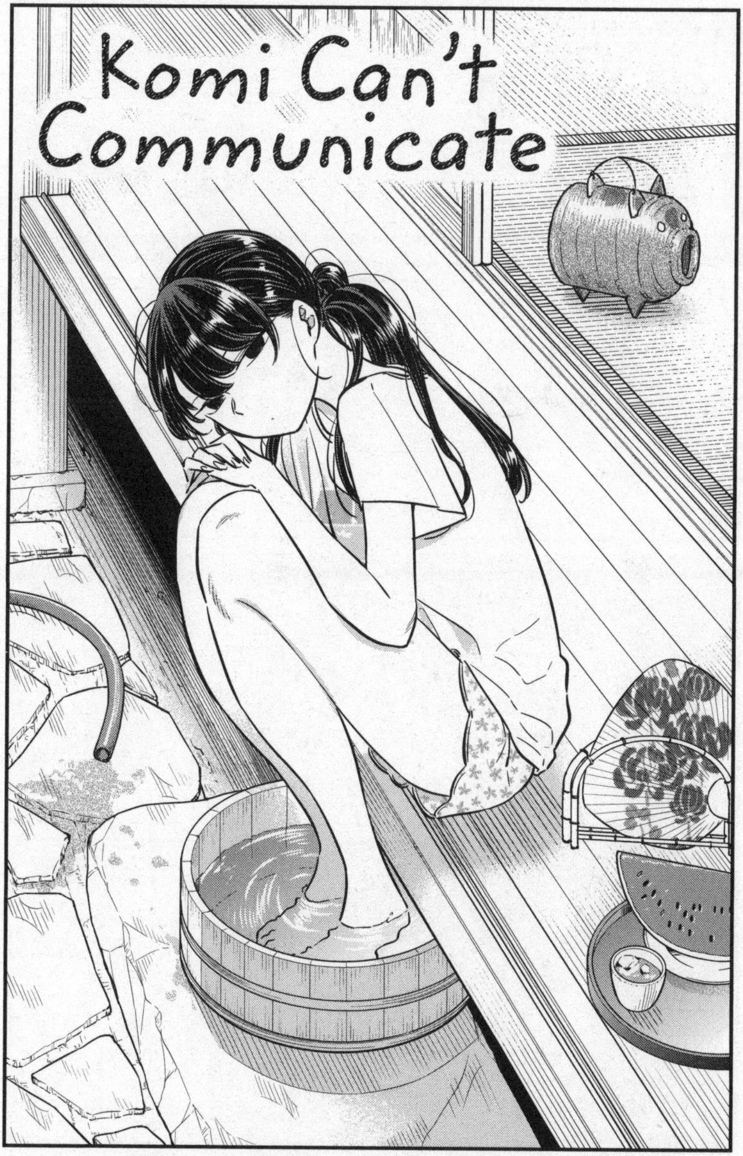
Komi Can't Communicate

Communication 49: A Hot Day

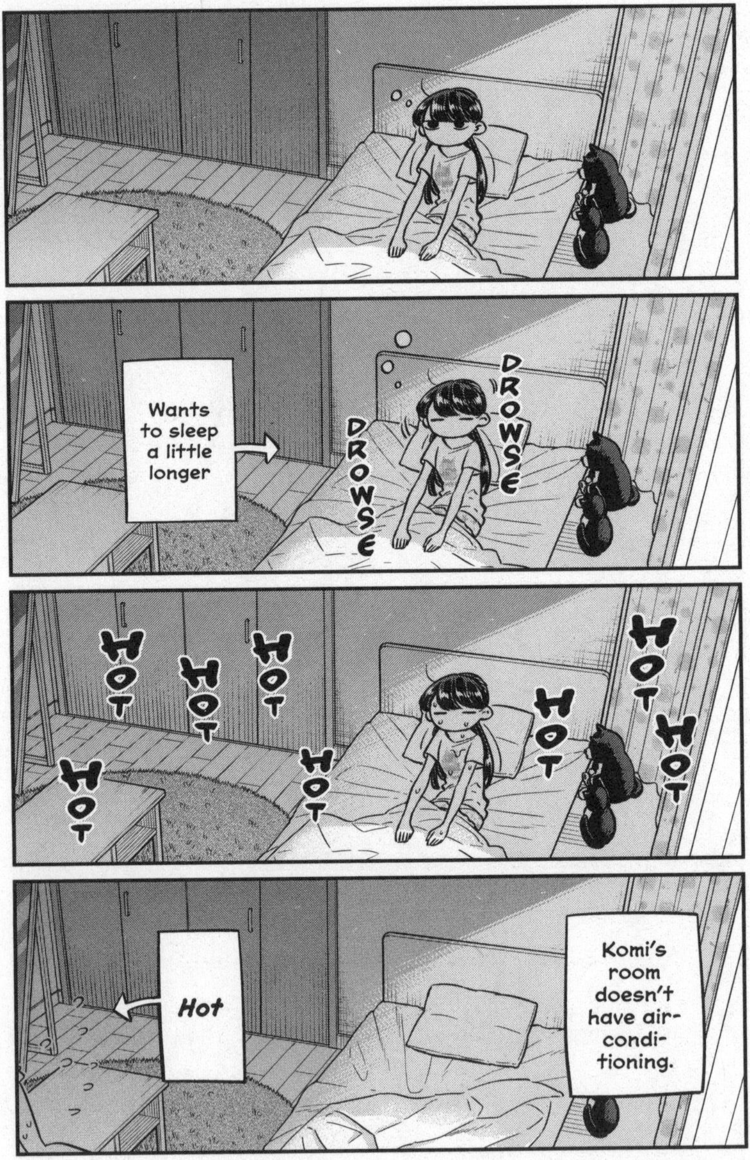
DROWSE
DROWSE
Wants to sleep a little longer
HOT HOT
HOT
HOT
HOT
HOT
HOT
HOT
Komi's room doesn't have air-conditioning.
Hot

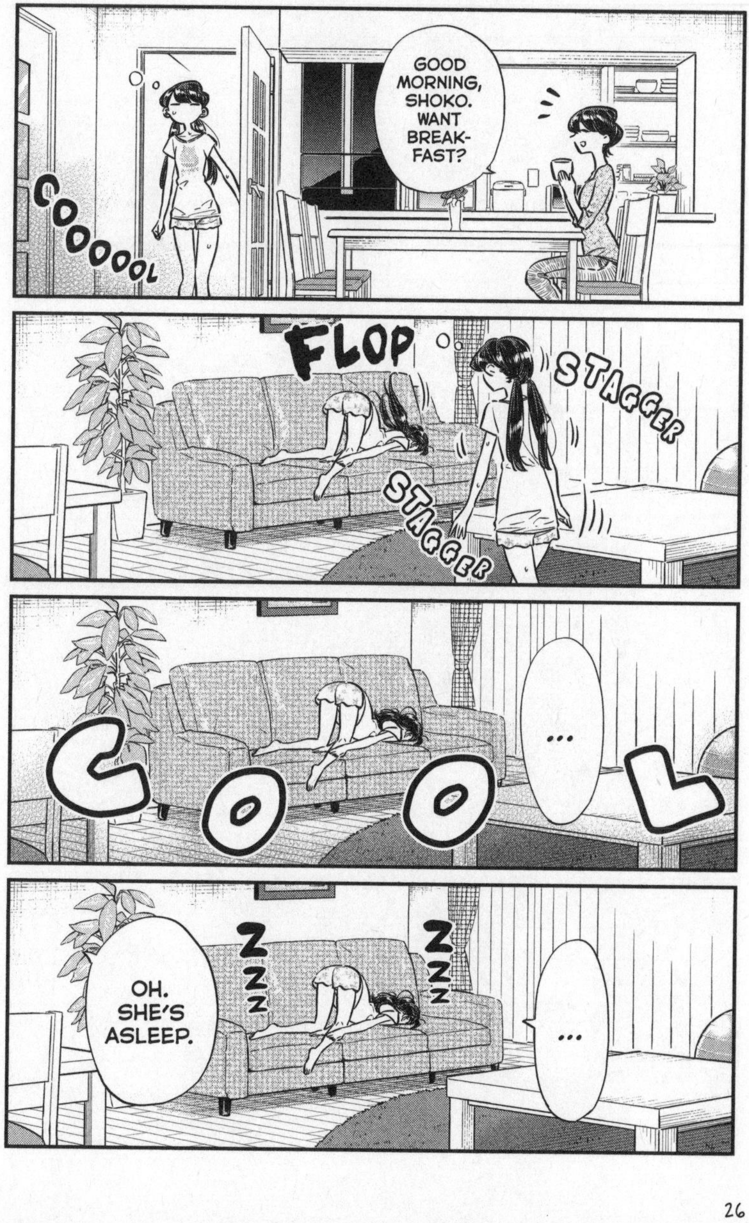
GOOD MORNING, SHOKO. WANT BREAK-FAST?
COOOOOOL
STAGGER
FLOP
STAGGER
...
COOL
...
ZZZ
ZZZ
OH. SHE'S ASLEEP.

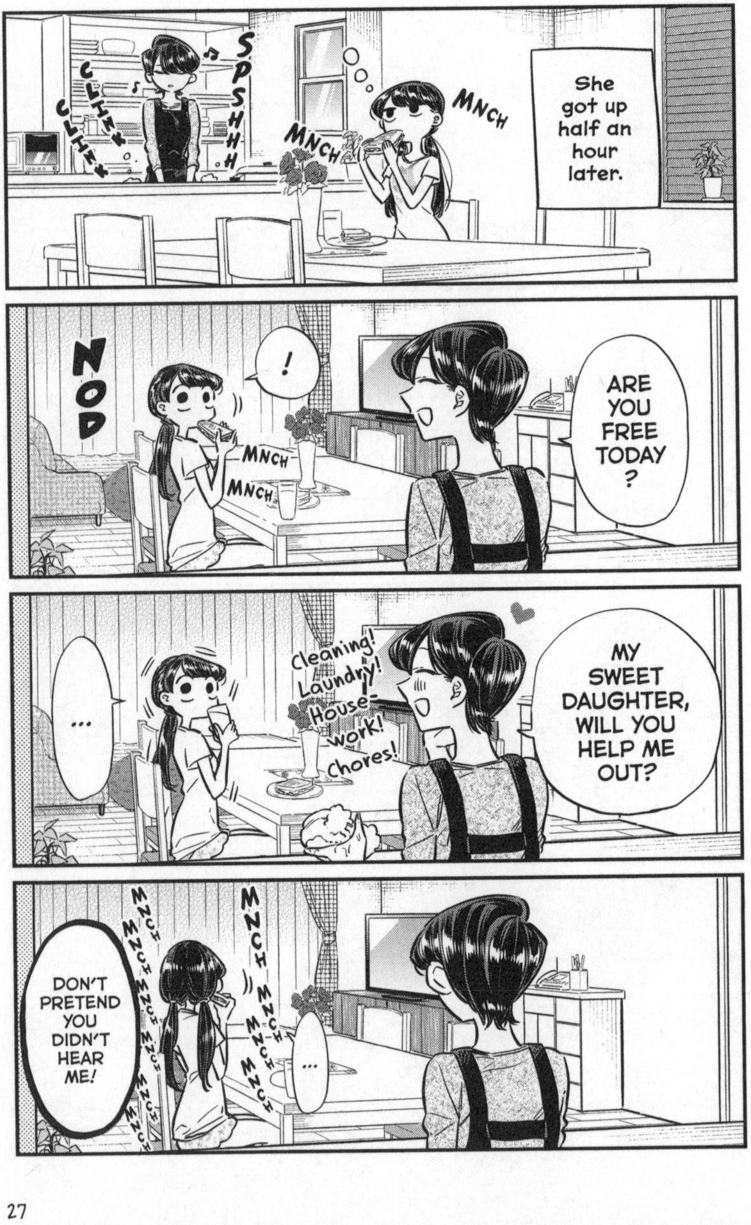
She got up half an hour later.
MNCH
SPSHHH
CLINK
CLINK
MNCH
ARE YOU FREE TODAY?
!
NOD
MNCH
MNCH
MY SWEET DAUGHTER, WILL YOU HELP ME OUT?
Cleaning! Laundry! House-work! Chores!
...
MNCH MNCH MNCH MNCH MNCH
...
MNCH MNCH MNCH MNCH MNCH MNCH
DON'T PRETEND YOU DIDN'T HEAR ME!

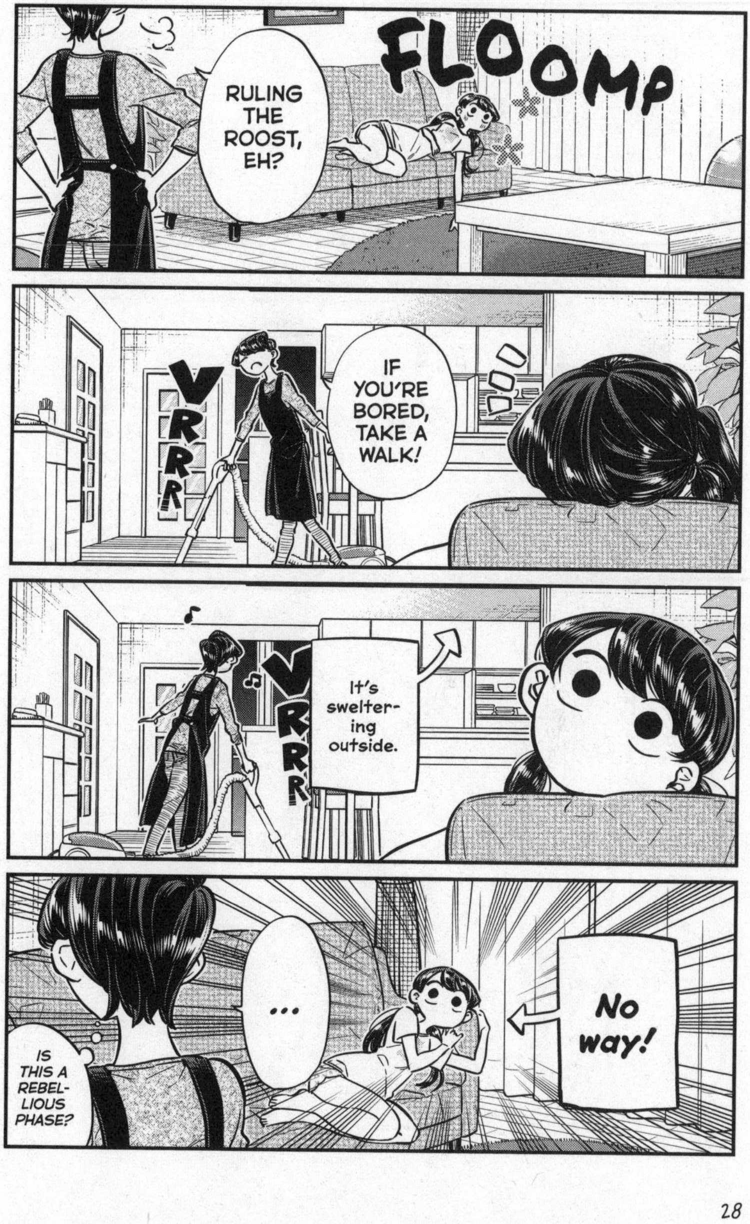
FLOOMP
RULING THE ROOST, EH?
IF YOU'RE BORED, TAKE A WALK!
VRRR
It's sweltering outside.
VRRR
No way!
...
IS THIS A REBELLIOUS PHASE?

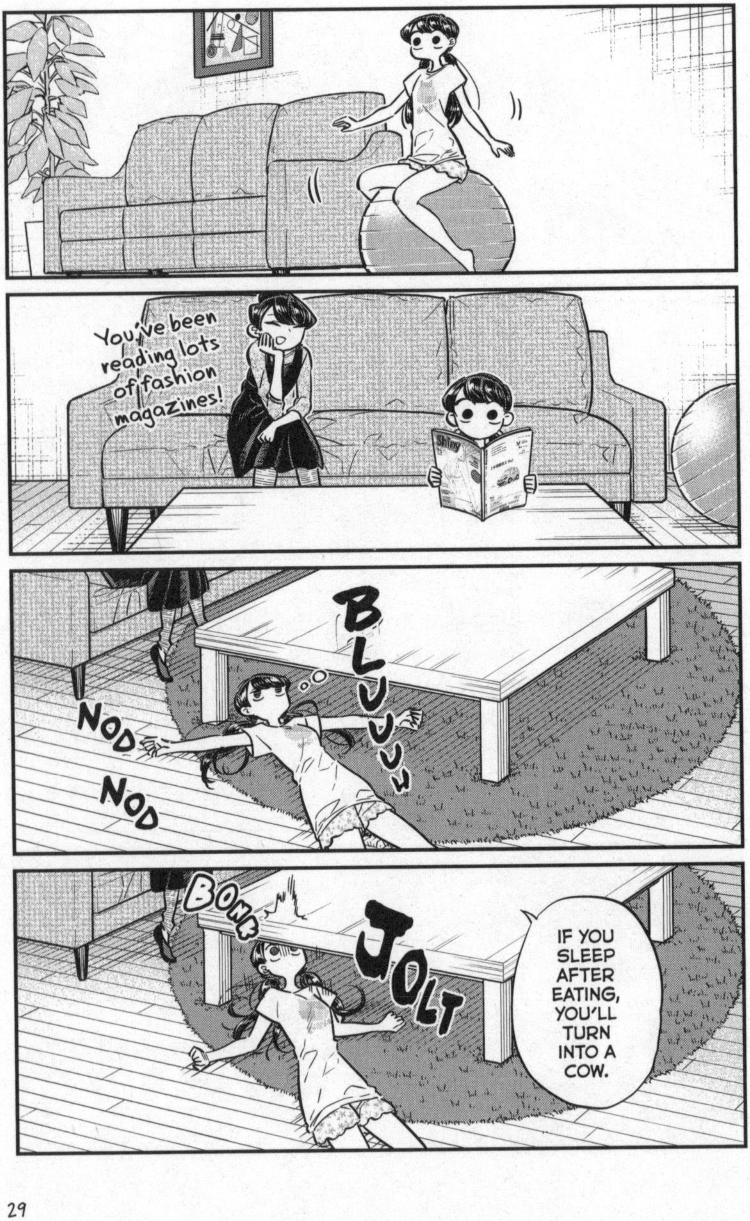
You've been reading lots of fashion magazines!
BLUUUUH
NOD NOD
BONK
JOLT
IF YOU SLEEP AFTER EATING, YOU'LL TURN INTO A COW.

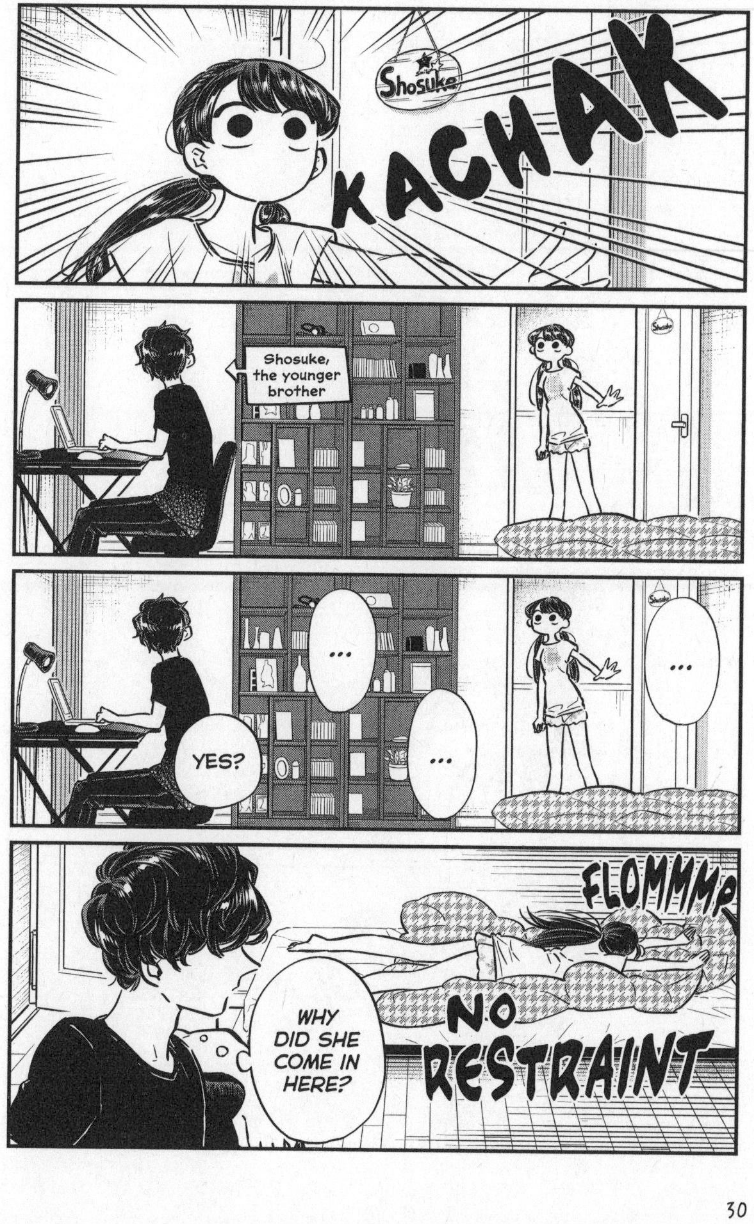
Shosuke
KACHAK
Shosuke
Shosuke, the younger brother
Shosuke
...
...
...
YES?
FLOMMMP
NO RESTRAINT
WHY DID SHE COME IN HERE?

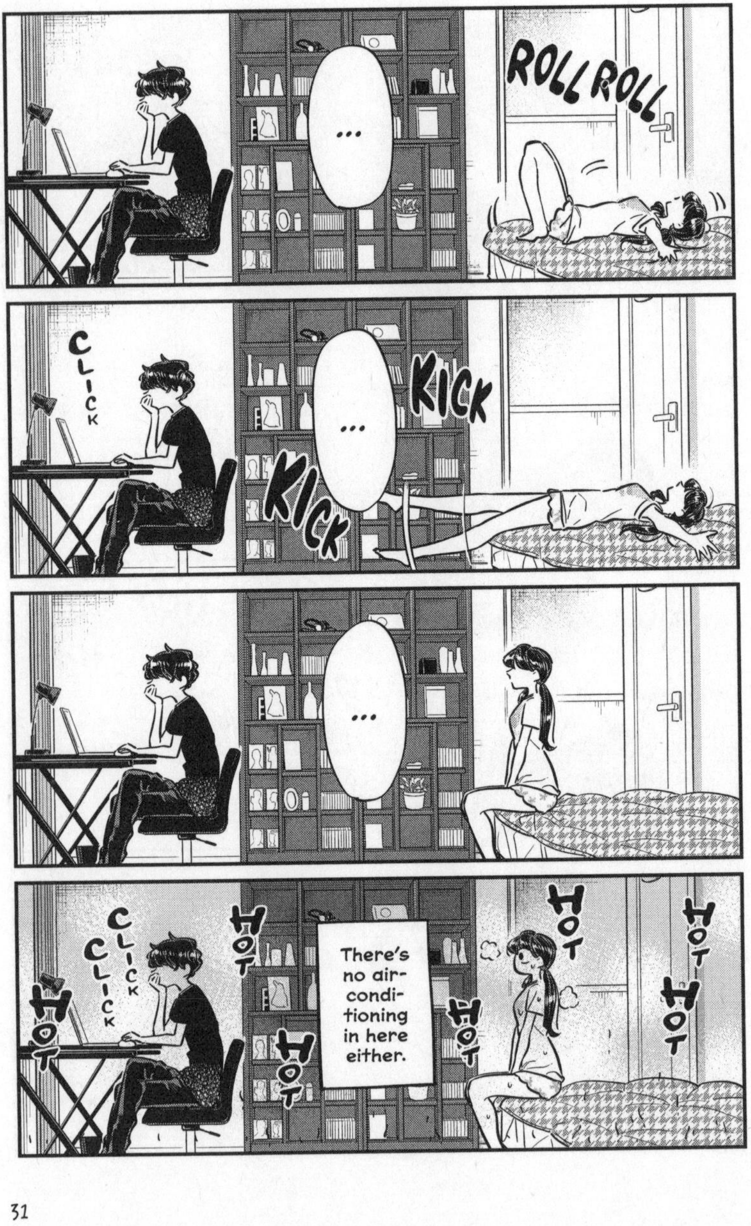
ROLL ROLL
...
KICK
KICK
...
CLICK
...
HOT
HOT
HOT
HOT
HOT
There's no air-conditioning in here either.
HOT
HOT
CLICK
CLICK

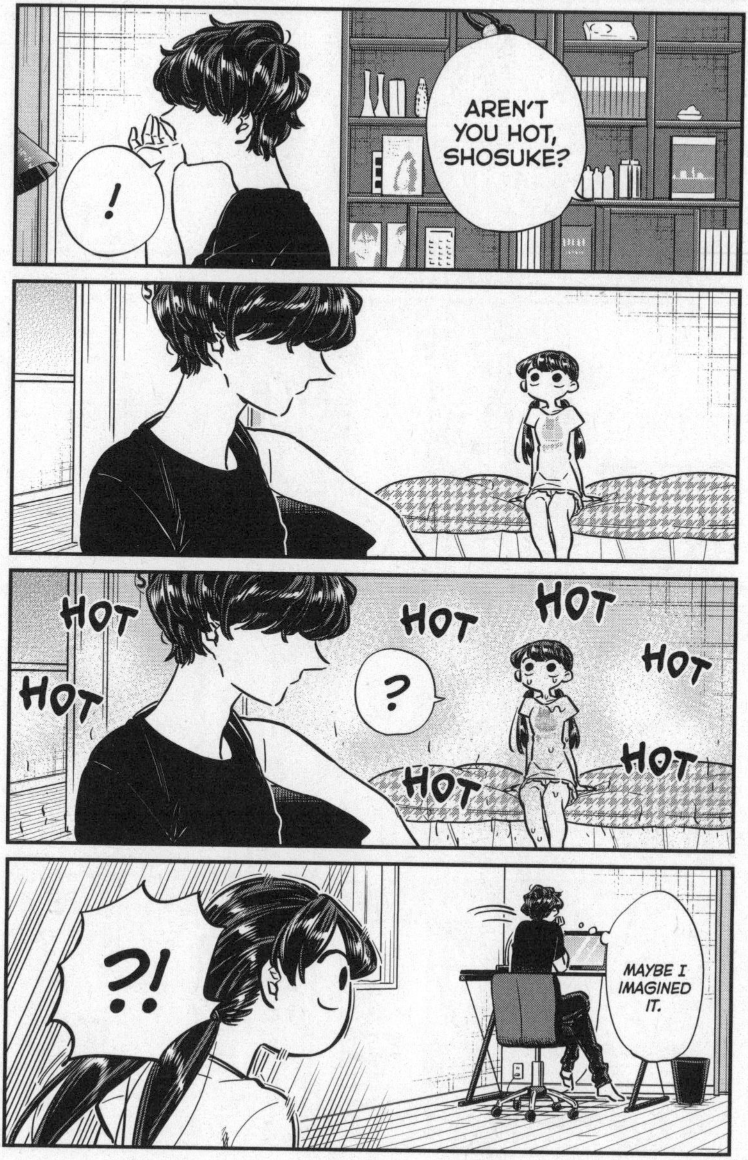
AREN'T YOU HOT, SHOSUKE?
!
HOT
HOT
HOT
HOT
HOT
HOT
HOT
?
MAYBE I IMAGINED IT.
?!

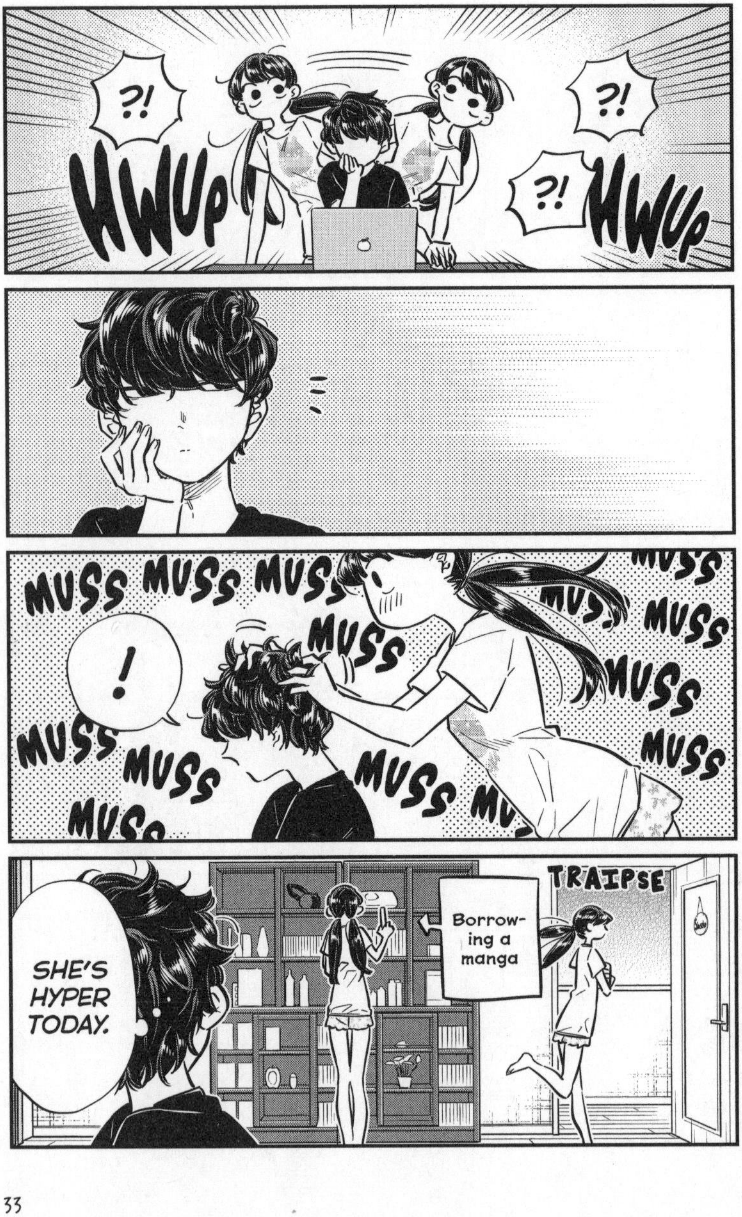
?!
?!
HWUP
?!
HWUP
!
MUSS
MUSS
MUSS
MUSS
MUSS
MUSS
MUSS
MUSS
MUSS
MUSS
TRAIPSE
Borrow-
ing a
manga
SHE'S
HYPER
TODAY.

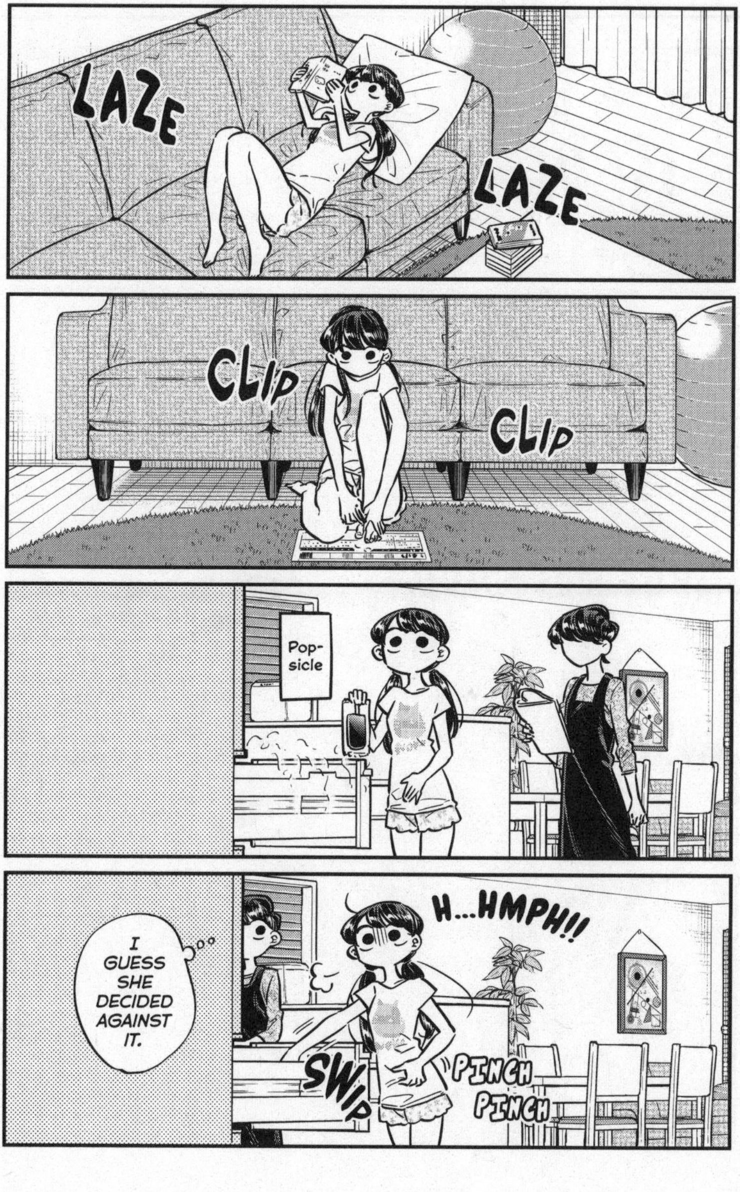
LAZE
LAZE
CLIP
CLIP
Pop-sicle
H...HMPH!!
I GUESS SHE DECIDED AGAINST IT.
PINCH PINCH
SWIP

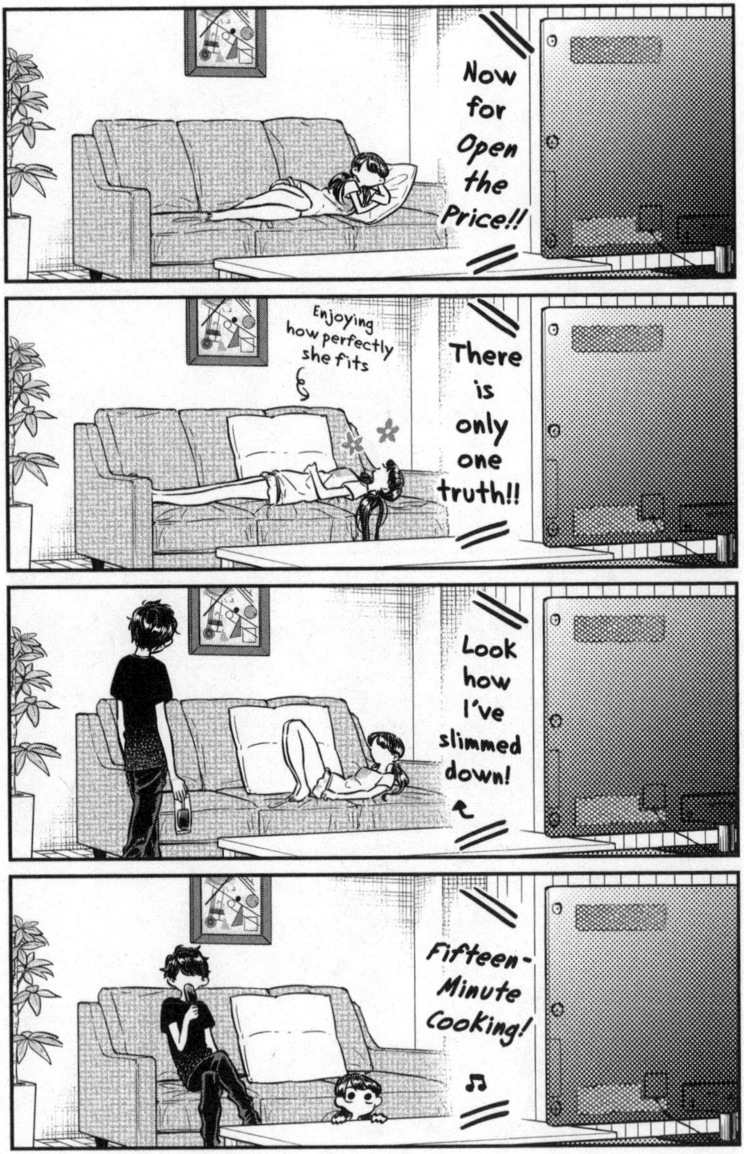
Now for Open the Price!!
There is only one truth!!
Enjoying how perfectly she fits
Look how I've slimmed down!
Fifteen-Minute Cooking!
♫

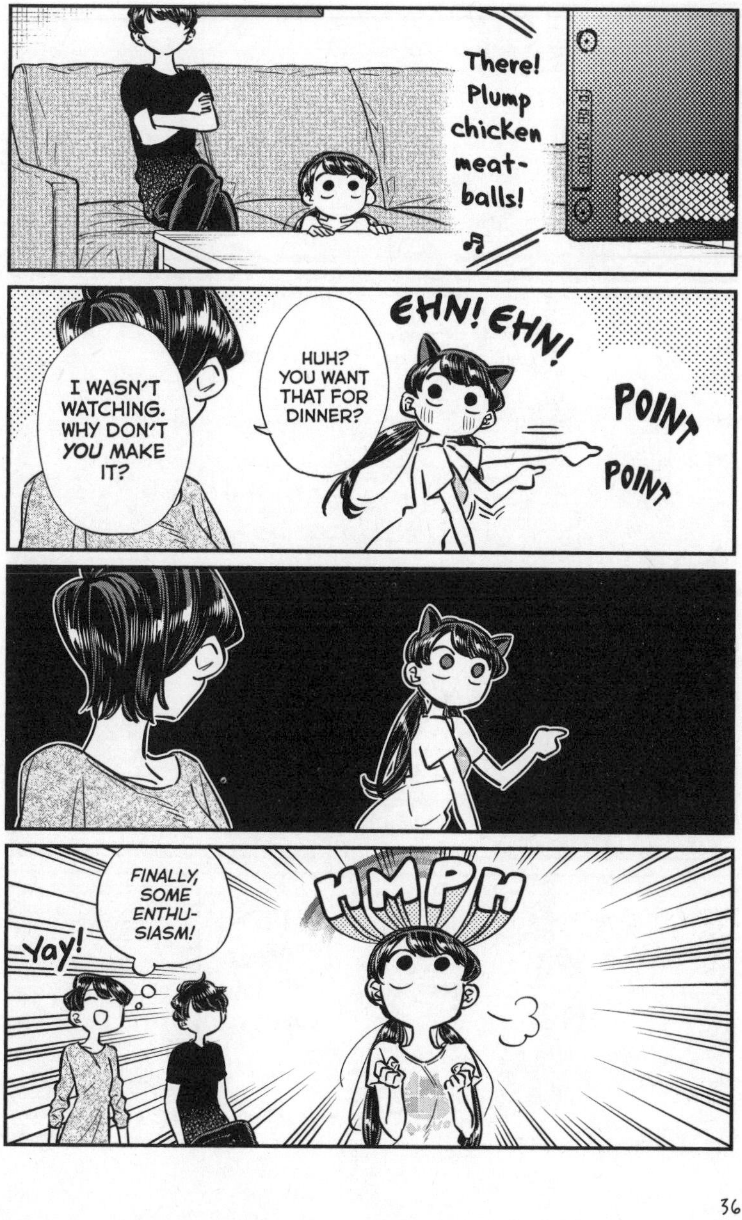
There! Plump chicken meat-balls!
EHN! EHN!
POINT
POINT
HUH? YOU WANT THAT FOR DINNER?
I WASN'T WATCHING. WHY DON'T *YOU* MAKE IT?
HMPH
FINALLY, SOME ENTHU-SIASM!
Yay!

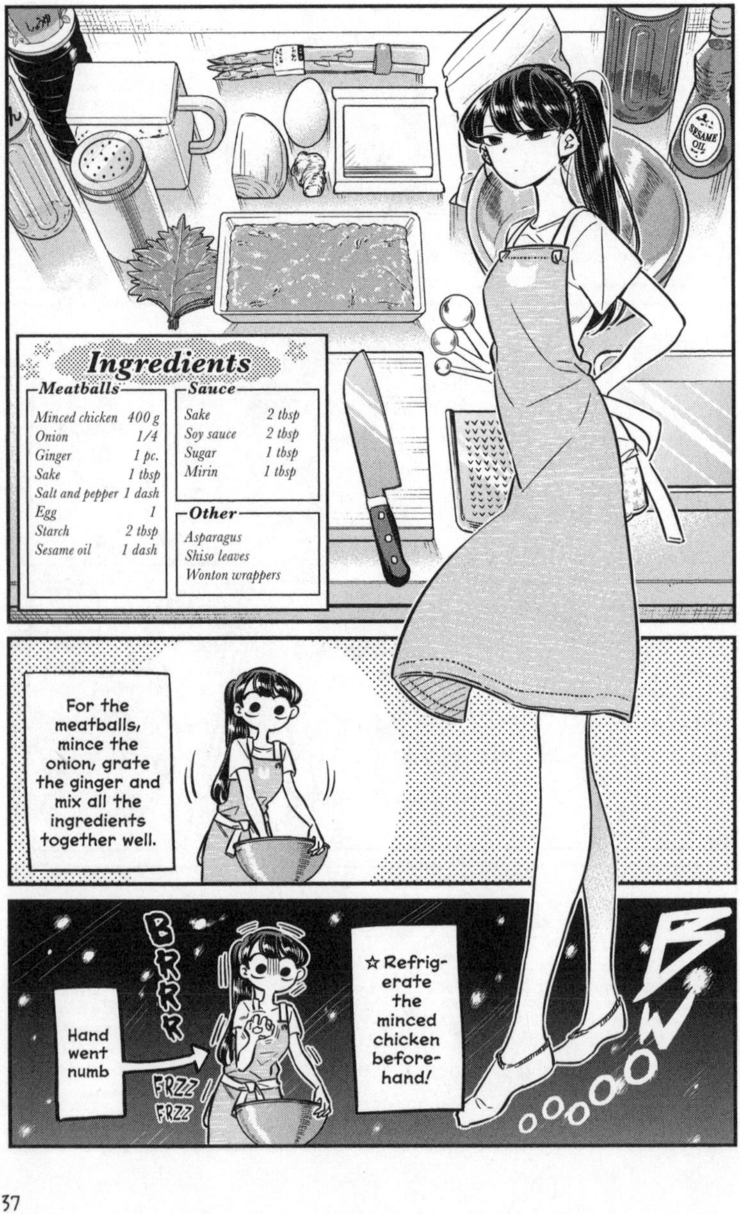
SESAME OIL
Ingredients
Meatballs
Minced chicken 400 g
Onion 1/4
Ginger 1 pc.
Sake 1 tbsp
Salt and pepper 1 dash
Egg 1
Starch 2 tbsp
Sesame oil 1 dash
Sauce
Sake 2 tbsp
Soy sauce 2 tbsp
Sugar 1 tbsp
Mirin 1 tbsp
Other
Asparagus
Shiso leaves
Wonton wrappers
For the meatballs, mince the onion, grate the ginger and mix all the ingredients together well.
BWOOOOOO
☆ Refrigerate the minced chicken beforehand!
BRRRR
Hand went numb
FRZZ FRZZ

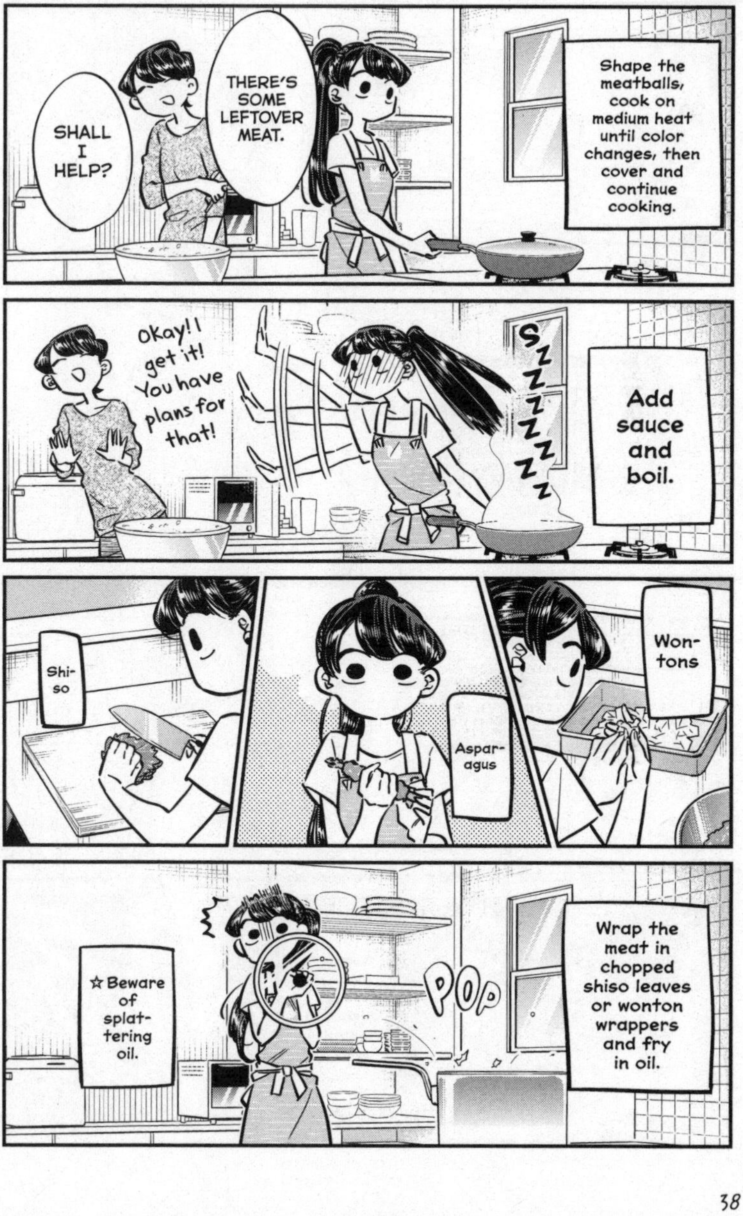
Shape the meatballs, cook on medium heat until color changes, then cover and continue cooking.
THERE'S SOME LEFTOVER MEAT.
SHALL I HELP?
Add sauce and boil.
SZZZZZZZ
Okay!! I get it! You have plans for that!
Won-tons
Aspar-agus
Shi-so
Wrap the meat in chopped shiso leaves or wonton wrappers and fry in oil.
POP
☆Beware of splat-tering oil.

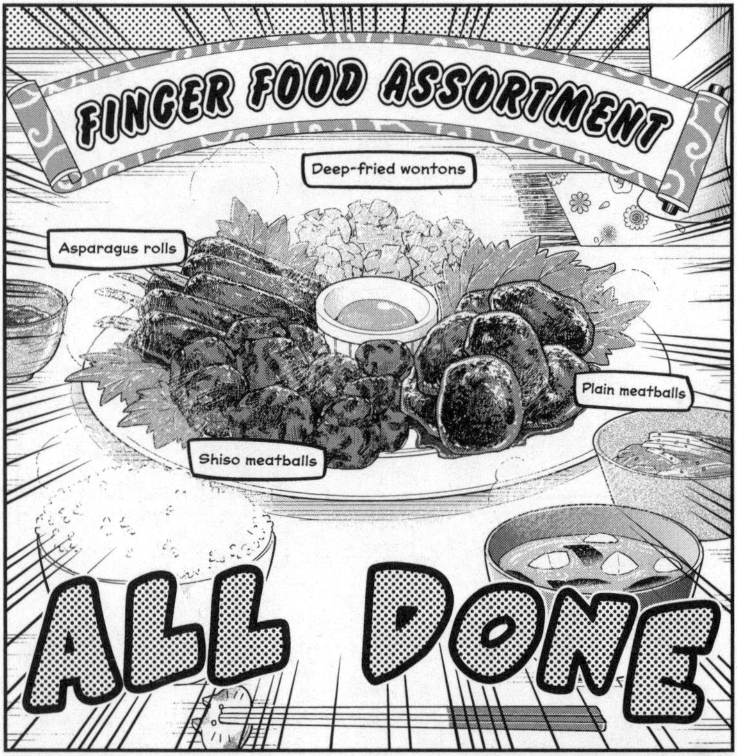
FINGER FOOD ASSORTMENT
Deep-fried wontons
Plain meatballs
Asparagus rolls
Shiso meatballs
ALL DONE

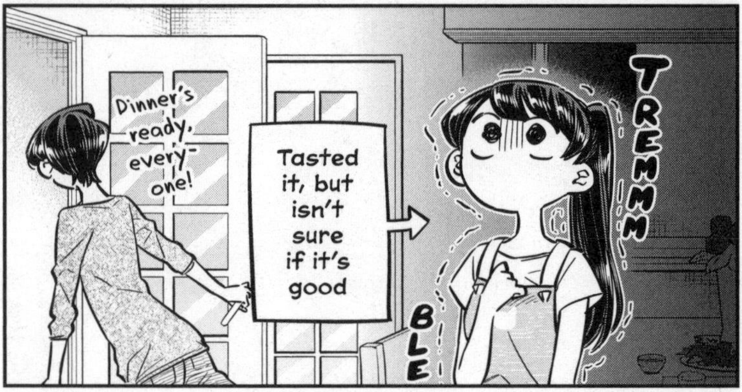
TREMMM
BLE
Tasted it, but isn't sure if it's good
Dinner's ready, every-one!

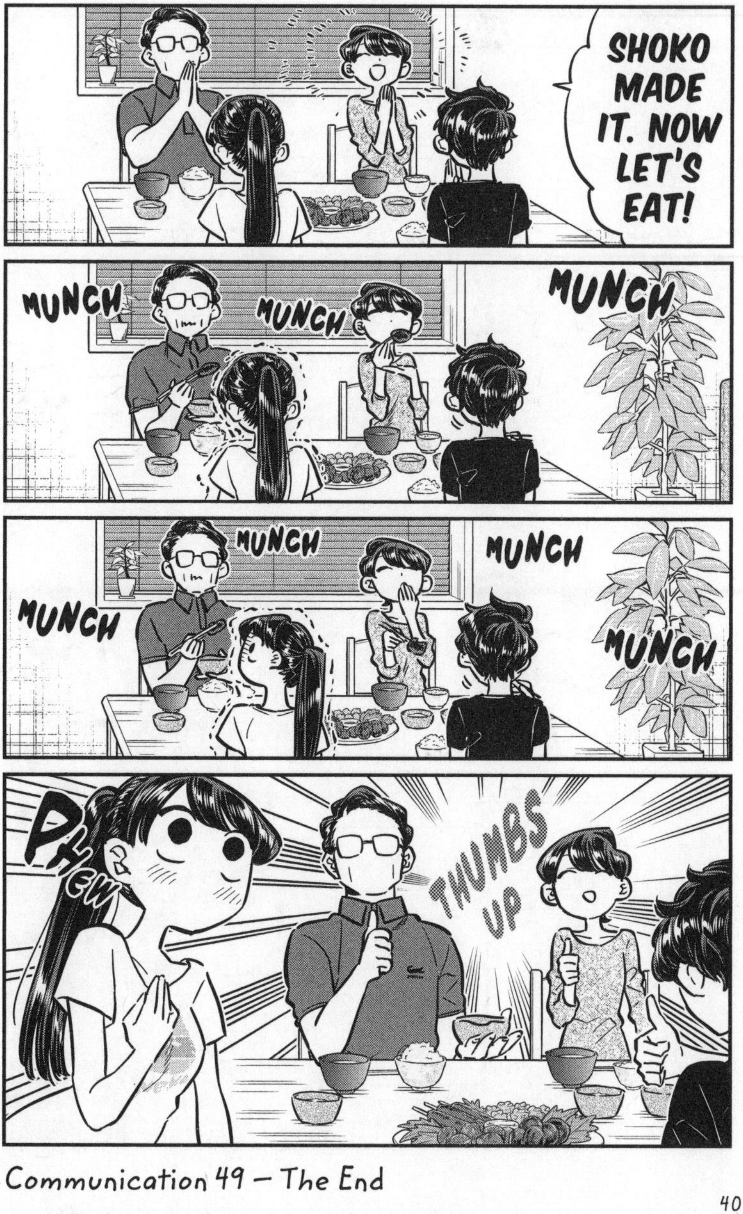
SHOKO MADE IT. NOW LET'S EAT!
MUNCH
MUNCH
MUNCH
MUNCH
MUNCH
MUNCH
MUNCH
THUMBS UP
PHEW

Communication 49 — The End

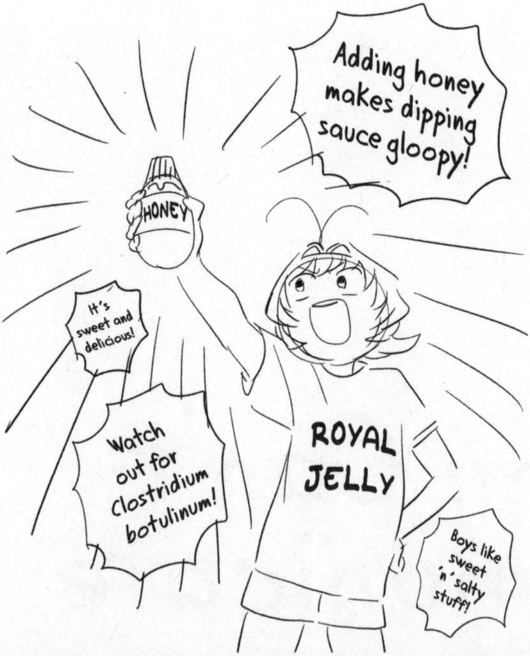
Adding honey makes dipping sauce gloopy!
HONEY
It's sweet and delicious!
ROYAL JELLY
Watch out for Clostridium botulinum!
Boys like sweet 'n' salty stuff!

Komi Can't
Communicate

Komi Can't Communicate

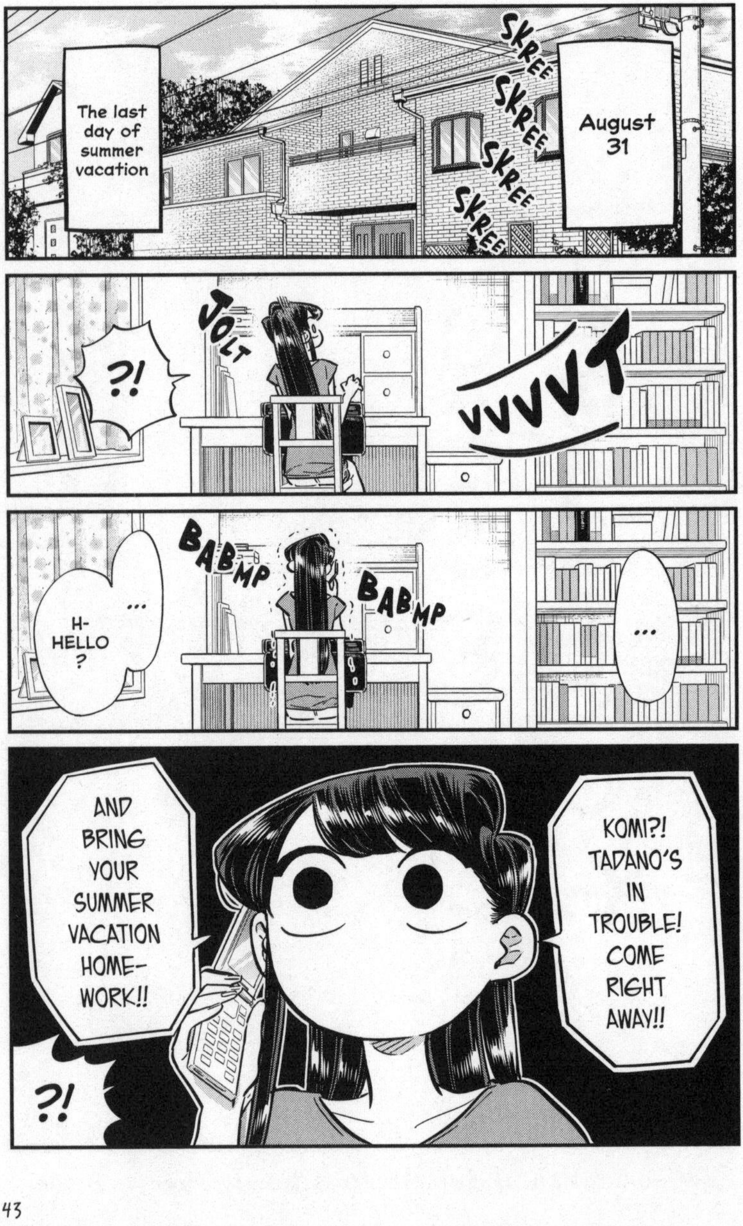

August 31
SKREE SKREE SKREE SKREE
The last day of summer vacation
VVVVT
JOLT
?!
...
BABMP BABMP
... H-HELLO?
KOMI?! TADANO'S IN TROUBLE! COME RIGHT AWAY!!
AND BRING YOUR SUMMER VACATION HOME-WORK!!
?!

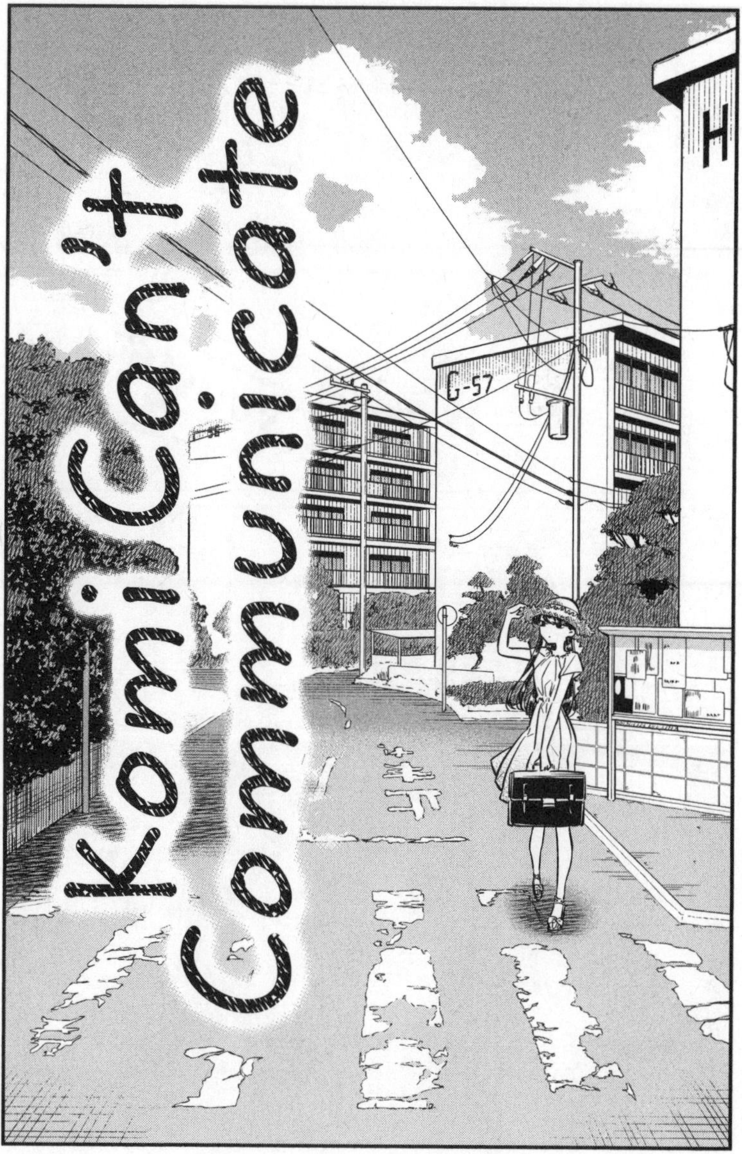
Komi Can't Communicate
H
G-57

Communication 50: Summer Vacation Is Over

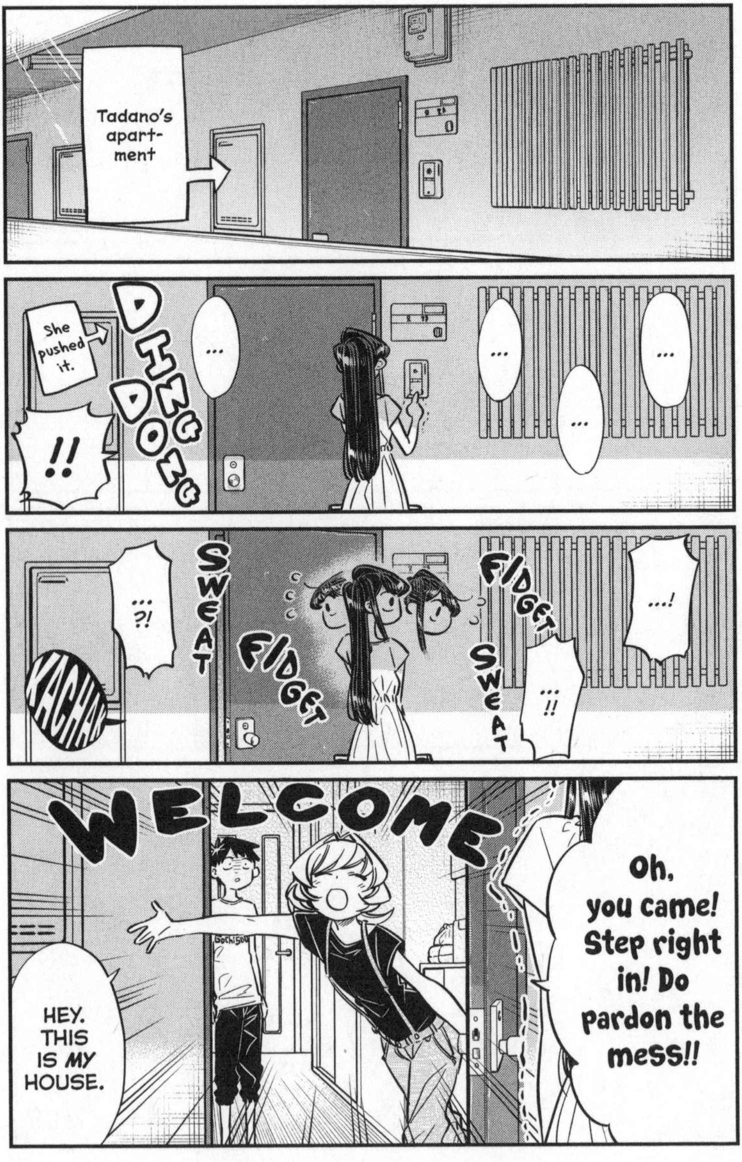

Tadano's apartment
...
...
...
...
DING DONG
She pushed it.
!!
...!
FIDGET
SWEAT
... !!
FIDGET
SWEAT
... ?!
KACHA
WELCOME
Oh, you came! Step right in! Do pardon the mess!!
HEY. THIS IS *MY* HOUSE.

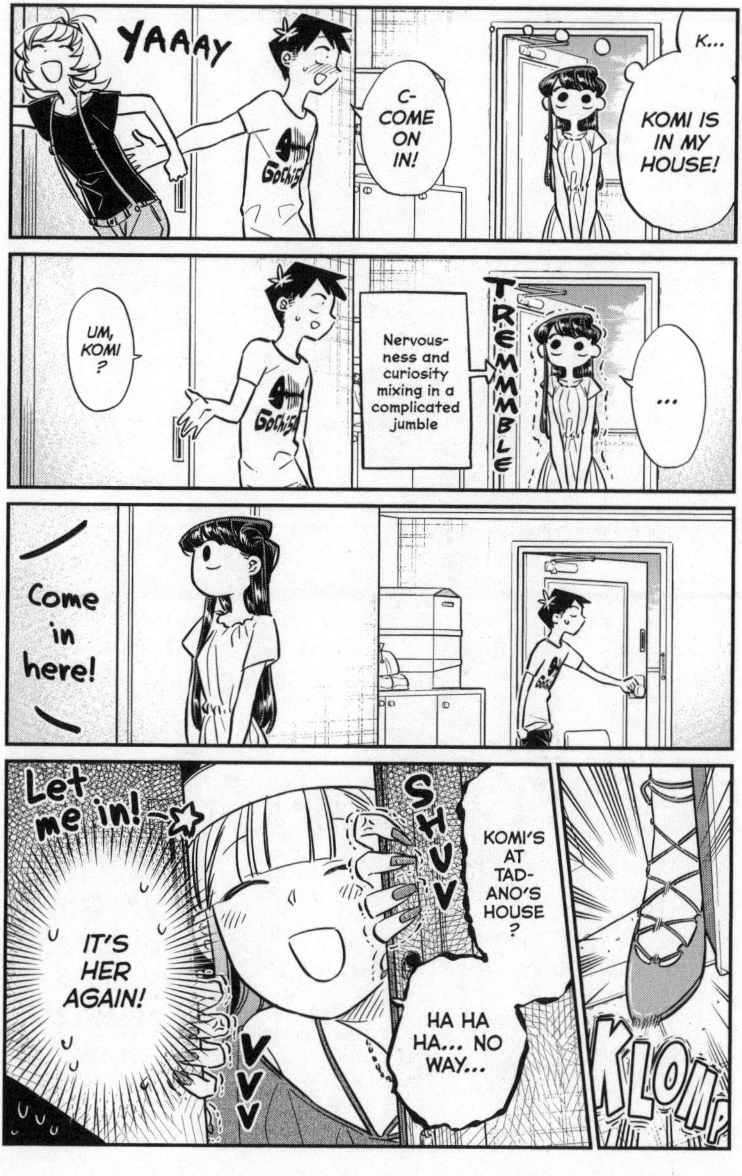
K...
KOMI IS IN MY HOUSE!
C-COME ON IN!
YAAAY
...
TREMMMBLE
Nervousness and curiosity mixing in a complicated jumble
UM, KOMI?
Come in here!
KLOMP
SHUV
KOMI'S AT TADANO'S HOUSE?
HA HA HA... NO WAY...
Let me in!
IT'S HER AGAIN!

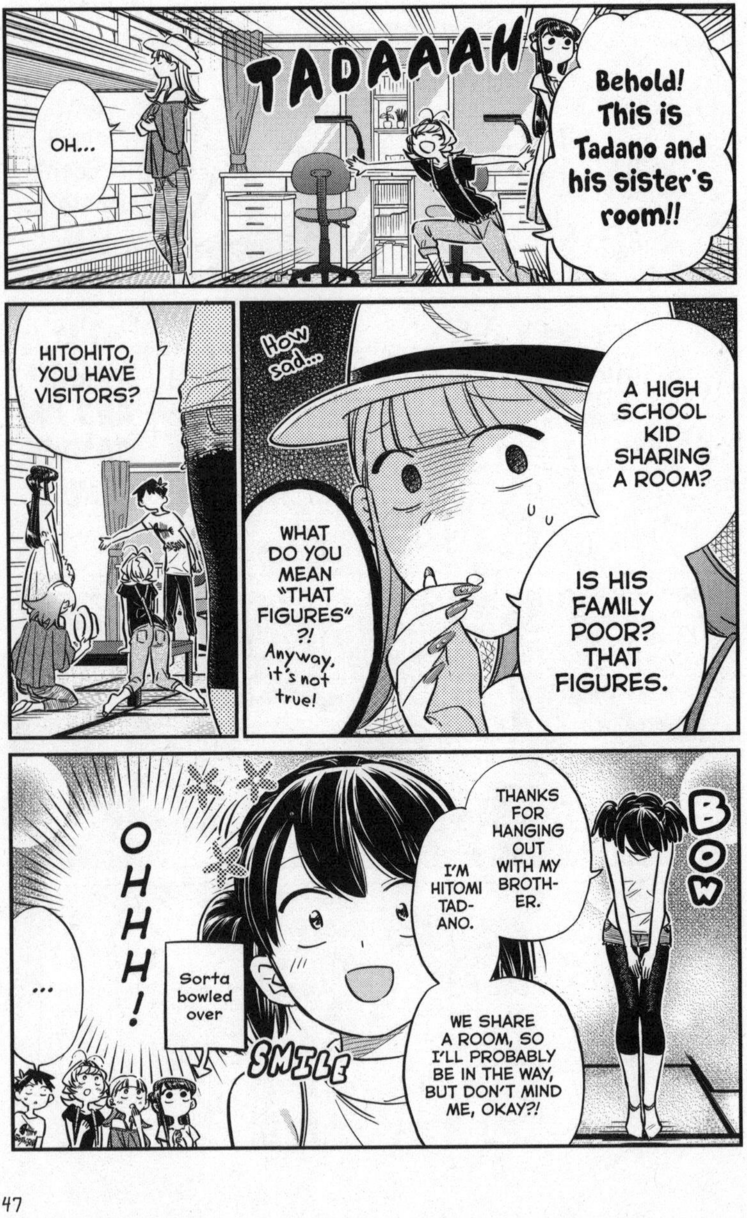
Behold! This is Tadano and his sister's room!!
TADAAAH
OH...
How sad...
A HIGH SCHOOL KID SHARING A ROOM?
IS HIS FAMILY POOR? THAT FIGURES.
WHAT DO YOU MEAN "THAT FIGURES"?! Anyway, it's not true!
HITOHITO, YOU HAVE VISITORS?
BOW
THANKS FOR HANGING OUT WITH MY BROTHER.
I'M HITOMI TADANO.
WE SHARE A ROOM, SO I'LL PROBABLY BE IN THE WAY, BUT DON'T MIND ME, OKAY?!
SMILE
Sorta bowled over
OHHH!
...

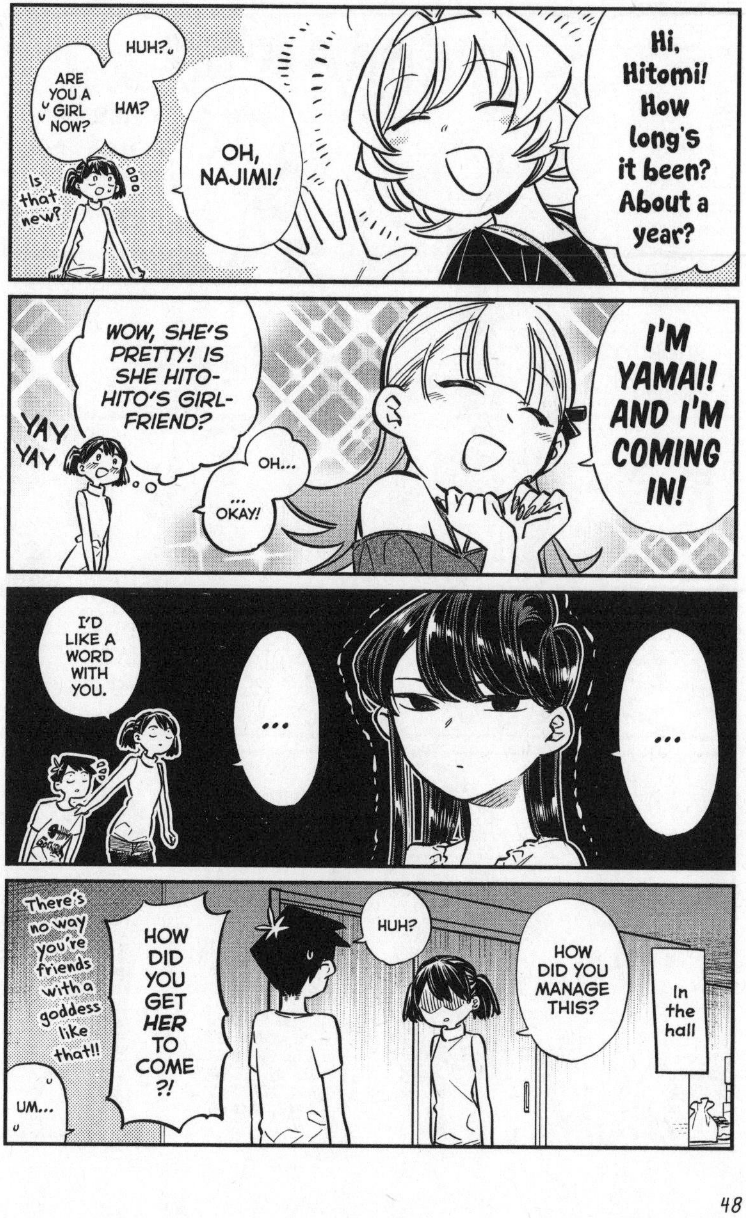
Hi, Hitomi! How long's it been? About a year?
OH, NAJIMI!
HUH?
HM?
ARE YOU A GIRL NOW?
Is that new?
I'M YAMAI! AND I'M COMING IN!
OH... ...OKAY!
WOW, SHE'S PRETTY! IS SHE HITO-HITO'S GIRL-FRIEND?
YAY YAY
...
...
I'D LIKE A WORD WITH YOU.
In the hall
HOW DID YOU MANAGE THIS?
HUH?
HOW DID YOU GET HER TO COME?!
There's no way you're friends with a goddess like that!!
UM...

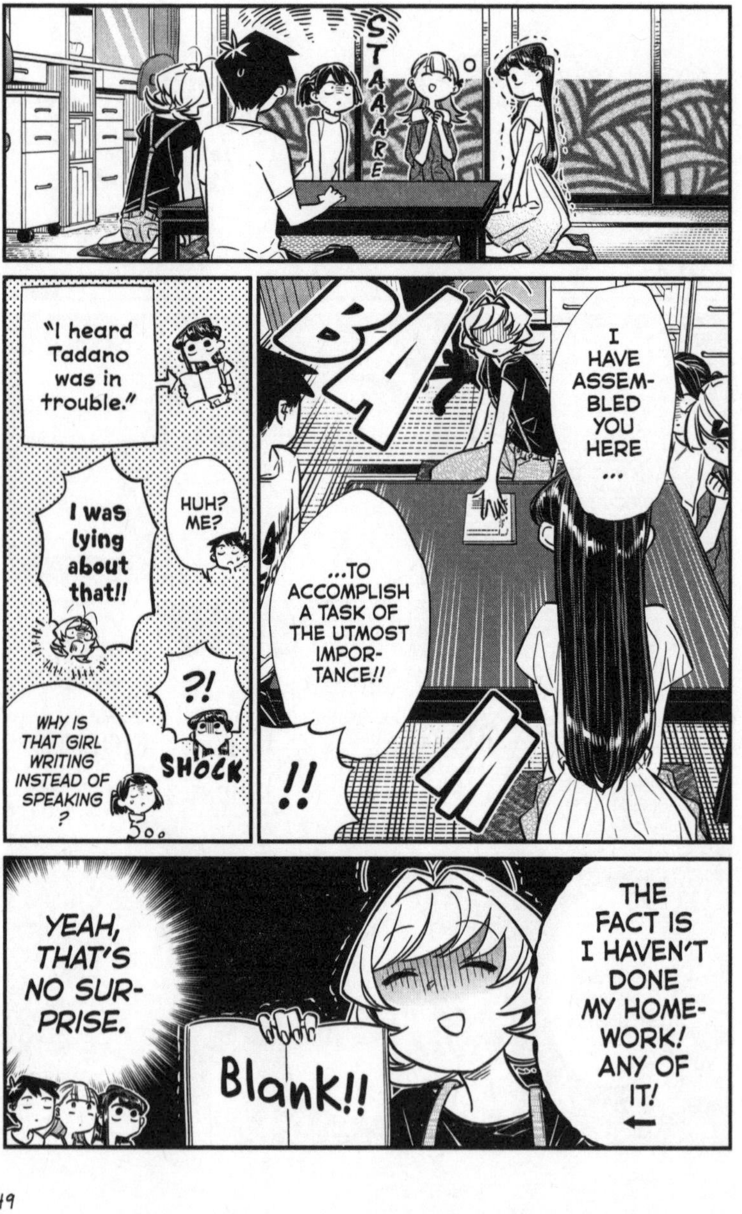
STAAARE
BAM
I HAVE ASSEMBLED YOU HERE...
...TO ACCOMPLISH A TASK OF THE UTMOST IMPORTANCE!!
!!
"I heard Tadano was in trouble."
HUH? ME?
I was lying about that!!
?!
SHOCK
WHY IS THAT GIRL WRITING INSTEAD OF SPEAKING?
THE FACT IS I HAVEN'T DONE MY HOMEWORK! ANY OF IT!
Blank!!
YEAH, THAT'S NO SURPRISE.

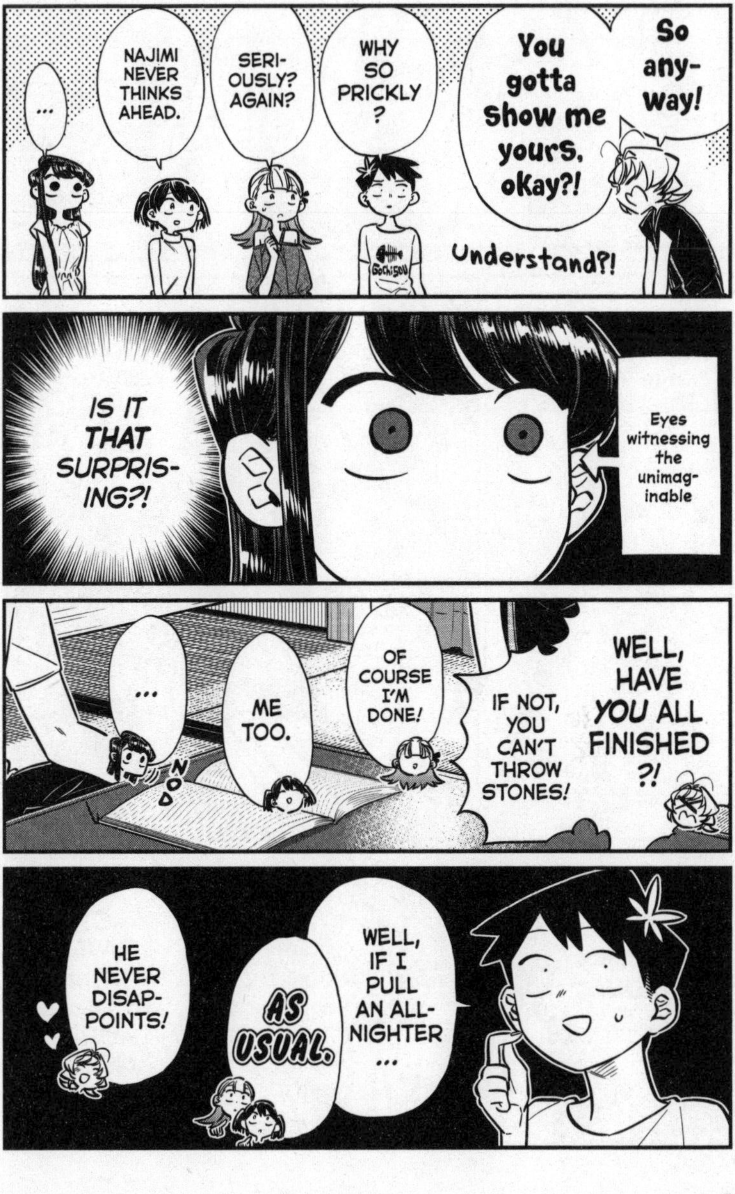
So anyway!
You gotta show me yours, okay?!
Understand?!
WHY SO PRICKLY?
GOCHISOU
SERIOUSLY? AGAIN?
NAJIMI NEVER THINKS AHEAD.
...
Eyes witnessing the unimaginable
IS IT THAT SURPRISING?!
WELL, HAVE YOU ALL FINISHED?!
IF NOT, YOU CAN'T THROW STONES!
OF COURSE I'M DONE!
ME TOO.
...
NOD
WELL, IF I PULL AN ALL-NIGHTER...
AS USUAL.
HE NEVER DISAPPOINTS!

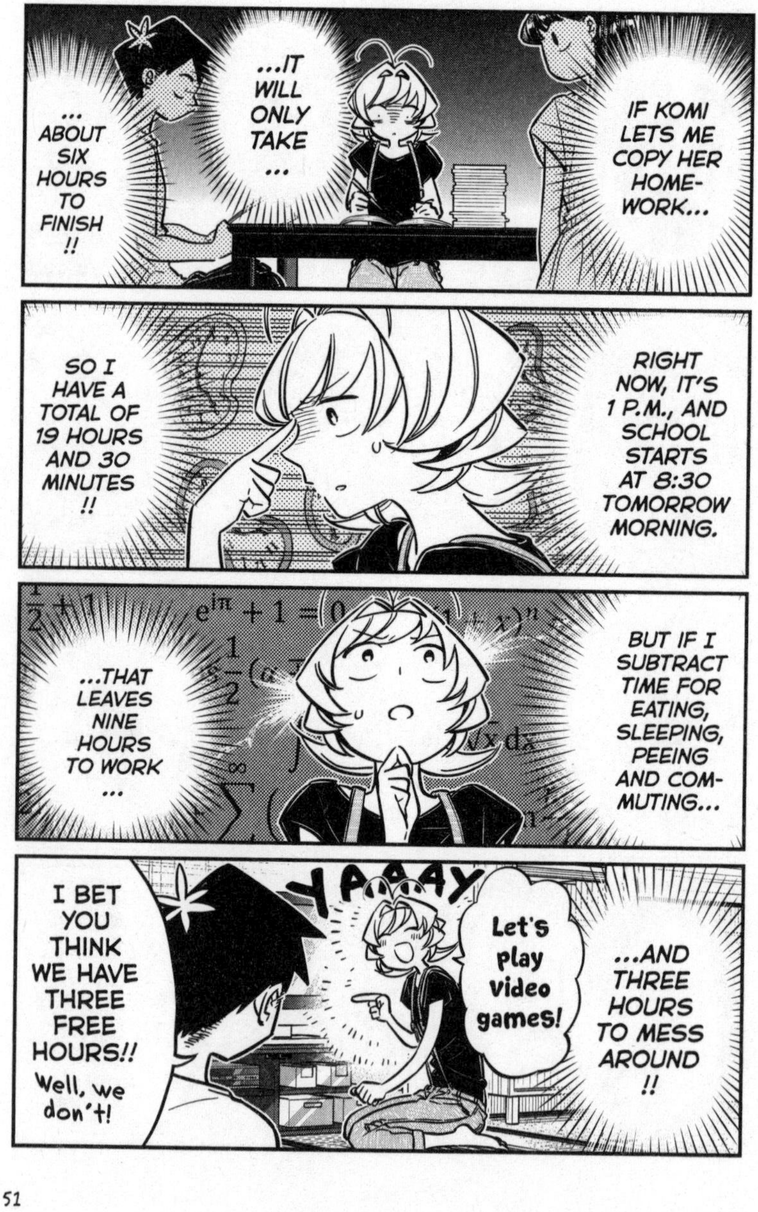
IF KOMI LETS ME COPY HER HOME-WORK...
...IT WILL ONLY TAKE ...
... ABOUT SIX HOURS TO FINISH !!
RIGHT NOW, IT'S 1 P.M., AND SCHOOL STARTS AT 8:30 TOMORROW MORNING.
SO I HAVE A TOTAL OF 19 HOURS AND 30 MINUTES !!
BUT IF I SUBTRACT TIME FOR EATING, SLEEPING, PEEING AND COM-MUTING...
...THAT LEAVES NINE HOURS TO WORK ...
...AND THREE HOURS TO MESS AROUND !!
Let's play video games!
YAAAY
I BET YOU THINK WE HAVE THREE FREE HOURS!!
Well, we don't!

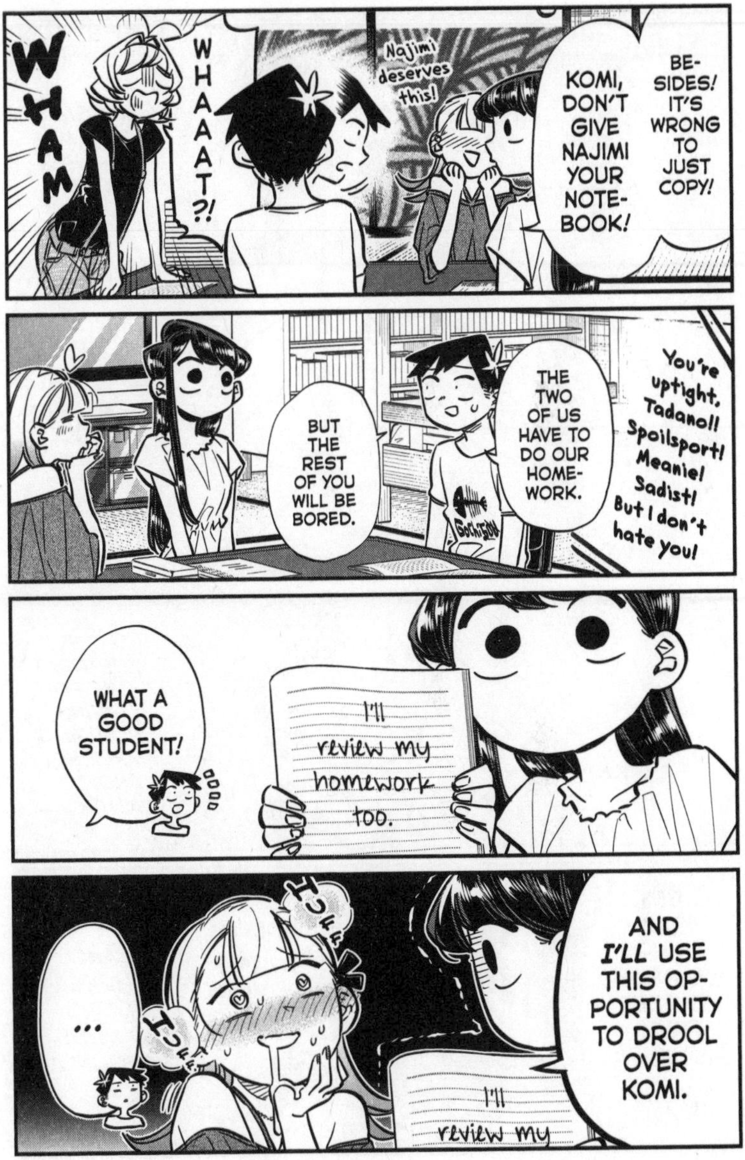
BE-SIDES! IT'S WRONG TO JUST COPY!
KOMI, DON'T GIVE NAJIMI YOUR NOTE-BOOK!
Najimi deserves this!
WHAAAAT?!
WHAM
You're uptight, Tadano!! Spoilsport! Meanie! Sadist! But I don't hate you!
THE TWO OF US HAVE TO DO OUR HOME-WORK.
BUT THE REST OF YOU WILL BE BORED.
I'll review my homework too.
WHAT A GOOD STUDENT!
AND I'LL USE THIS OP-PORTUNITY TO DROOL OVER KOMI.
I'll review my
HUFF
HUFF
...

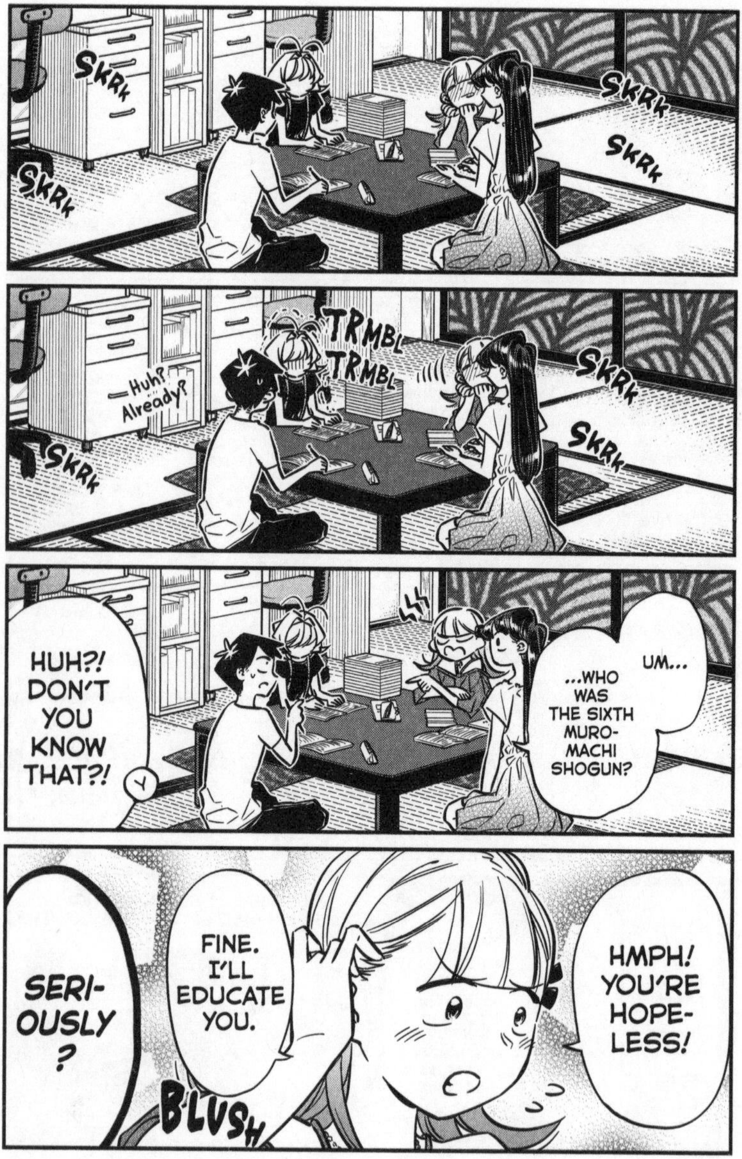
SKRK
SKRK
SKRK
SKRK
SKRK
SKRK
TRMBL TRMBL
—Huh? ...Already?
SKRK
UM... ...WHO WAS THE SIXTH MURO-MACHI SHOGUN?
HUH?! DON'T YOU KNOW THAT?!
HMPH! YOU'RE HOPE-LESS!
FINE. I'LL EDUCATE YOU.
SERI-OUSLY?
BLUSH

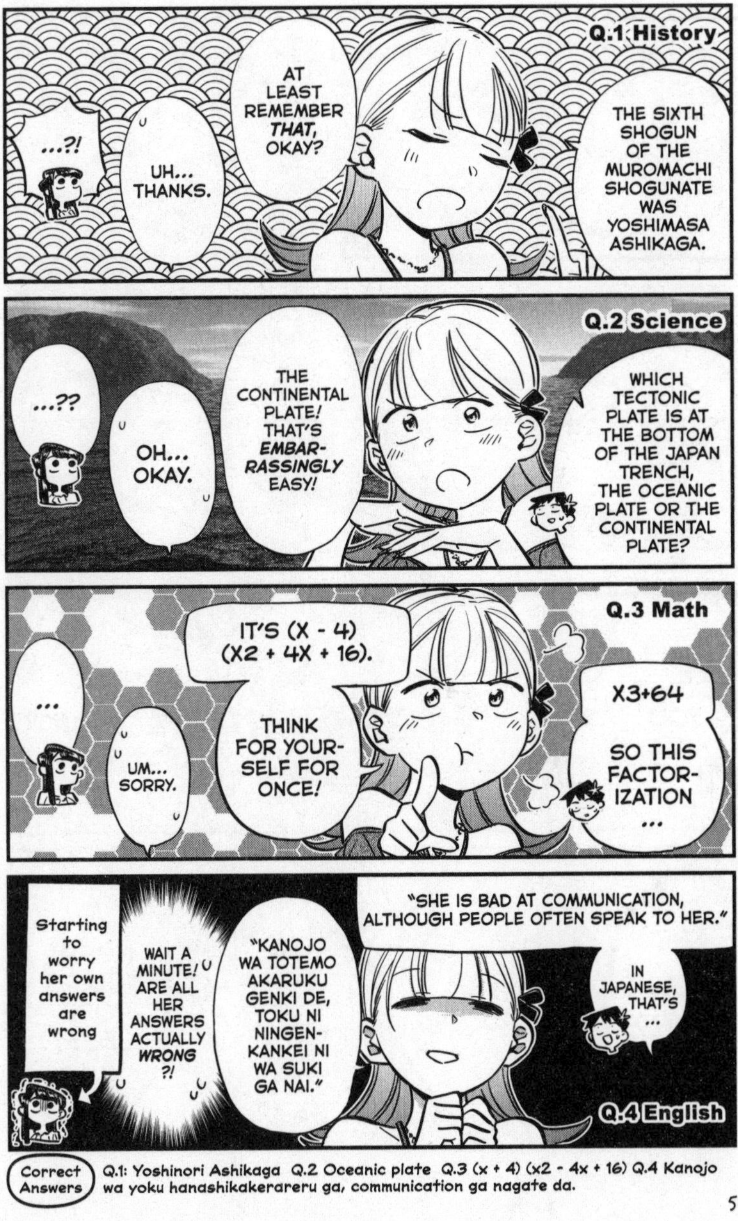
Q.1 History
THE SIXTH SHOGUN OF THE MUROMACHI SHOGUNATE WAS YOSHIMASA ASHIKAGA.
AT LEAST REMEMBER *THAT*, OKAY?
UH... THANKS.
...?!
Q.2 Science
WHICH TECTONIC PLATE IS AT THE BOTTOM OF THE JAPAN TRENCH, THE OCEANIC PLATE OR THE CONTINENTAL PLATE?
THE CONTINENTAL PLATE! THAT'S *EMBARRASSINGLY* EASY!
OH... OKAY.
...??
Q.3 Math
X3+64
SO THIS FACTORIZATION...
IT'S (X - 4) (X2 + 4X + 16).
THINK FOR YOURSELF FOR ONCE!
UM... SORRY.
...
Q.4 English
"SHE IS BAD AT COMMUNICATION, ALTHOUGH PEOPLE OFTEN SPEAK TO HER."
IN JAPANESE, THAT'S...
"KANOJO WA TOTEMO AKARUKU GENKI DE, TOKU NI NINGEN-KANKEI NI WA SUKI GA NAI."
WAIT A MINUTE! ARE ALL HER ANSWERS ACTUALLY *WRONG* ?!
Starting to worry her own answers are wrong

Correct Answers Q.1: Yoshinori Ashikaga Q.2 Oceanic plate Q.3 (x + 4) (x2 - 4x + 16) Q.4 Kanojo wa yoku hanashikakerareru ga, communication ga nagate da.

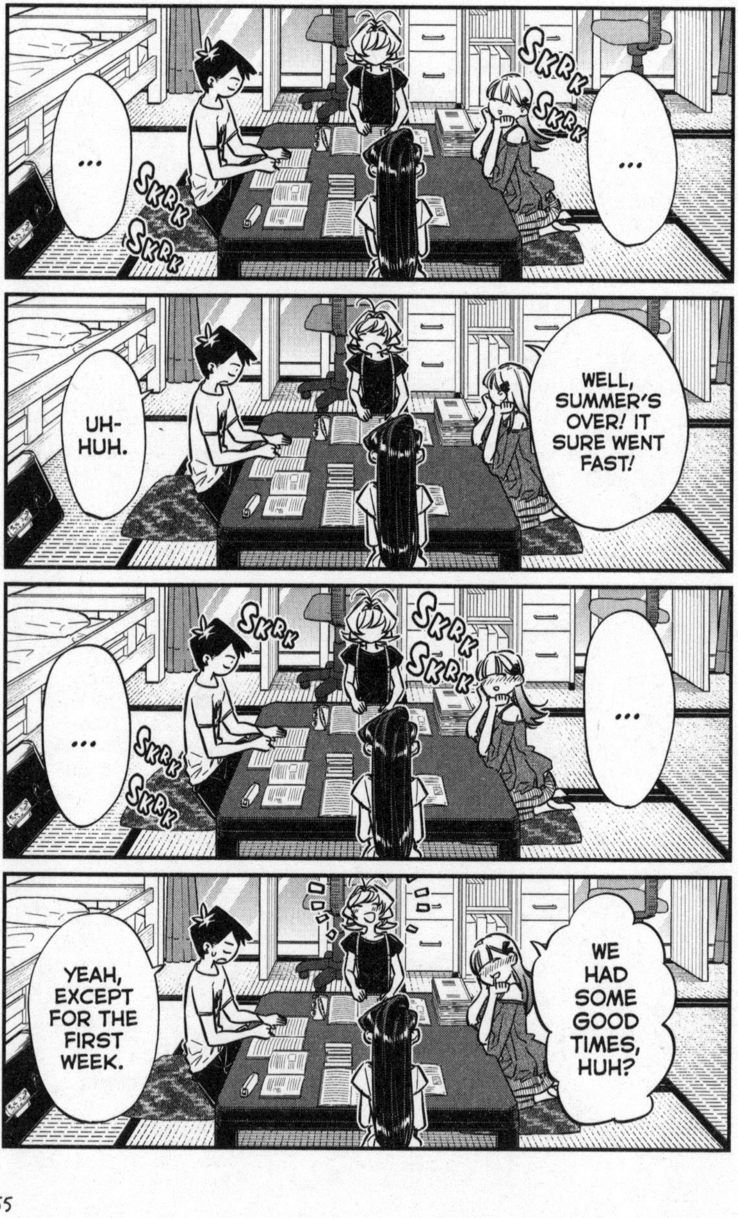
SKRK
SKRK
...
...
SKRK
SKRK
WELL, SUMMER'S OVER! IT SURE WENT FAST!
UH-HUH.
SKRK
SKRK
...
SKRK
...
SKRK
SKRK
WE HAD SOME GOOD TIMES, HUH?
YEAH, EXCEPT FOR THE FIRST WEEK.

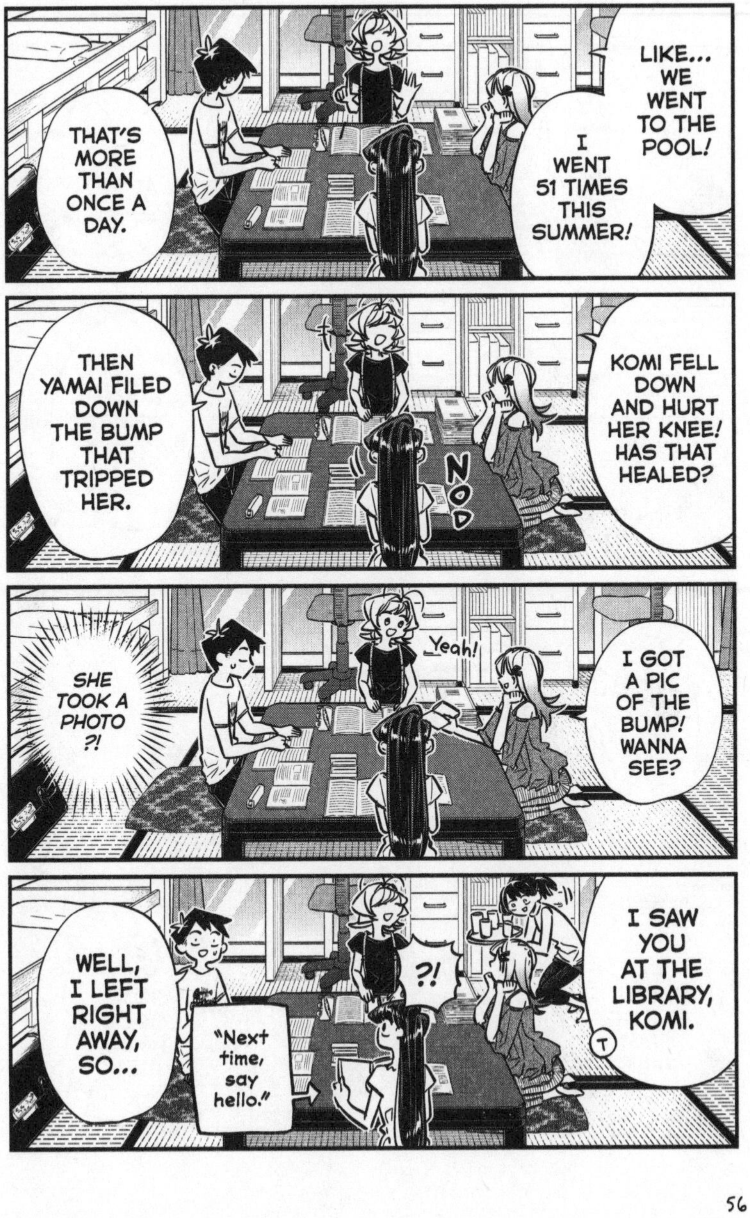
LIKE... WE WENT TO THE POOL!
I WENT 51 TIMES THIS SUMMER!
THAT'S MORE THAN ONCE A DAY.
KOMI FELL DOWN AND HURT HER KNEE! HAS THAT HEALED?
NOD
THEN YAMAI FILED DOWN THE BUMP THAT TRIPPED HER.
I GOT A PIC OF THE BUMP! WANNA SEE?
Yeah!
SHE TOOK A PHOTO ?!
I SAW YOU AT THE LIBRARY, KOMI.
?!
"Next time, say hello."
WELL, I LEFT RIGHT AWAY, SO...

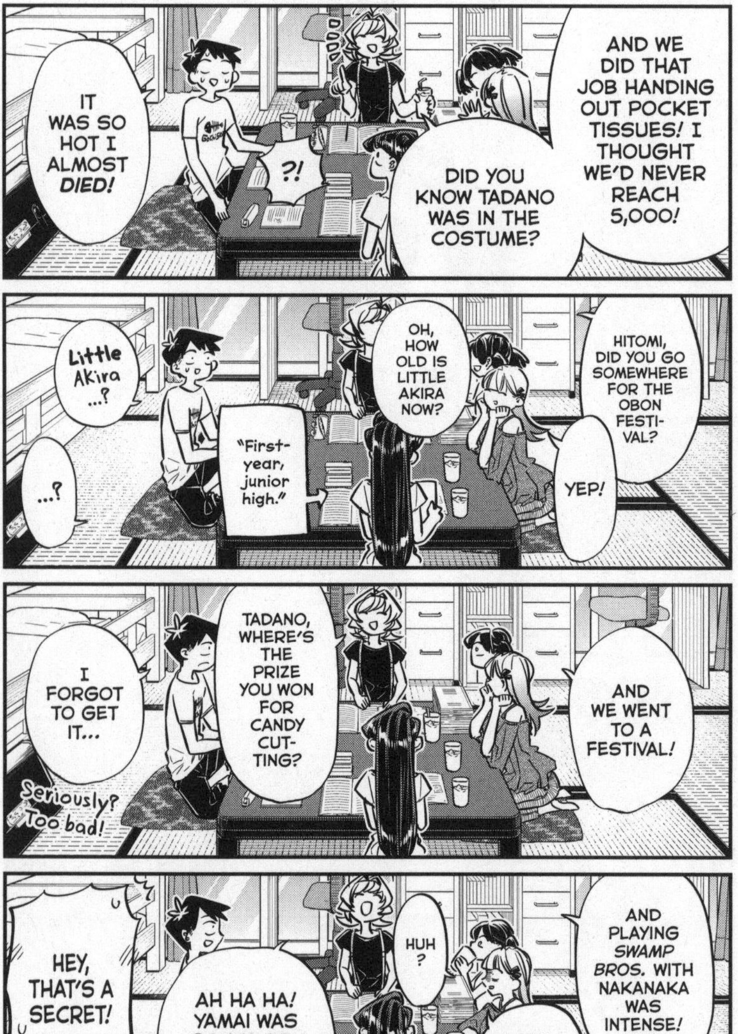
AND WE DID THAT JOB HANDING OUT POCKET TISSUES! I THOUGHT WE'D NEVER REACH 5,000!
DID YOU KNOW TADANO WAS IN THE COSTUME?
?!
IT WAS SO HOT I ALMOST *DIED!*
HITOMI, DID YOU GO SOMEWHERE FOR THE OBON FESTIVAL?
OH, HOW OLD IS LITTLE AKIRA NOW?
YEP!
"First-year, junior high."
Little Akira...?
...?
AND WE WENT TO A FESTIVAL!
TADANO, WHERE'S THE PRIZE YOU WON FOR CANDY CUTTING?
I FORGOT TO GET IT...
Seriously? Too bad!
AND PLAYING *SWAMP BROS.* WITH NAKANAKA WAS INTENSE!
HUH?
YOU GUYS WENT TO NAKANAKA'S?
AH HA HA! YAMAI WAS GONNA ASK KOMI OUT, BUT IT NEVER HAPPENED!
HEY, THAT'S A SECRET!
AH HA HA

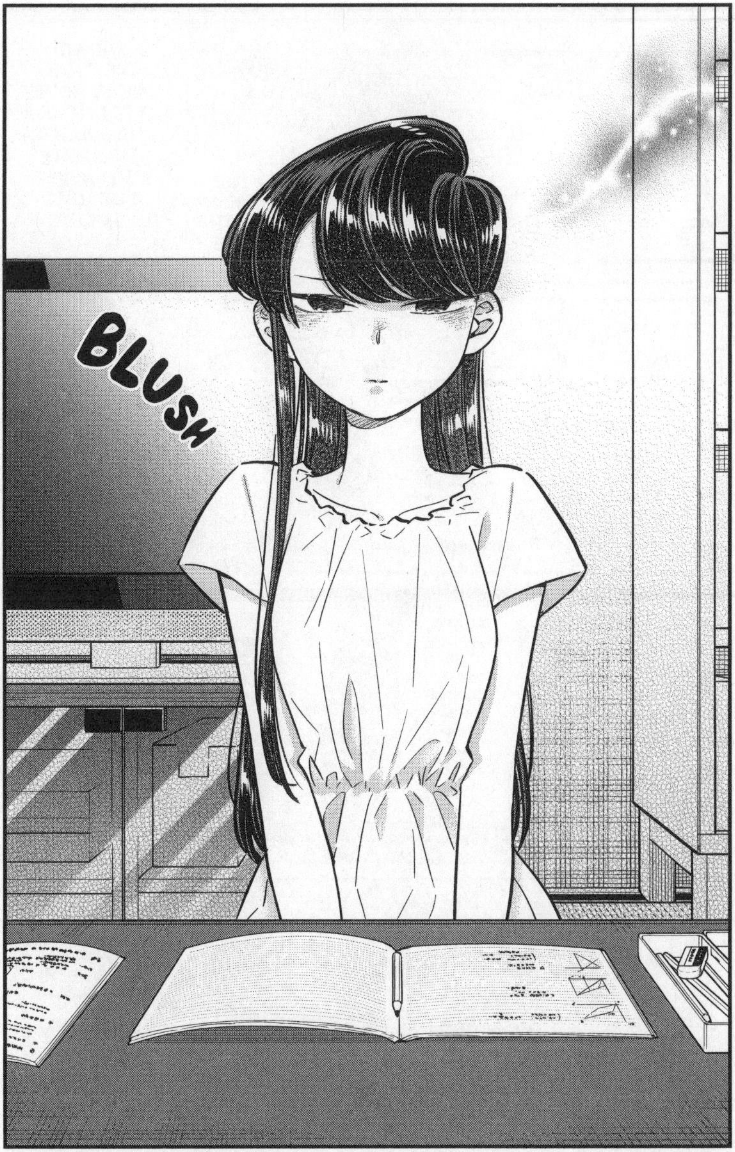
BLUSH

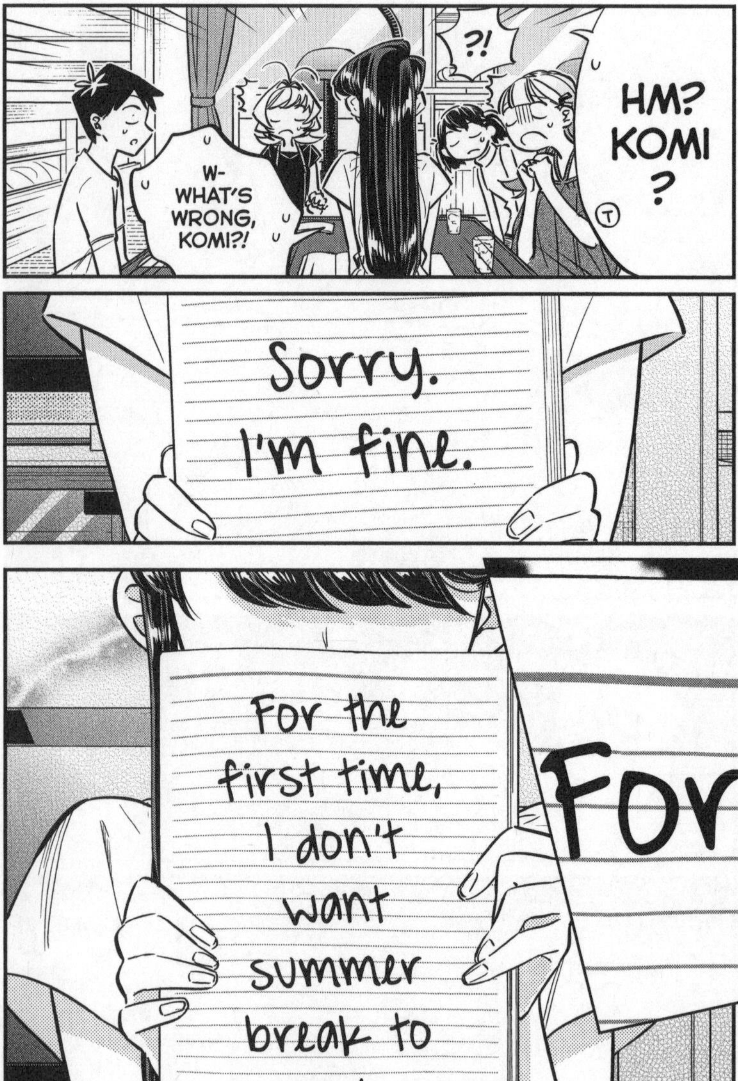
HM? KOMI ?
?!
W- WHAT'S WRONG, KOMI?!
Sorry. I'm fine.
For
For the first time, I don't want summer break to end.

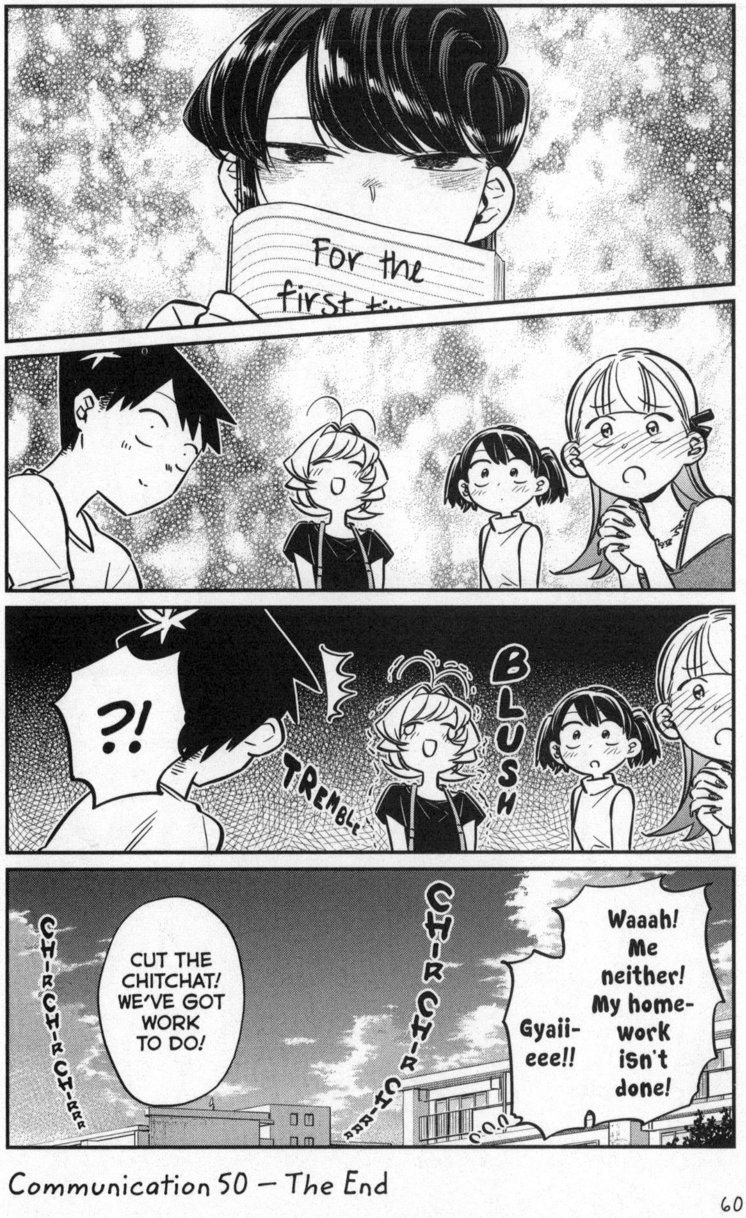
For the
first
BLUSH
TREMBLE
?!
Waaah! Me neither! My home-work isn't done!
Gyaii-eee!!
CHIR-CHIR-CHIR-CHIRRR
CUT THE CHITCHAT! WE'VE GOT WORK TO DO!
CHIR-CHIR-CHIR-CHIRRR

Communication 50 — The End

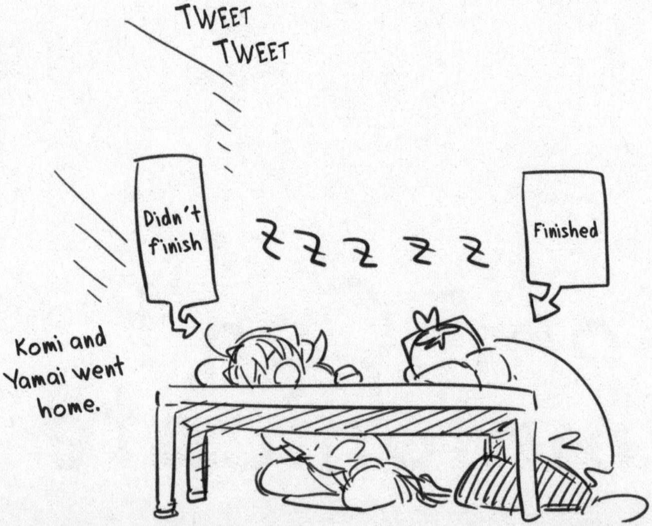
TWEET
TWEET
Finished
ZZZZZ
Didn't finish
Komi and Yamai went home.

Komi Can't
Communicate

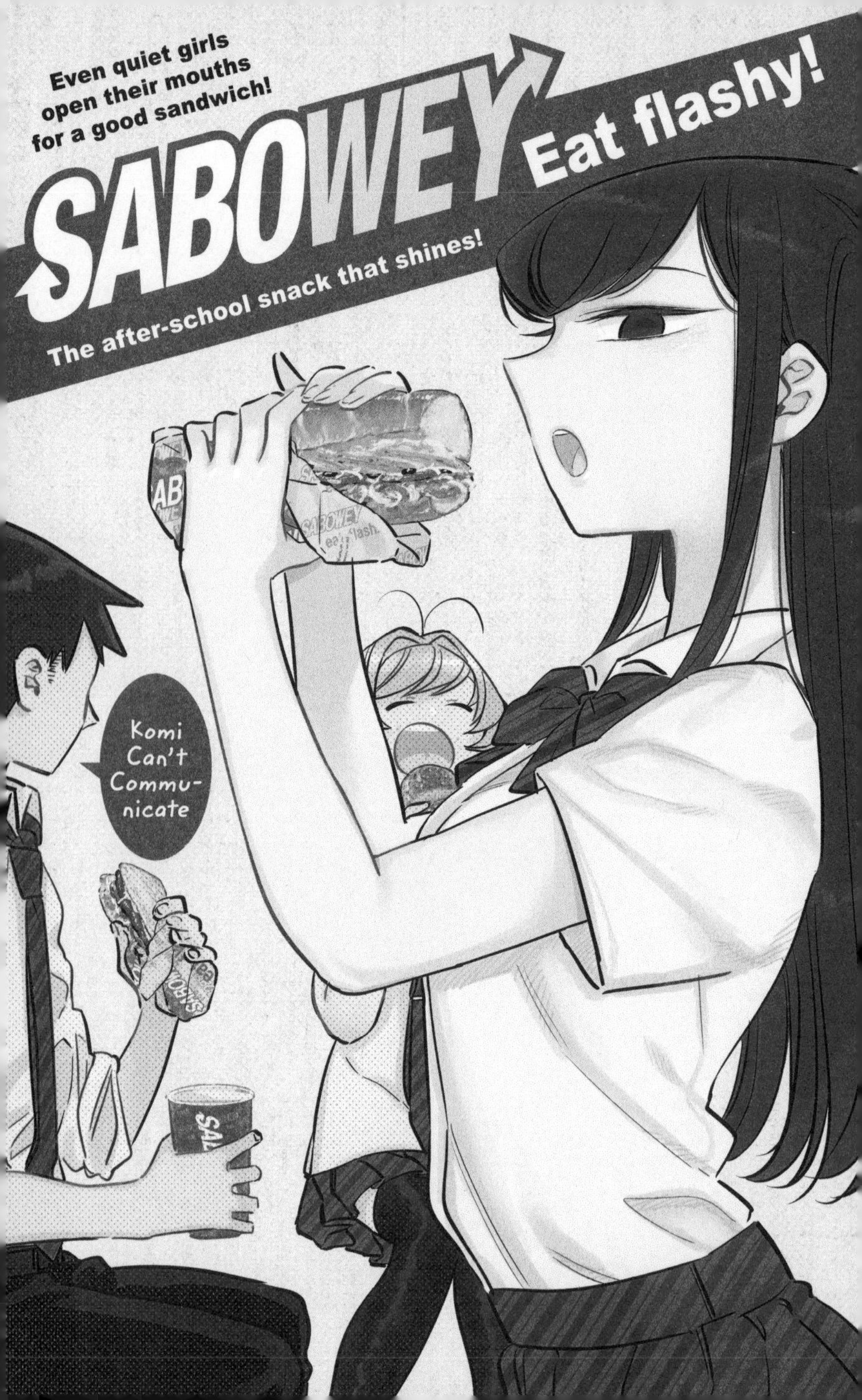
Even quiet girls open their mouths for a good sandwich!
SABOWEY
Eat flashy!
The after-school snack that shines!
Komi Can't Communicate
SABOWEY eat flash.

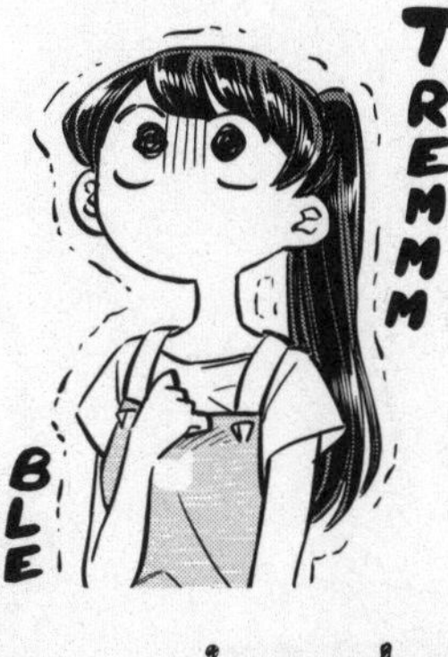
TREMMM
BLE

Komi Can't Communicate

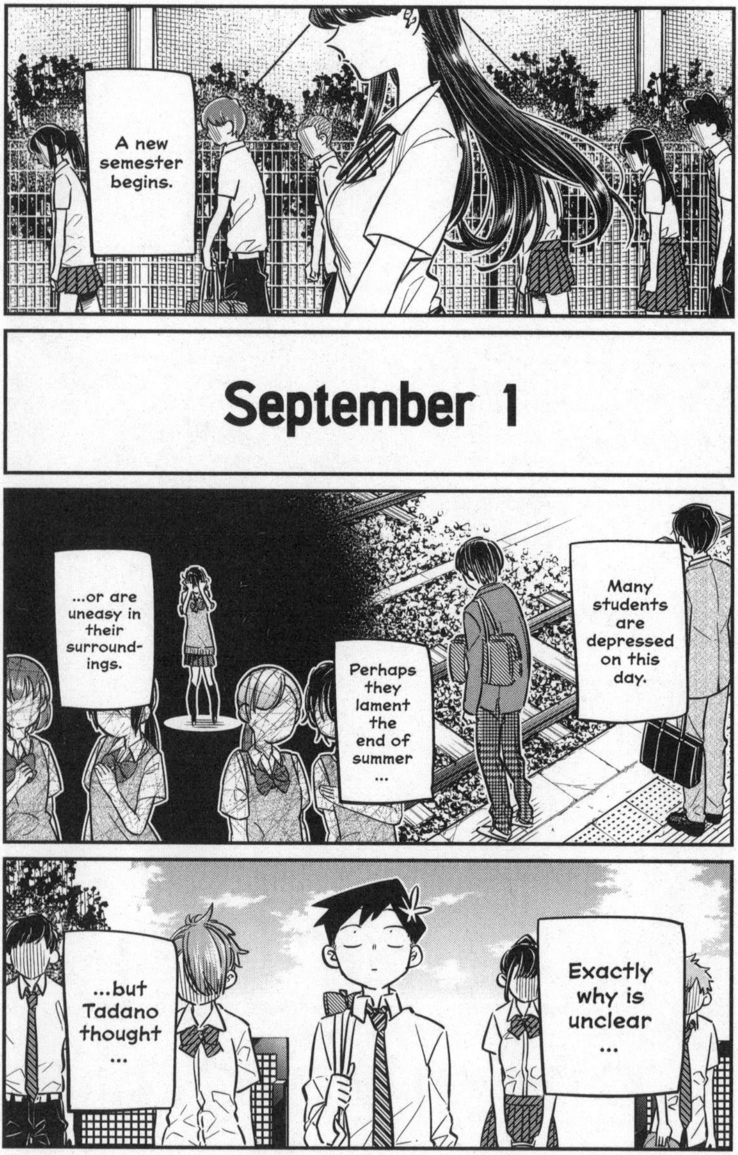
A new semester begins.
September 1
Many students are depressed on this day.
Perhaps they lament the end of summer...
...or are uneasy in their surroundings.
Exactly why is unclear...
...but Tadano thought...

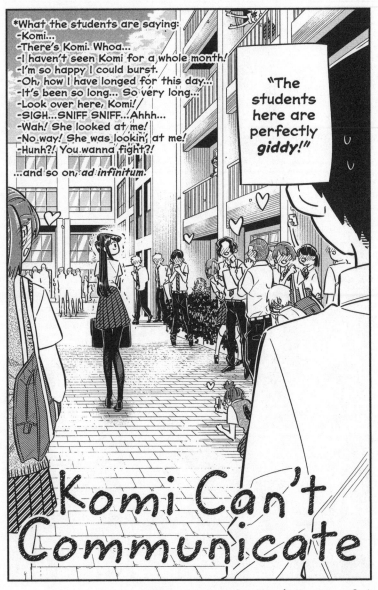

"The students here are perfectly *giddy!*"
*What the students are saying:
-Komi...
-There's Komi. Whoa...
-I haven't seen Komi for a whole month!
-I'm so happy I could burst.
-Oh, how I have longed for this day...
-It's been so long... So very long...
-Look over here, Komi!
-SIGH...SNIFF SNIFF...Ahhh...
-Wah! She looked at me!
-No way! She was lookin' at me!
-Hunh?! You wanna fight?!
...and so on, *ad infinitum.*
Komi Can't Communicate

Communication 51: A Country Girl

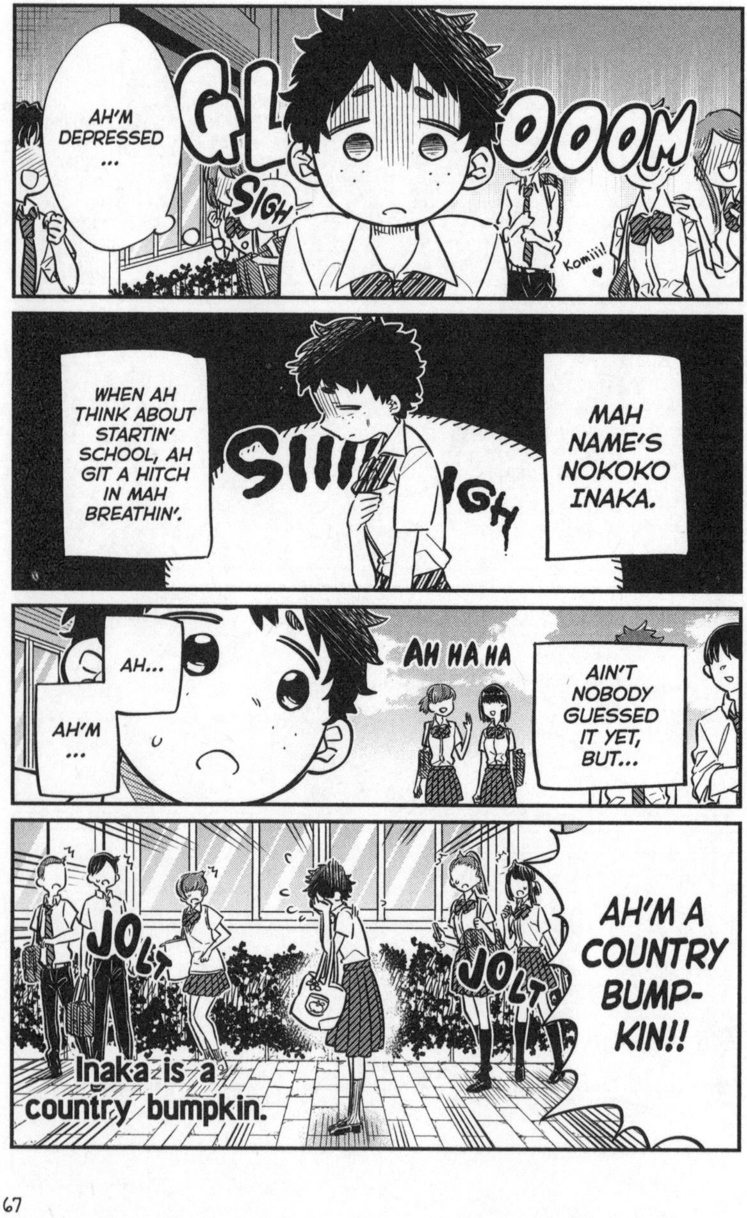
GLOOOM
Komiii!
AH'M DEPRESSED ...
SIGH
MAH NAME'S NOKOKO INAKA.
SIIIIGH
WHEN AH THINK ABOUT STARTIN' SCHOOL, AH GIT A HITCH IN MAH BREATHIN'.
AIN'T NOBODY GUESSED IT YET, BUT...
AH HA HA
AH...
AH'M ...
AH'M A COUNTRY BUMP-KIN!!
JOLT
JOLT
Inaka is a country bumpkin.

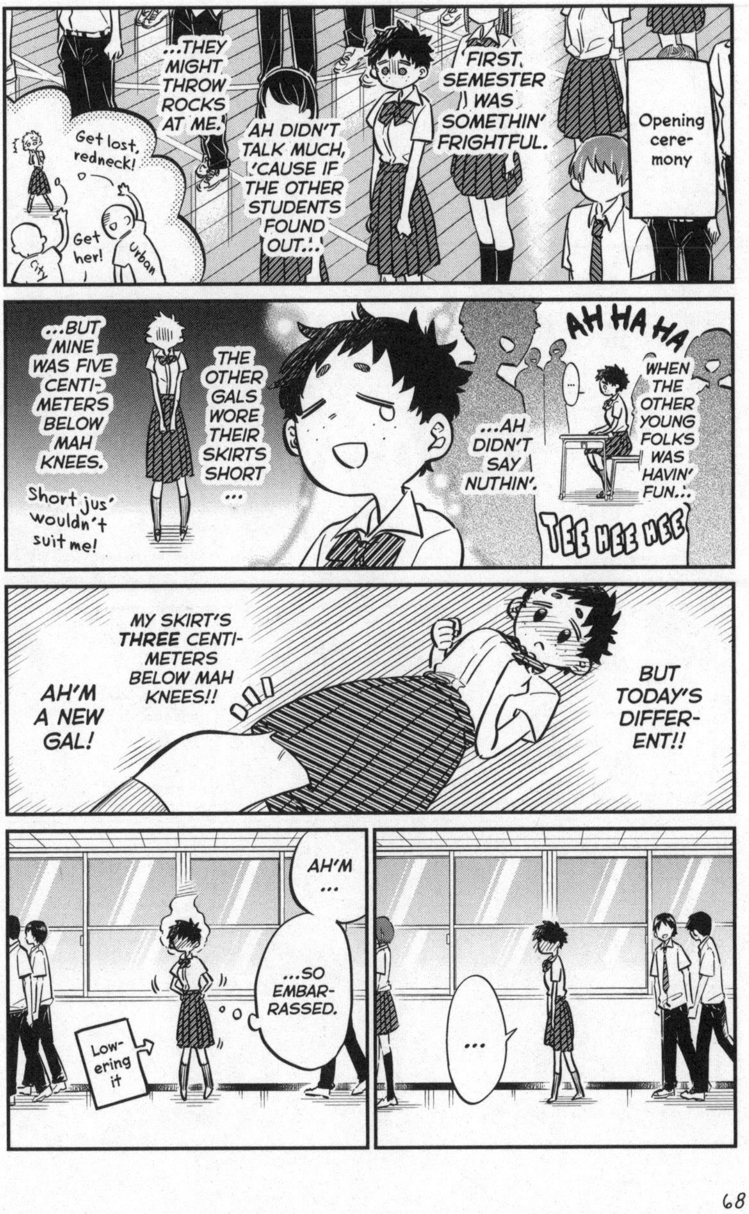
Opening ceremony
FIRST SEMESTER WAS SOMETHIN' FRIGHTFUL.
AH DIDN'T TALK MUCH, 'CAUSE IF THE OTHER STUDENTS FOUND OUT...
...THEY MIGHT THROW ROCKS AT ME.
Get lost, redneck!
Get her!
Urban
City
AH HA HA
WHEN THE OTHER YOUNG FOLKS WAS HAVIN' FUN...
...
...AH DIDN'T SAY NUTHIN'.
TEE HEE HEE
THE OTHER GALS WORE THEIR SKIRTS SHORT...
...BUT MINE WAS FIVE CENTIMETERS BELOW MAH KNEES.
Short jus' wouldn't suit me!
BUT TODAY'S DIFFERENT!!
MY SKIRT'S **THREE** CENTIMETERS BELOW MAH KNEES!!
AH'M A NEW GAL!
...
AH'M ...
...SO EMBARRASSED.
Lowering it

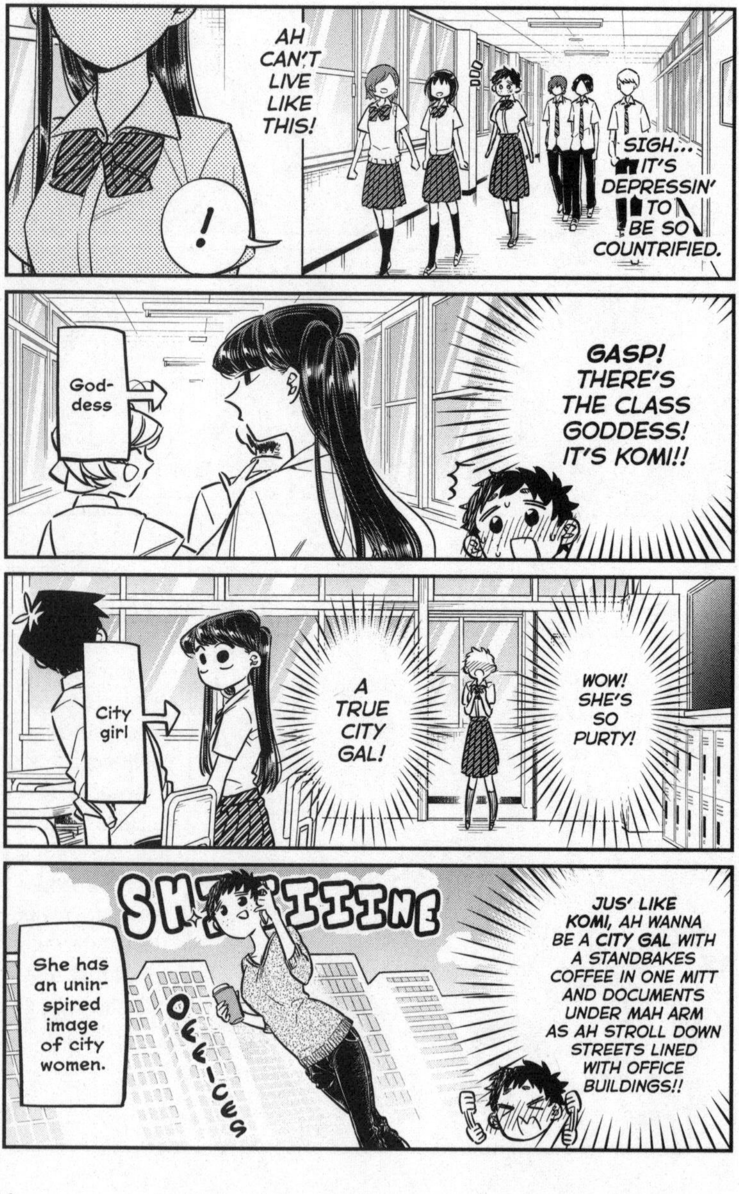
AH CAN'T LIVE LIKE THIS!
SIGH... IT'S DEPRESSIN' TO BE SO COUNTRIFIED.
!
GASP! THERE'S THE CLASS GODDESS! IT'S KOMI!!
God-dess
WOW! SHE'S SO PURTY!
A TRUE CITY GAL!
City girl
JUS' LIKE KOMI, AH WANNA BE A CITY GAL WITH A STANDBAKES COFFEE IN ONE MITT AND DOCUMENTS UNDER MAH ARM AS AH STROLL DOWN STREETS LINED WITH OFFICE BUILDINGS!!
SH IIIINE
OFFICES
She has an unin-spired image of city women.

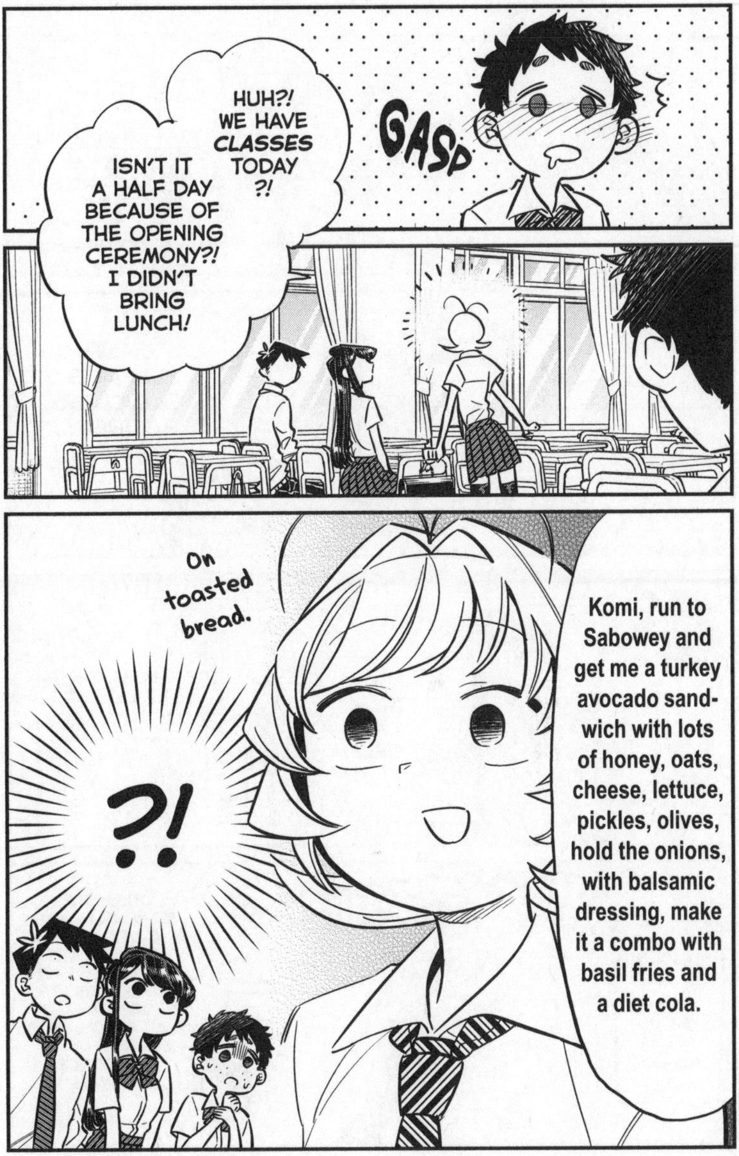
GASP
HUH?! WE HAVE CLASSES TODAY?!
ISN'T IT A HALF DAY BECAUSE OF THE OPENING CEREMONY?! I DIDN'T BRING LUNCH!
Komi, run to Sabowey and get me a turkey avocado sandwich with lots of honey, oats, cheese, lettuce, pickles, olives, hold the onions, with balsamic dressing, make it a combo with basil fries and a diet cola.
On toasted bread.
?!

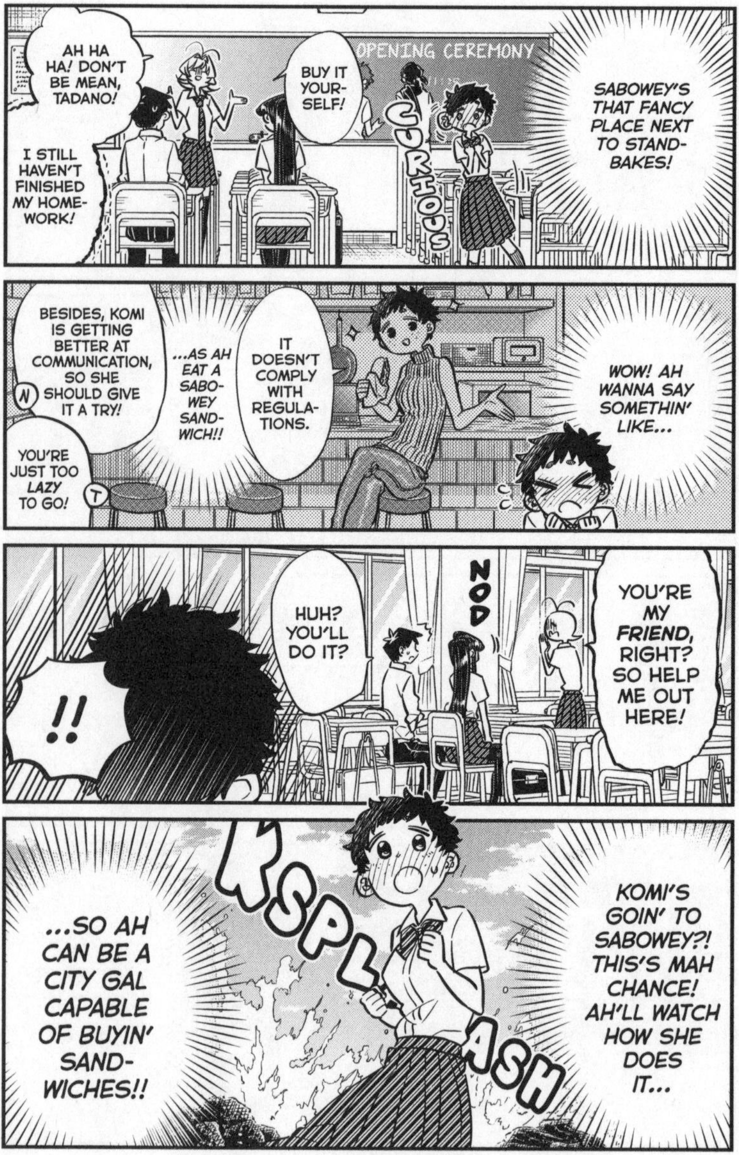

SABOWEY'S THAT FANCY PLACE NEXT TO STAND-BAKES!
OPENING CEREMONY
CURIOUS
BUY IT YOURSELF!
AH HA HA! DON'T BE MEAN, TADANO!
I STILL HAVEN'T FINISHED MY HOMEWORK!
WOW! AH WANNA SAY SOMETHIN' LIKE...
IT DOESN'T COMPLY WITH REGULATIONS.
...AS AH EAT A SABOWEY SANDWICH!!
BESIDES, KOMI IS GETTING BETTER AT COMMUNICATION, SO SHE SHOULD GIVE IT A TRY!
N
YOU'RE JUST TOO *LAZY* TO GO!
T
YOU'RE MY *FRIEND*, RIGHT? SO HELP ME OUT HERE!
NOD
HUH? YOU'LL DO IT?
!!
KOMI'S GOIN' TO SABOWEY?! THIS'S MAH CHANCE! AH'LL WATCH HOW SHE DOES IT...
KSPLASH
...SO AH CAN BE A CITY GAL CAPABLE OF BUYIN' SANDWICHES!!

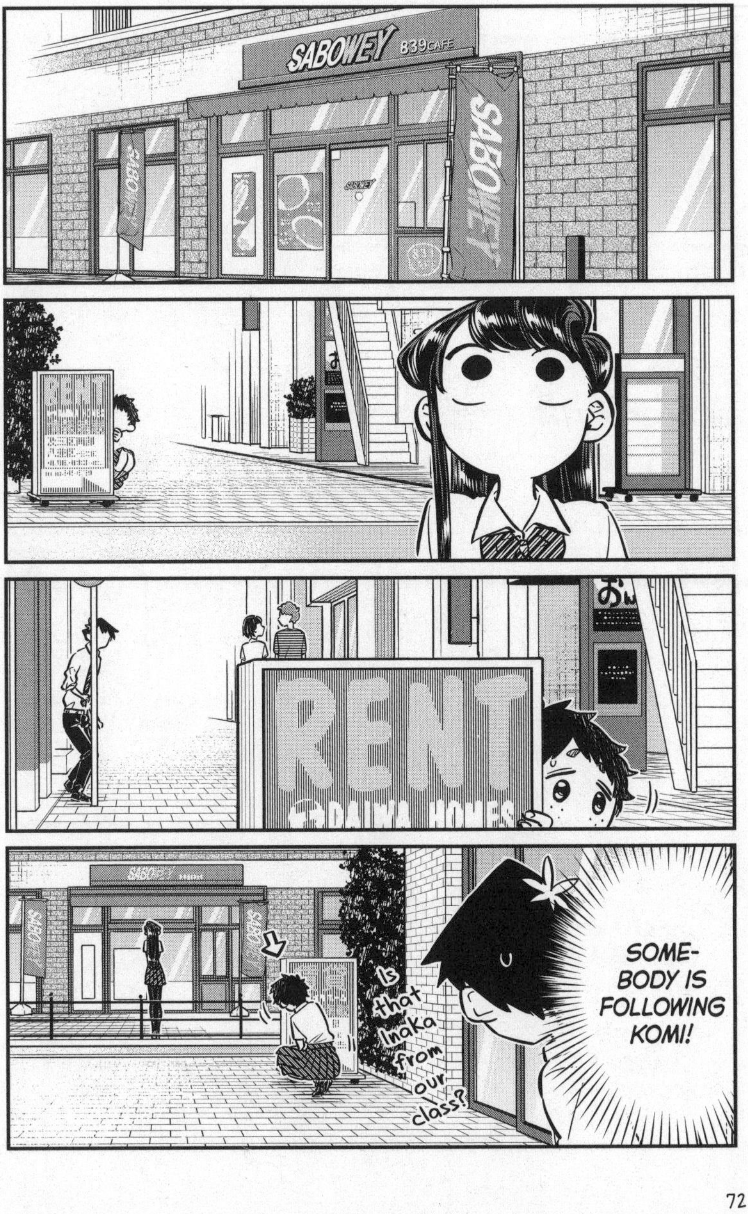

SABOWEY
839CAFE
SABOWEY
RENT
DAIWA HOMES
SOME-BODY IS FOLLOWING KOMI!
Is that Inaka from our class?

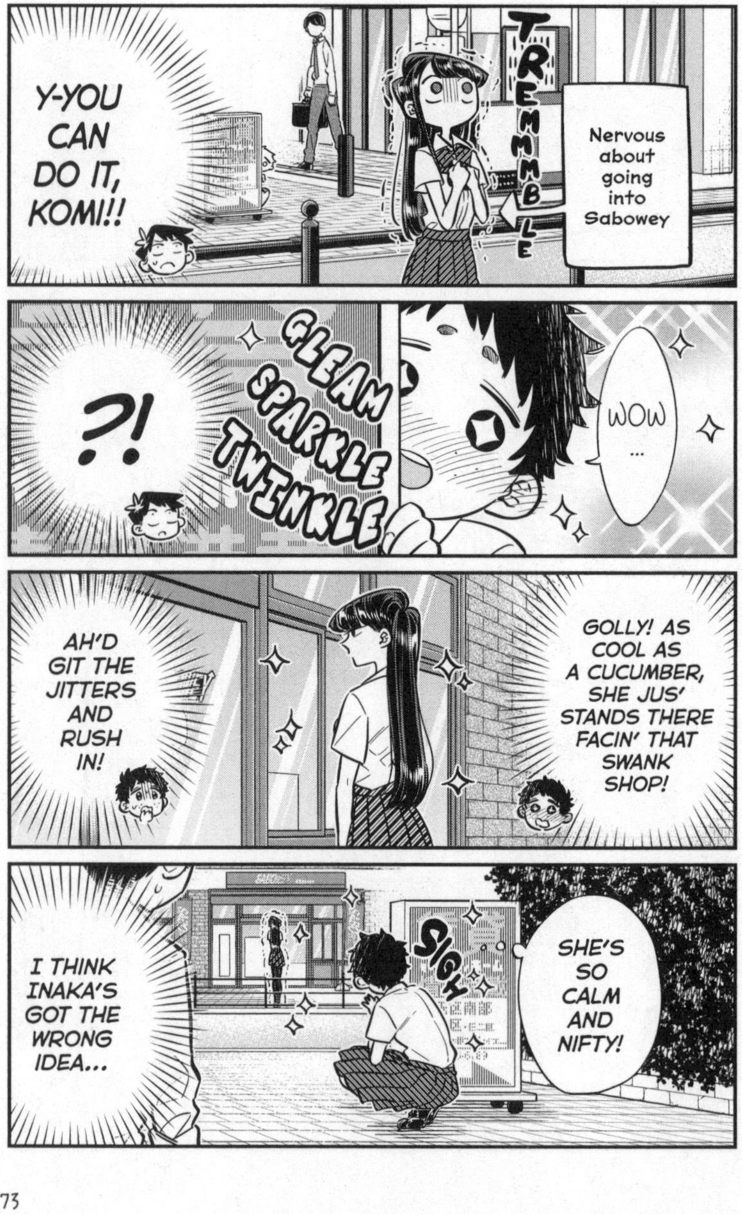
TREMMMBLE
Nervous about going into Sabowey
Y-YOU CAN DO IT, KOMI!!
WOW ...
GLEAM SPARKLE TWINKLE
?!
GOLLY! AS COOL AS A CUCUMBER, SHE JUS' STANDS THERE FACIN' THAT SWANK SHOP!
AH'D GIT THE JITTERS AND RUSH IN!
SHE'S SO CALM AND NIFTY!
SIGH
I THINK INAKA'S GOT THE WRONG IDEA...

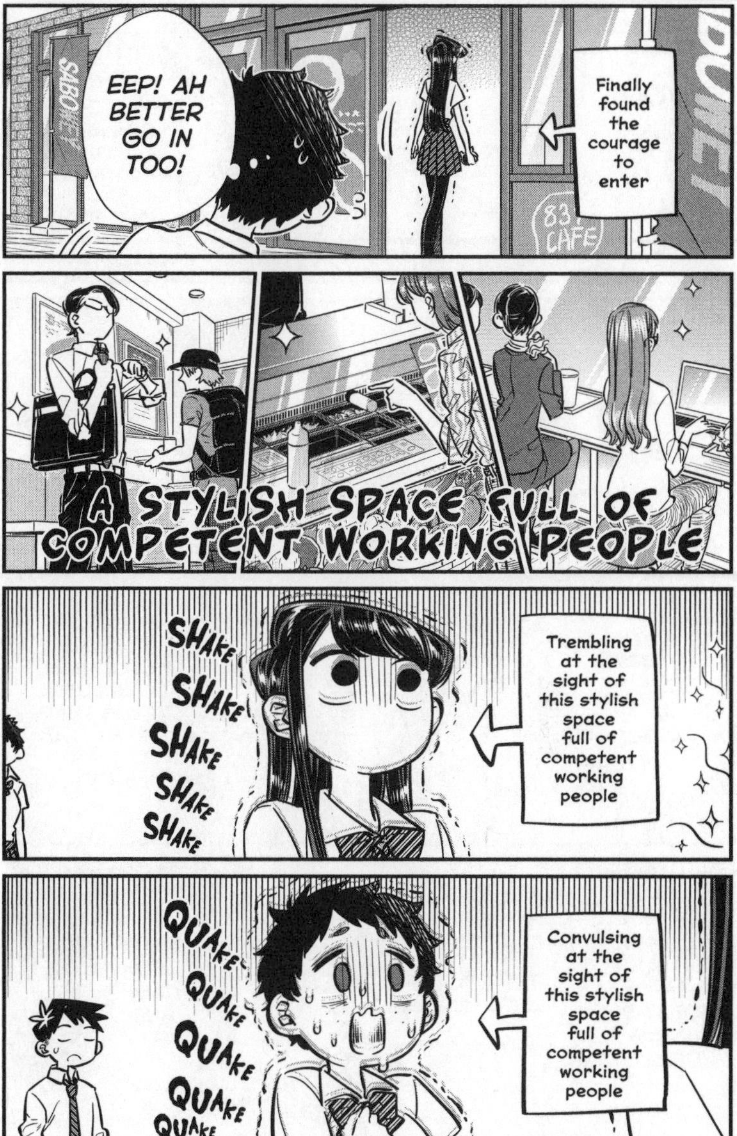
Finally found the courage to enter
EEP! AH BETTER GO IN TOO!
A STYLISH SPACE FULL OF COMPETENT WORKING PEOPLE
Trembling at the sight of this stylish space full of competent working people
SHAKE SHAKE SHAKE SHAKE SHAKE
Convulsing at the sight of this stylish space full of competent working people
QUAKE QUAKE QUAKE QUAKE QUAKE

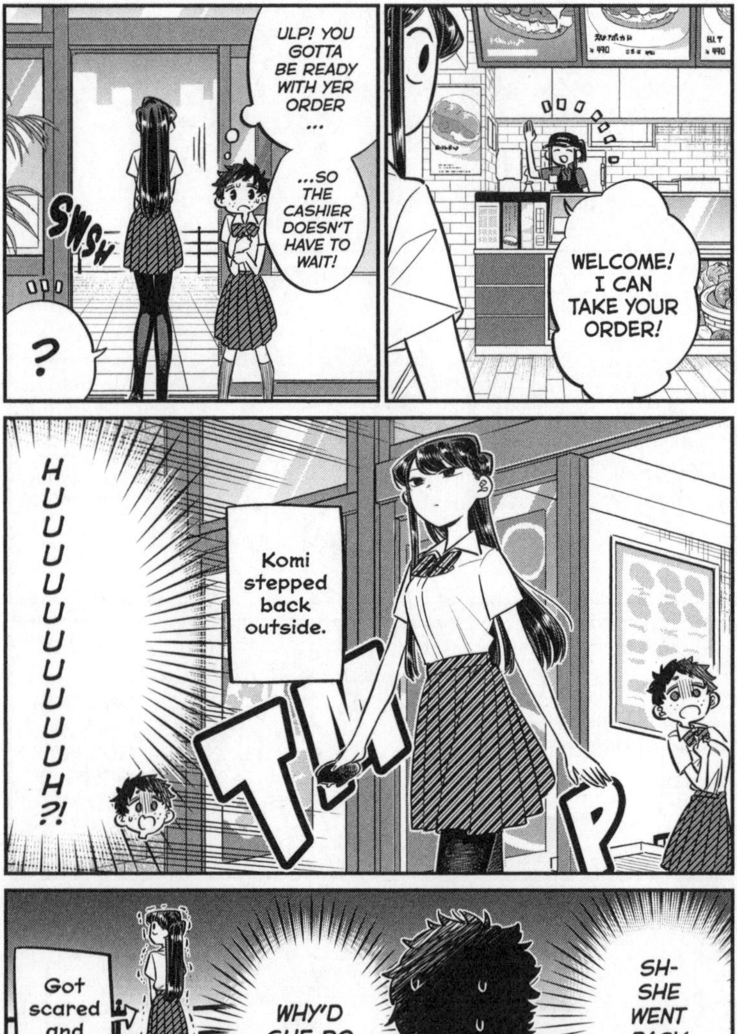
BLT
¥490
WELCOME! I CAN TAKE YOUR ORDER!
ULP! YOU GOTTA BE READY WITH YER ORDER ...
...SO THE CASHIER DOESN'T HAVE TO WAIT!
SWSH
?
Komi stepped back outside.
TMP
HUUUUUUUUUUUUH?!
SH-SHE WENT BACK OUT?!
WHY'D SHE DO THAT?!
Got scared and fled

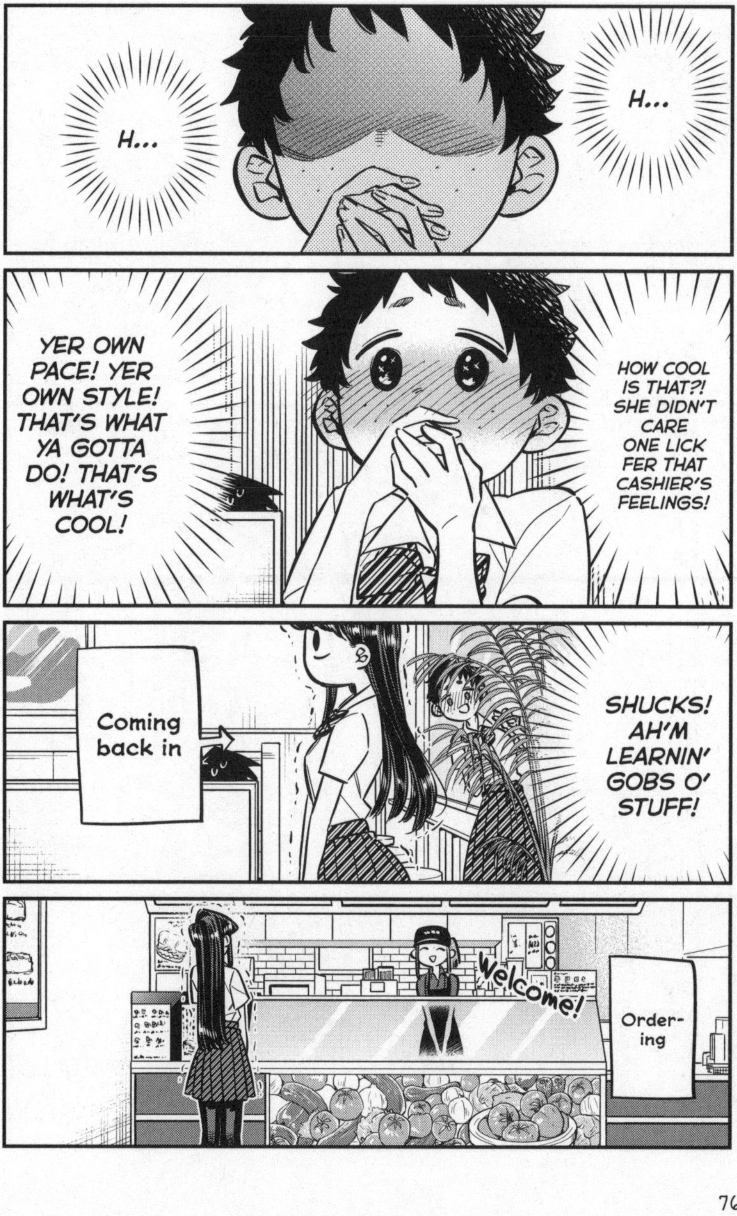
H...
H...
HOW COOL IS THAT?! SHE DIDN'T CARE ONE LICK FER THAT CASHIER'S FEELINGS!
YER OWN PACE! YER OWN STYLE! THAT'S WHAT YA GOTTA DO! THAT'S WHAT'S COOL!
SHUCKS! AH'M LEARNIN' GOBS O' STUFF!
Coming back in
Order-ing
Welcome!

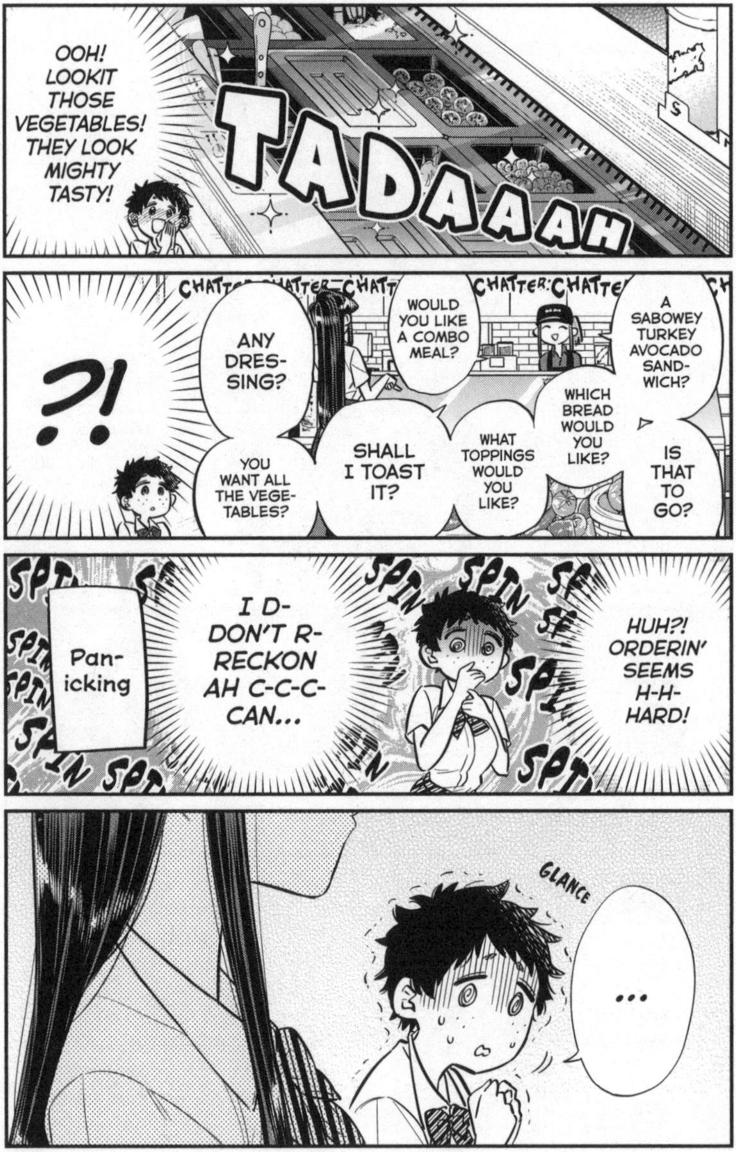
TADAAAAH
OOH! LOOKIT THOSE VEGETABLES! THEY LOOK MIGHTY TASTY!
CHATTER CHATTER CHATTER CHATTER CHATTER
A SABOWEY TURKEY AVOCADO SANDWICH?
IS THAT TO GO?
WOULD YOU LIKE A COMBO MEAL?
WHICH BREAD WOULD YOU LIKE?
WHAT TOPPINGS WOULD YOU LIKE?
SHALL I TOAST IT?
ANY DRESSING?
YOU WANT ALL THE VEGETABLES?
?!
HUH?! ORDERIN' SEEMS H-H-HARD!
I D-DON'T R-RECKON AH C-C-C-CAN...
Panicking
SPIN SPIN SPIN SPIN SPIN SPIN SPIN
GLANCE
...

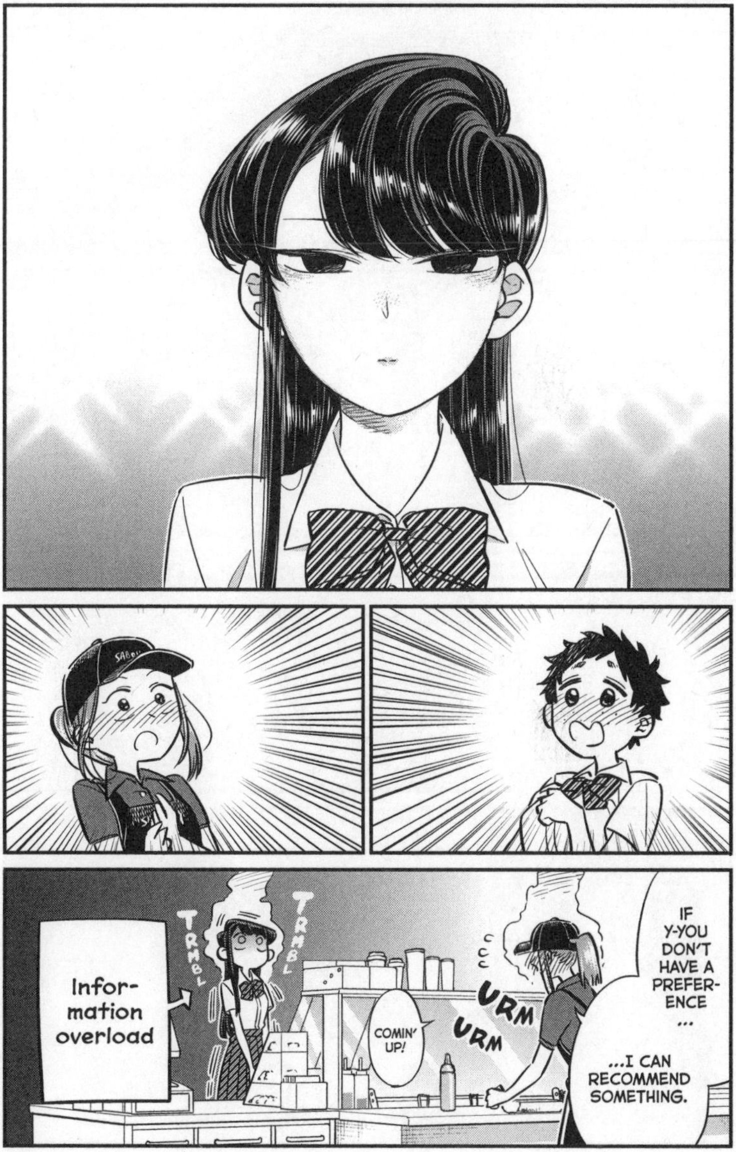
IF Y-YOU DON'T HAVE A PREFERENCE...
...I CAN RECOMMEND SOMETHING.
URM
URM
COMIN' UP!
TRMBL
TRMBL
Information overload

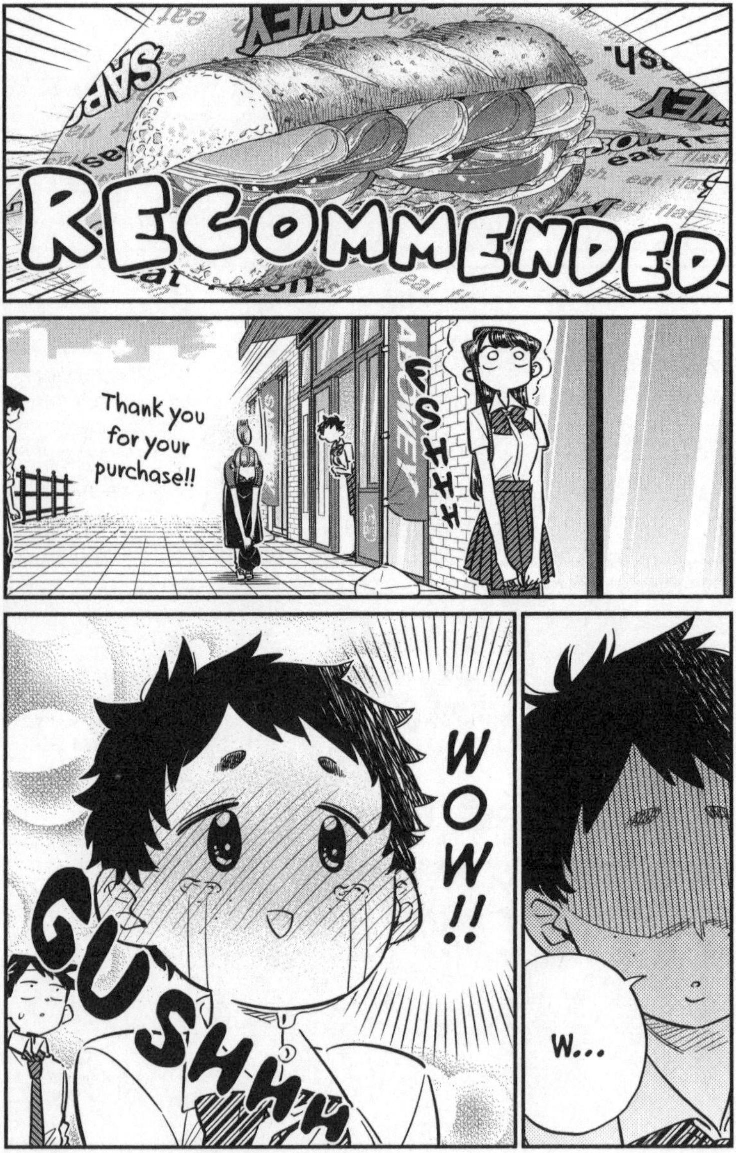
RECOMMENDED
FSHHH
Thank you for your purchase!!
W...
WOW!!
GUSHHHH

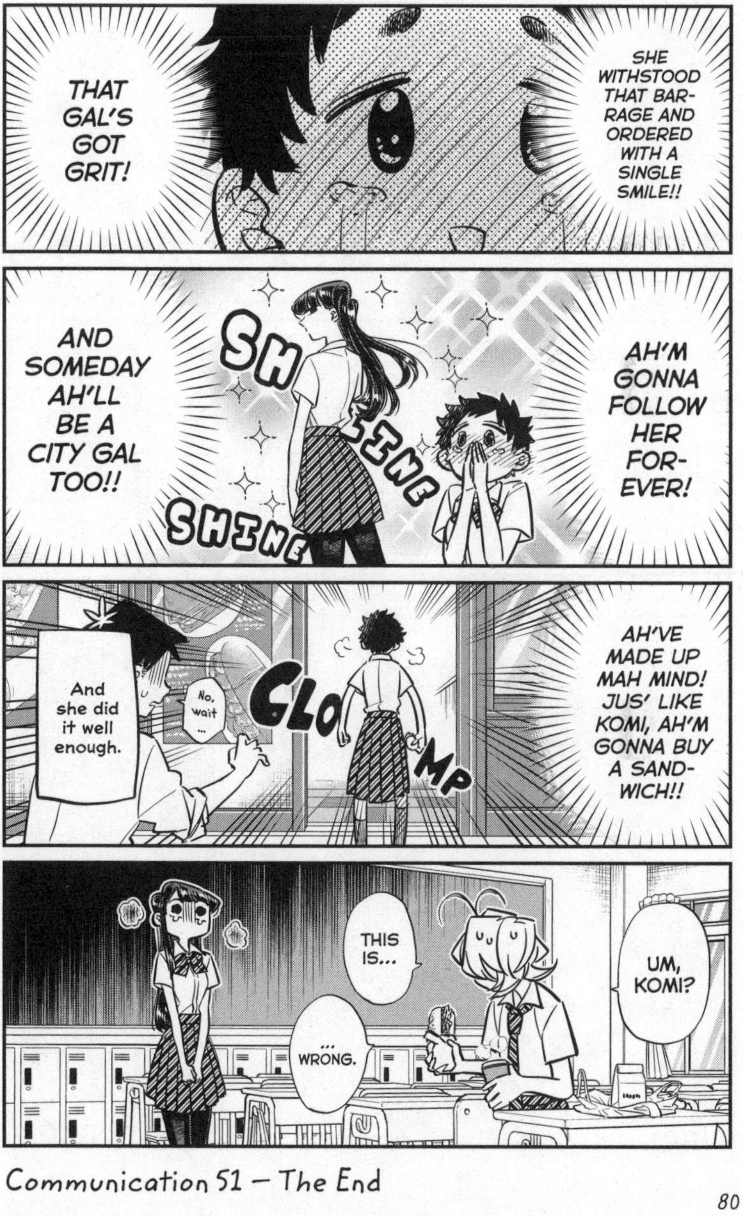
SHE WITHSTOOD THAT BARRAGE AND ORDERED WITH A SINGLE SMILE!!
THAT GAL'S GOT GRIT!
AH'M GONNA FOLLOW HER FOREVER!
SHINE
SHINE
AND SOMEDAY AH'LL BE A CITY GAL TOO!!
AH'VE MADE UP MAH MIND! JUS' LIKE KOMI, AH'M GONNA BUY A SANDWICH!!
CLOMP
No, wait ...
And she did it well enough.
UM, KOMI?
THIS IS...
... WRONG.

Communication 51 – The End

Komi Can't Communicate

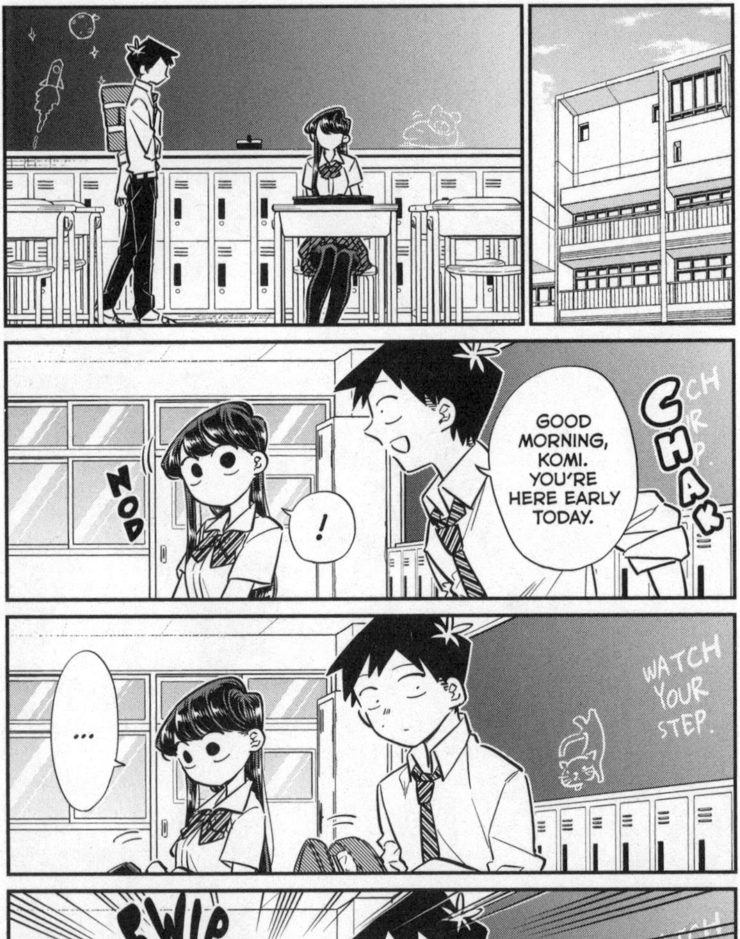
CHAK
GOOD MORNING, KOMI. YOU'RE HERE EARLY TODAY.
!
NOD
WATCH YOUR STEP.
...
WATCH YOUR STEP.
?!
FWIP

Komi Can't Communicate

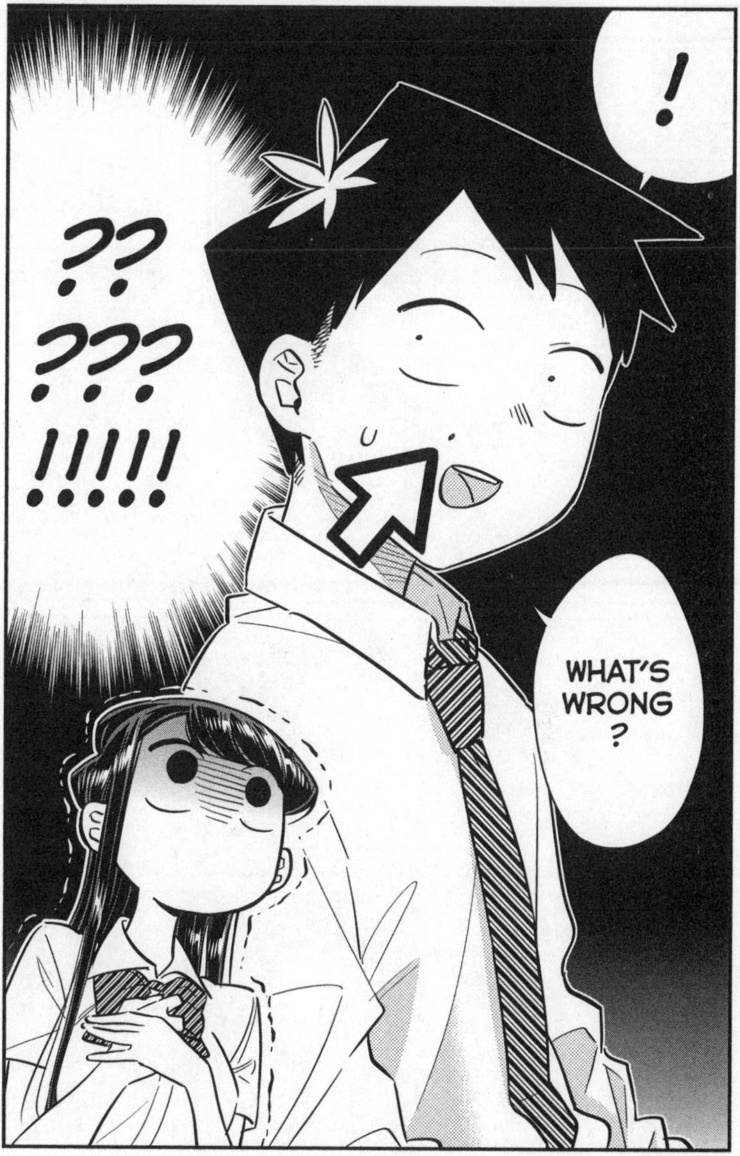
!
??
???
!!!!!
WHAT'S WRONG ?

Communication 52: Something on Your Face

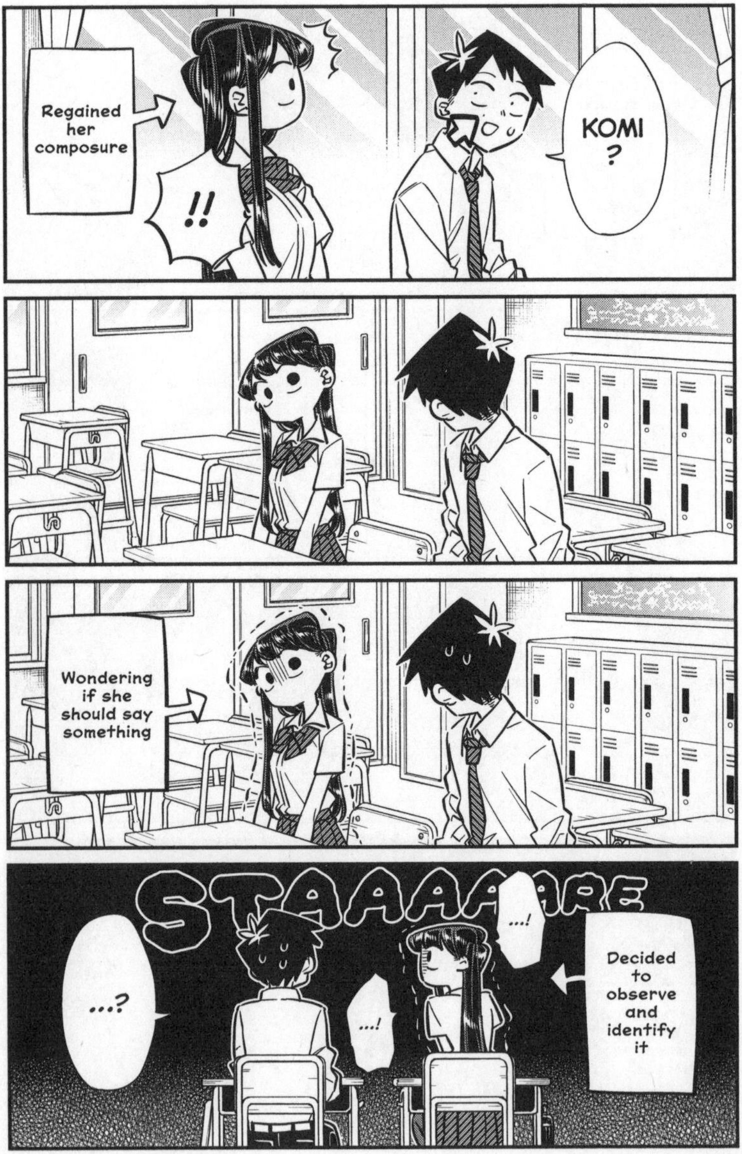

KOMI ?
!!
Regained her composure
Wondering if she should say something
STAAAAARE
Decided to observe and identify it
...!
...!
...?

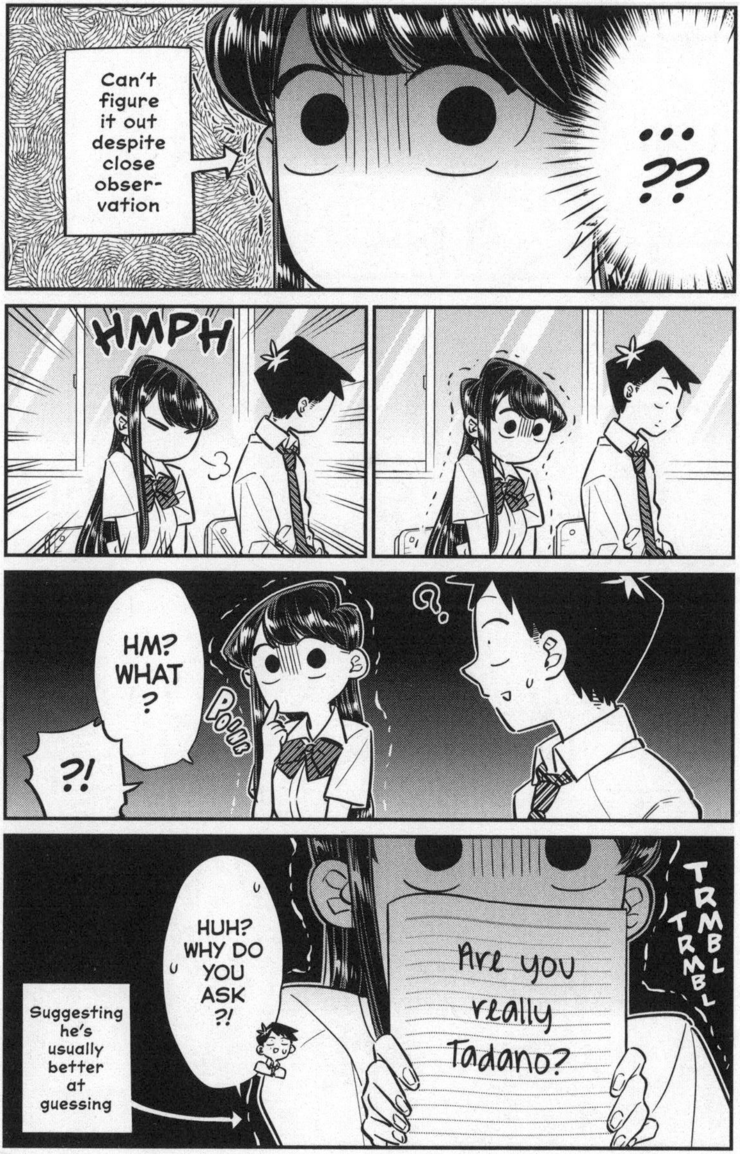
...??
Can't figure it out despite close observation
HMPH
?
Pouts
HM? WHAT?
?!
TRMBL TRMBL
Are you really Tadano?
HUH? WHY DO YOU ASK?!
Suggesting he's usually better at guessing

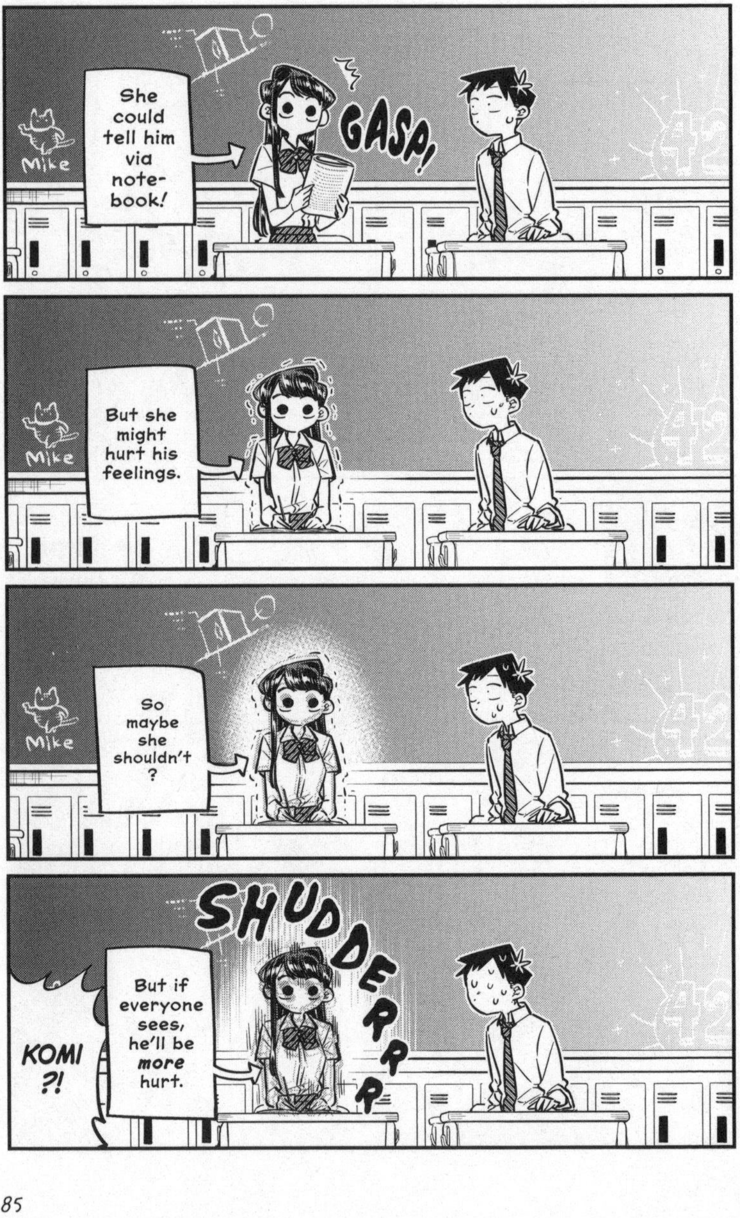

Mike
She could tell him via note-book!
GASP!
Mike
But she might hurt his feelings.
Mike
So maybe she shouldn't?
SHUDDERRR
But if everyone sees, he'll be *more* hurt.
KOMI?!

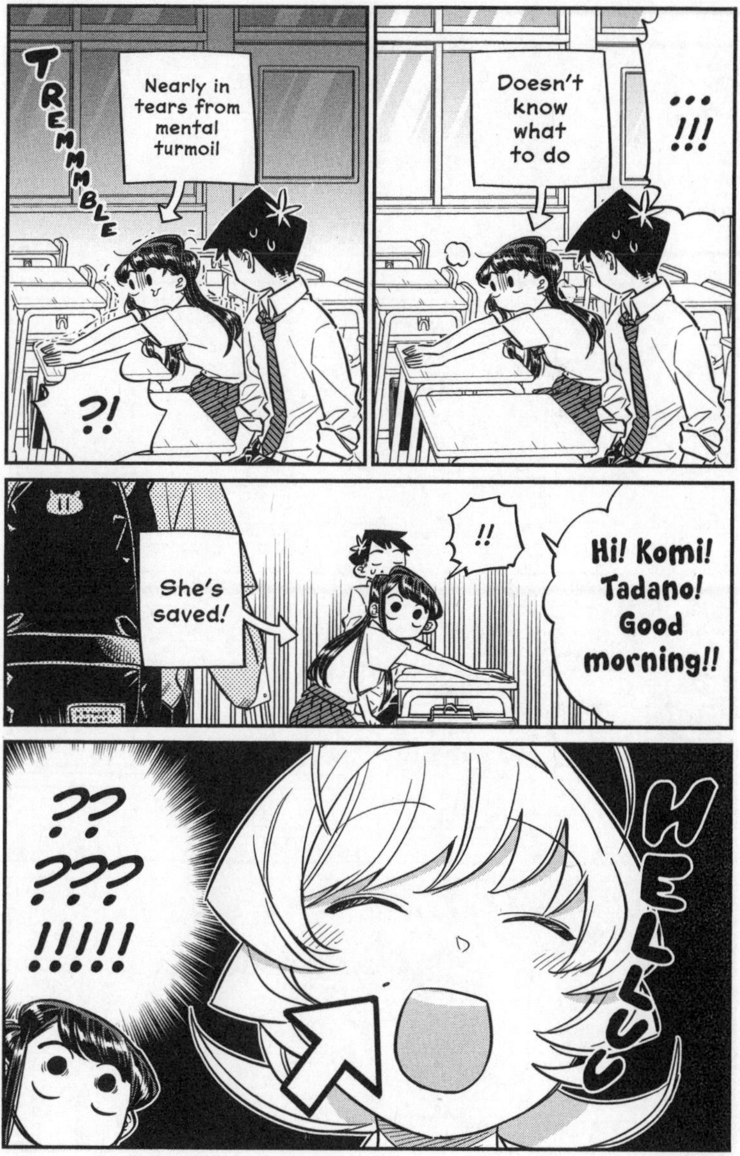
Doesn't know what to do
...!!!
Nearly in tears from mental turmoil
TREMMMBLE
?!
Hi! Komi! Tadano! Good morning!!
!!
She's saved!
HELLUUU
?? ??? !!!!!

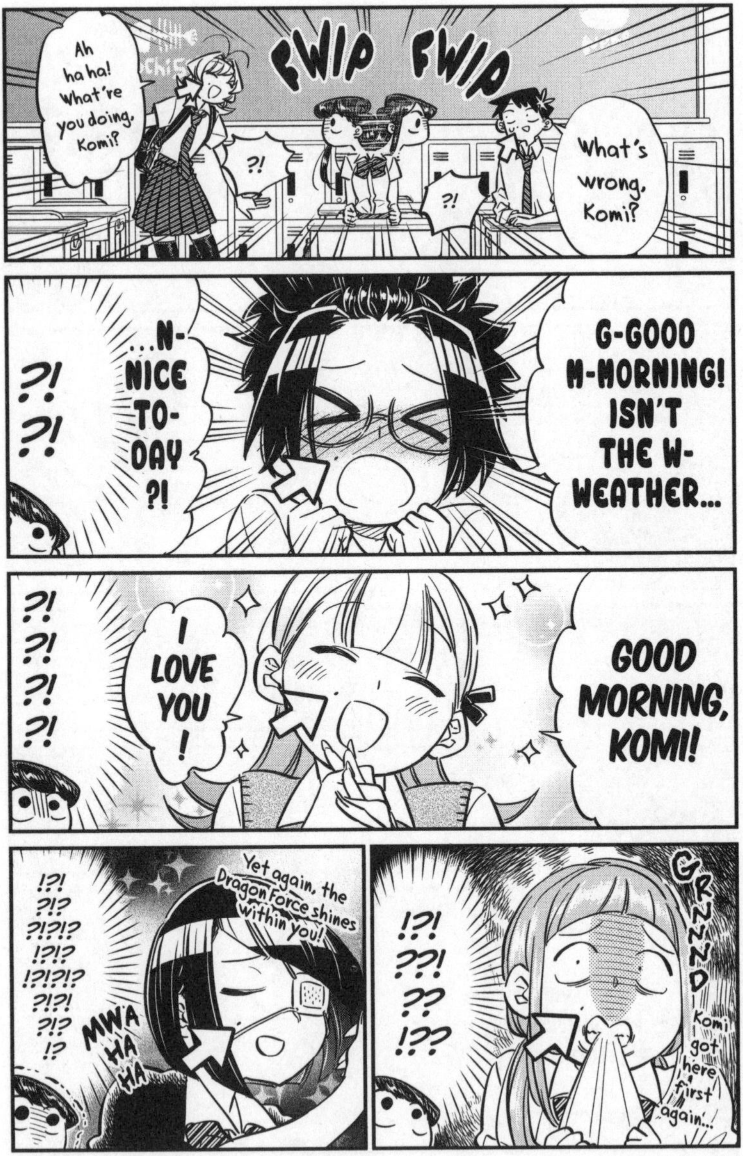
FWIP FWIP
What's wrong, Komi?
?!
Ah ha ha! What're you doing, Komi?
?!
G-GOOD M-MORNING! ISN'T THE W-WEATHER...
...N-NICE TO-DAY?!
?! ?!
GOOD MORNING, KOMI!
I LOVE YOU!
?! ?! ?! ?!
GRNNND
Komi got here first again...
!?! ??! ?? !??
Yet again, the Dragon Force shines within you!
MWA HA HA
!?! ?!? ?!?!? !?!? !?!?!? ?!?! ?!? !?

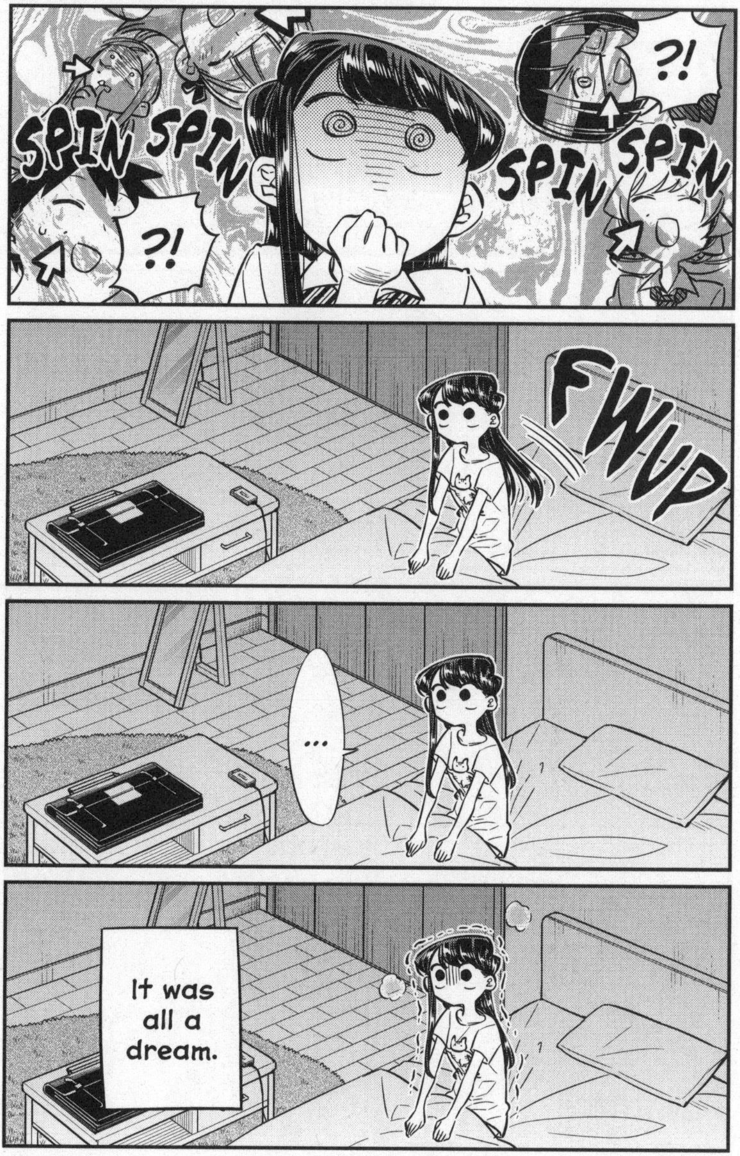
?!
SPIN SPIN
SPIN SPIN
?!
FWUP
...
It was all a dream.

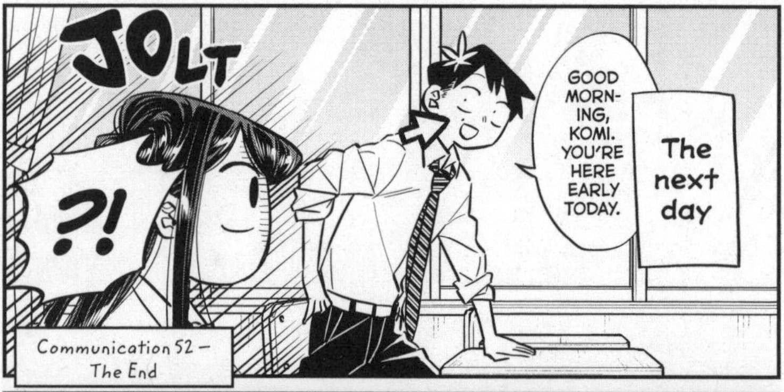
The next day
GOOD MORNING, KOMI. YOU'RE HERE EARLY TODAY.
JOLT
?!
Communication 52 — The End

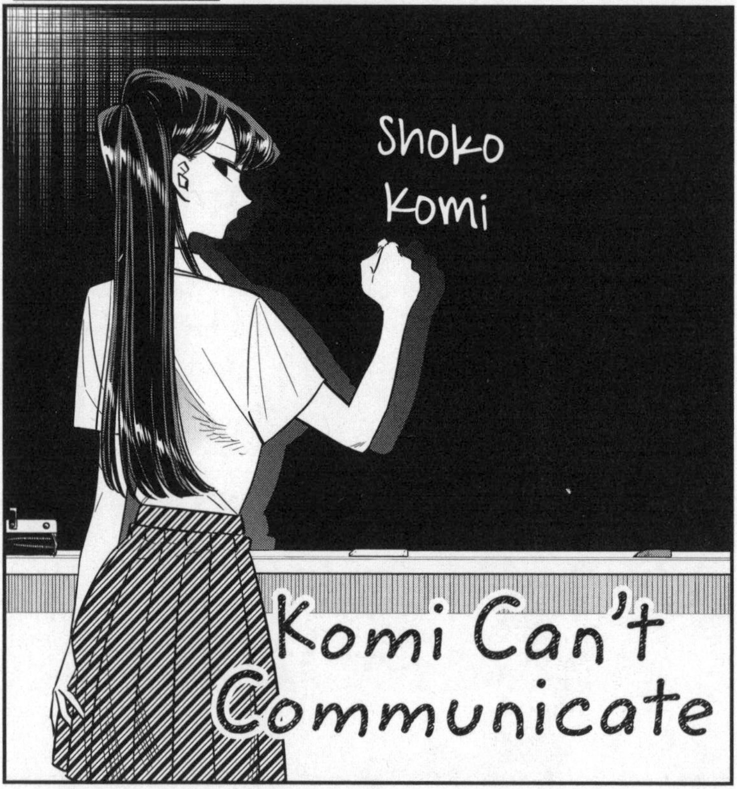
Shoko Komi
Komi Can't Communicate

Communication 53: First Names

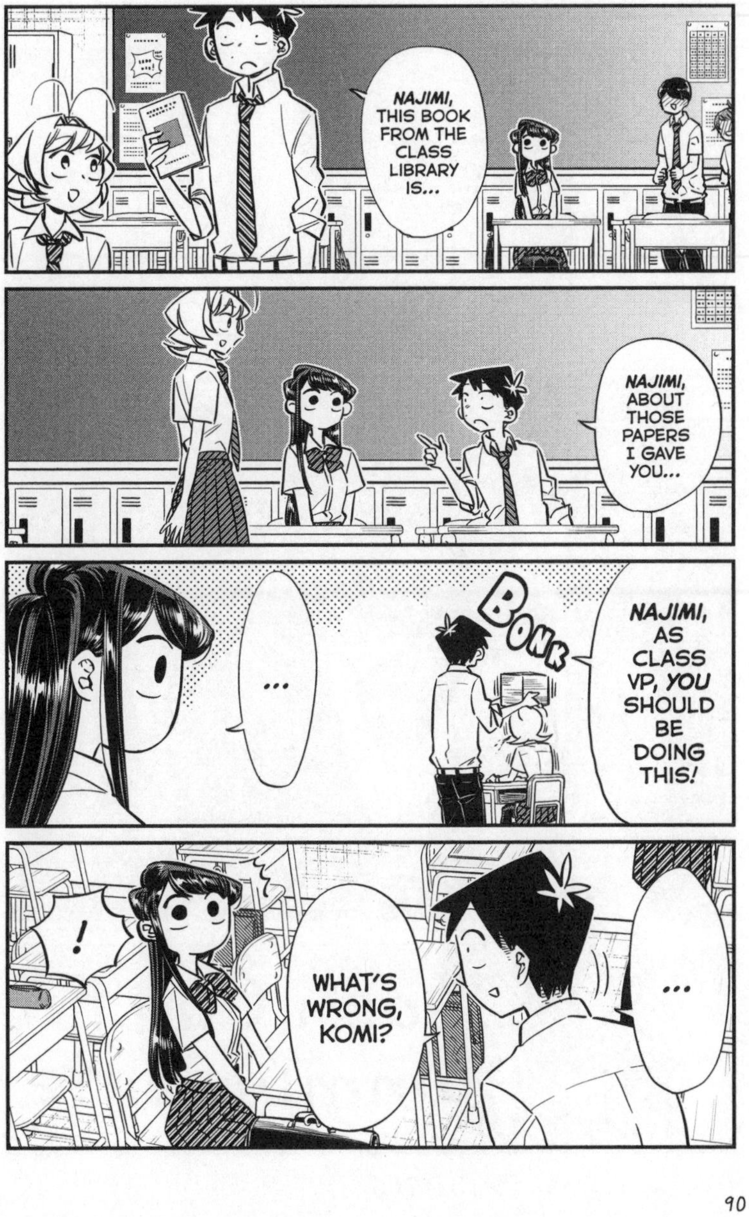
NAJIMI, THIS BOOK FROM THE CLASS LIBRARY IS...
NAJIMI, ABOUT THOSE PAPERS I GAVE YOU...
NAJIMI, AS CLASS VP, YOU SHOULD BE DOING THIS!
BONK
...
...
WHAT'S WRONG, KOMI?
!

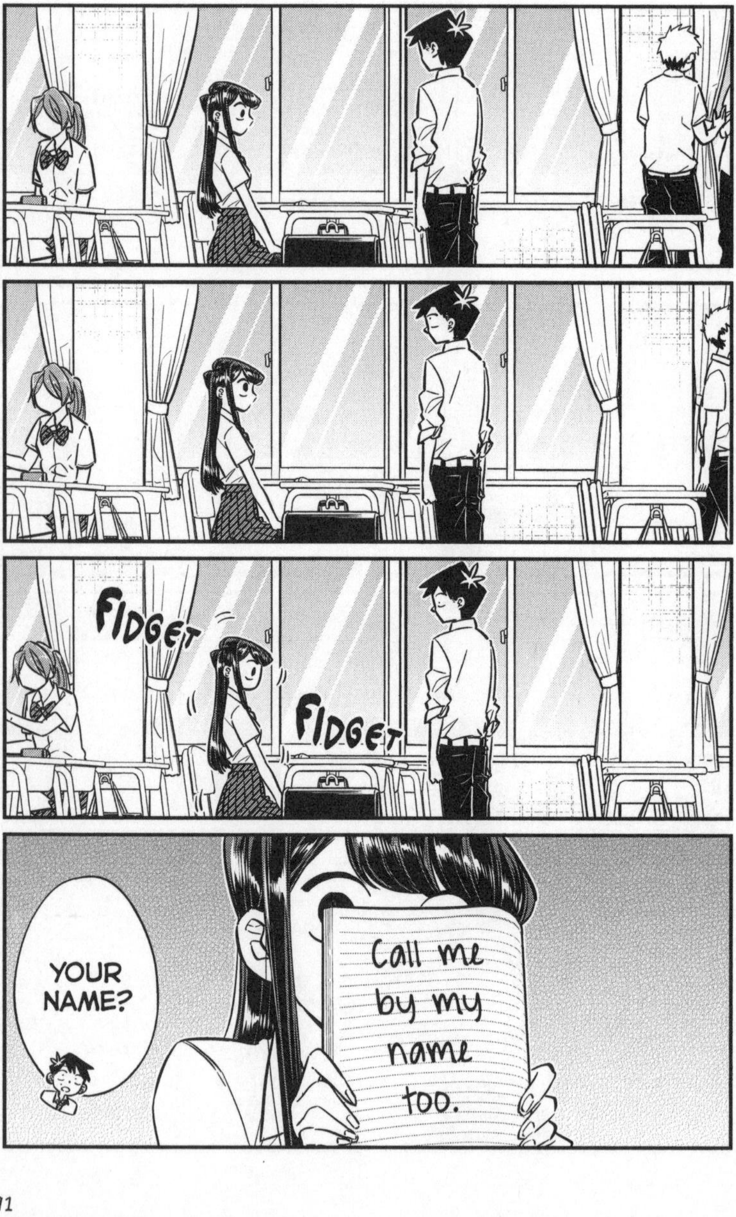
FIDGET
FIDGET
Call me by my name too.
YOUR NAME?

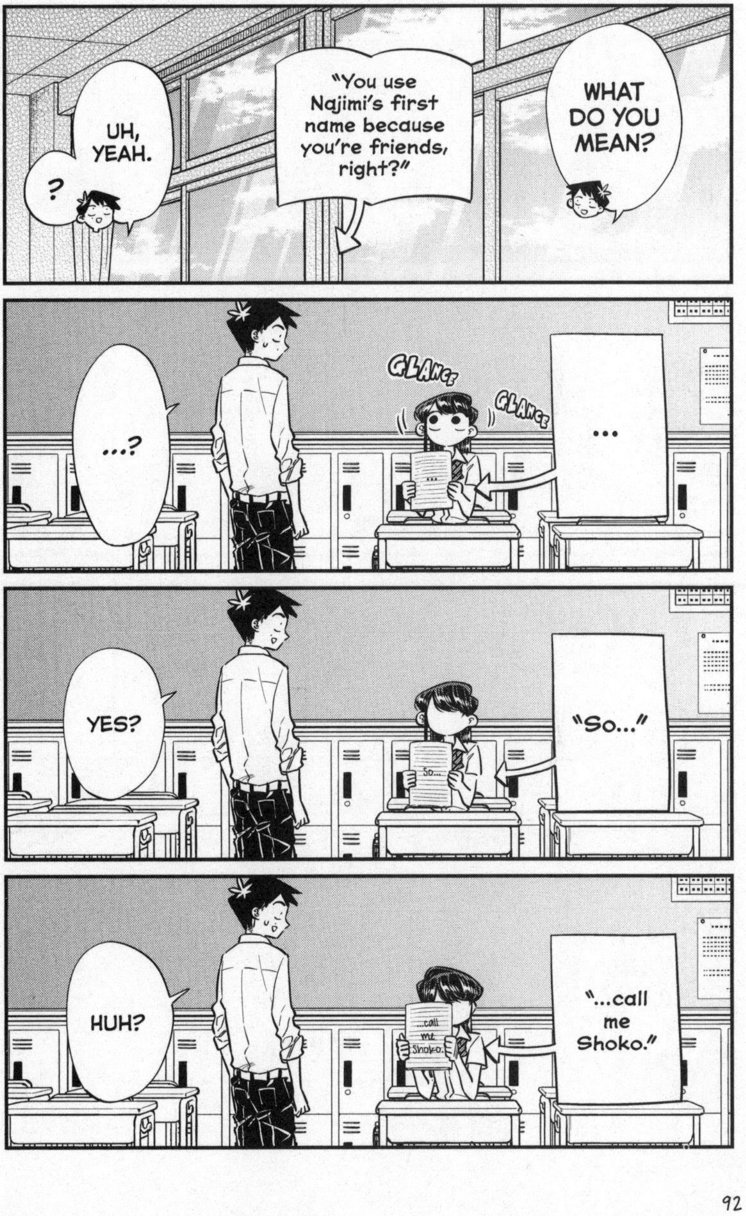
WHAT DO YOU MEAN?
"You use Najimi's first name because you're friends, right?"
UH, YEAH.
?
...
GLANCE
GLANCE
...
...?
"So..."
So...
YES?
"...call me Shoko."
...call me Shoko.
HUH?

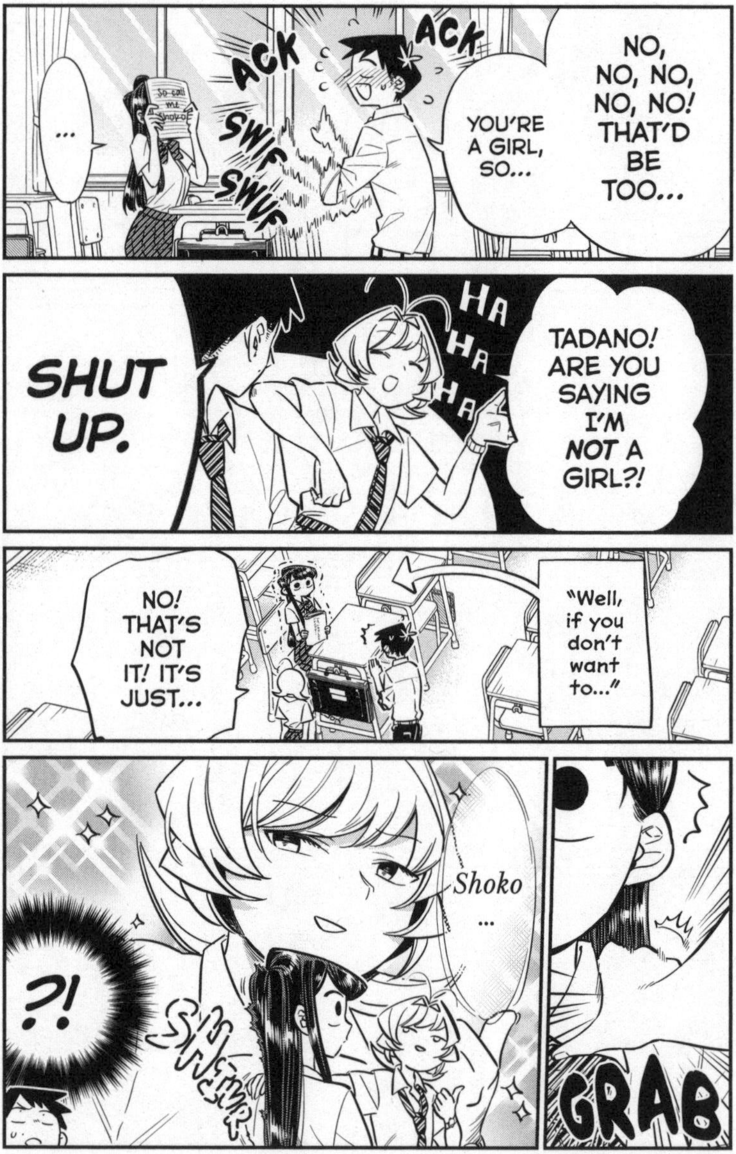
NO, NO, NO, NO, NO! THAT'D BE TOO...
YOU'RE A GIRL, SO...
ACK
ACK
SWIF
SWUF
So call me Shoko
...
TADANO! ARE YOU SAYING I'M *NOT* A GIRL?!
HA HA HA
SHUT UP.
"Well, if you don't want to..."
NO! THAT'S NOT IT! IT'S JUST...
GRAB
Shoko ...
?!

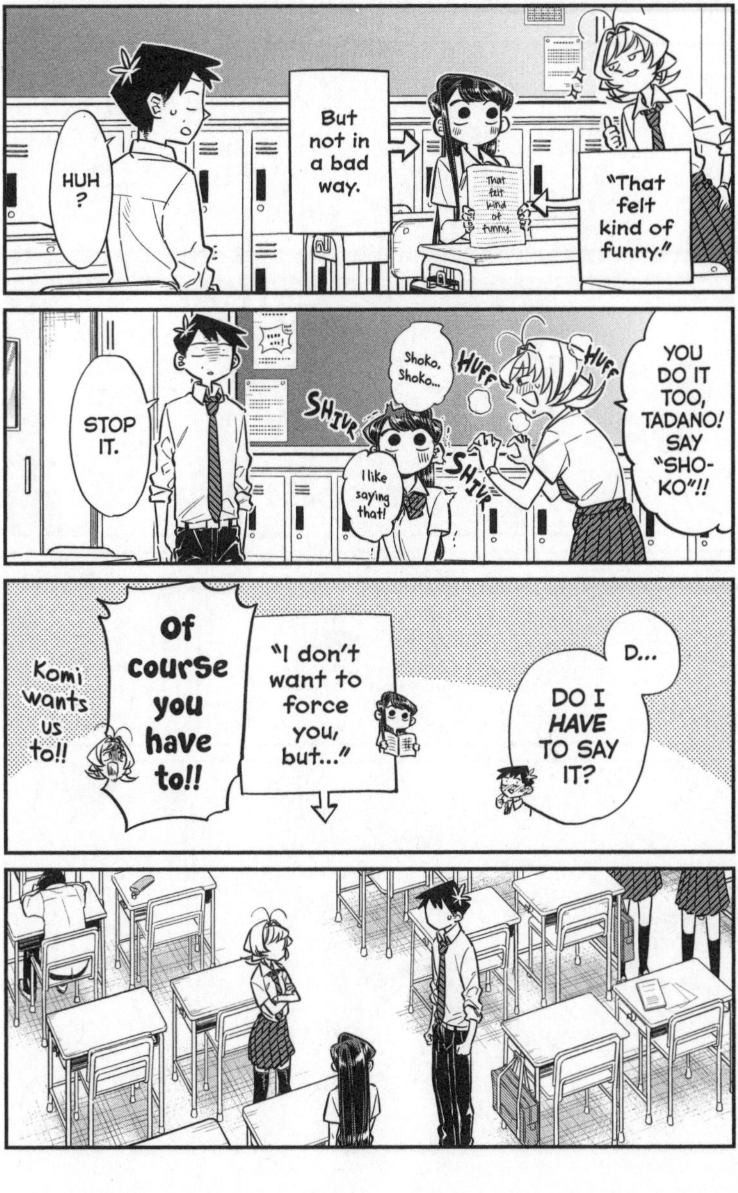
"That felt kind of funny."
That felt kind of funny.
But not in a bad way.
HUH?
YOU DO IT TOO, TADANO! SAY "SHO-KO"!!
HUFF
HUFF
Shoko, Shoko...
SHIVR
SHIVR
I like saying that!
STOP IT.
D...
DO I *HAVE* TO SAY IT?
"I don't want to force you, but..."
Of course you have to!!
Komi wants us to!!

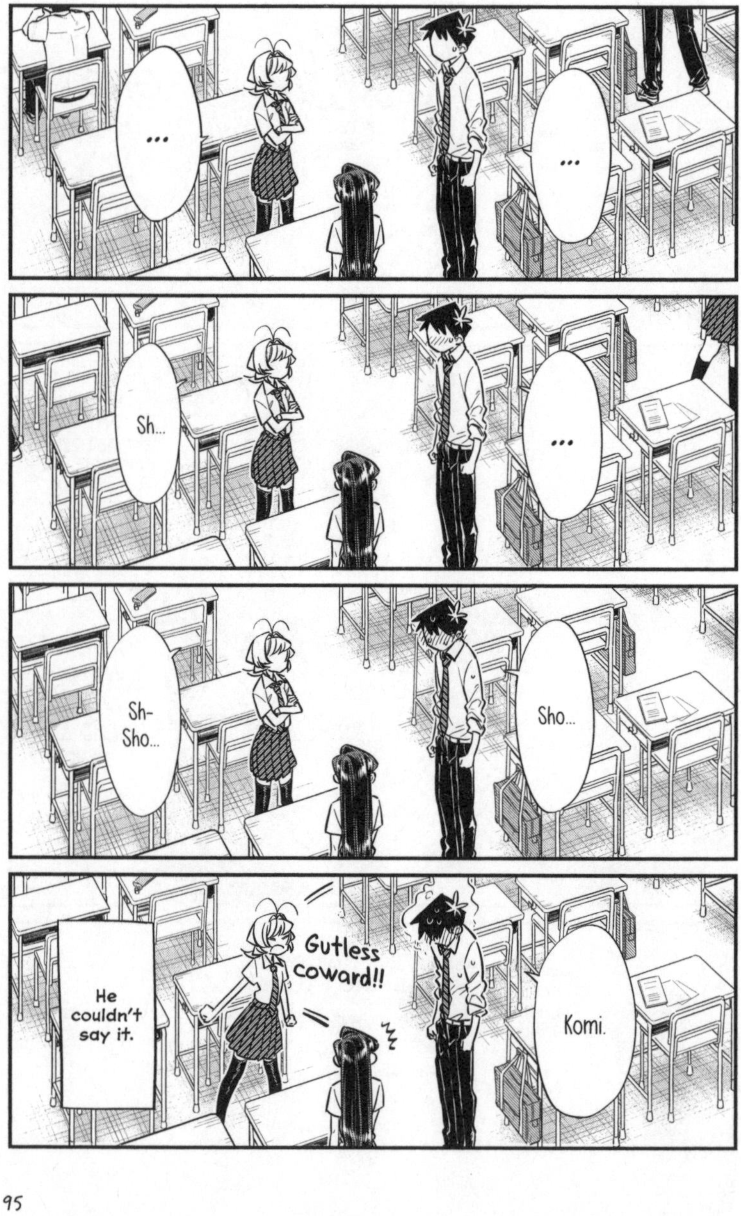
...
...
...
Sh...
Sho...
Sh-Sho...
Komi.
Gutless coward!!
He couldn't say it.

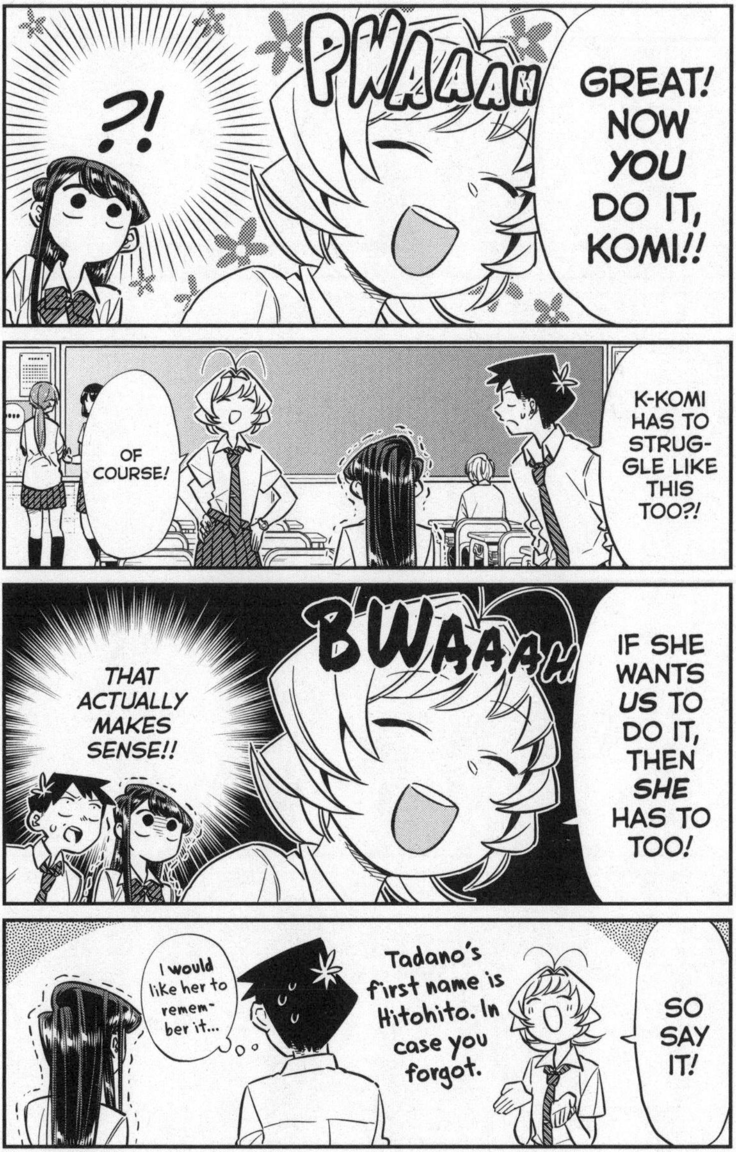
GREAT! NOW YOU DO IT, KOMI!!
PWAAAAH
?!
K-KOMI HAS TO STRUGGLE LIKE THIS TOO?!
OF COURSE!
IF SHE WANTS US TO DO IT, THEN SHE HAS TO TOO!
BWAAAAH
THAT ACTUALLY MAKES SENSE!!
SO SAY IT!
Tadano's first name is Hitohito. In case you forgot.
I would like her to remember it...

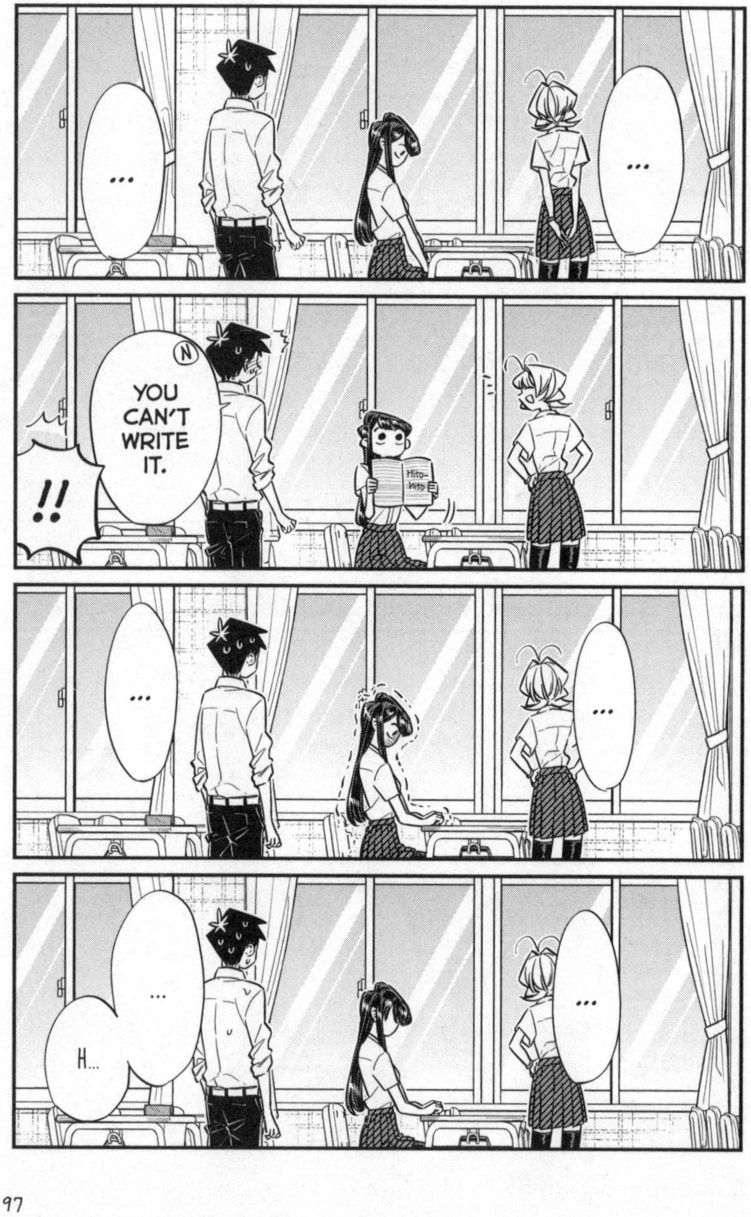
...
...
YOU CAN'T WRITE IT.
!!
Hito-hito
...
...
...
...
H...

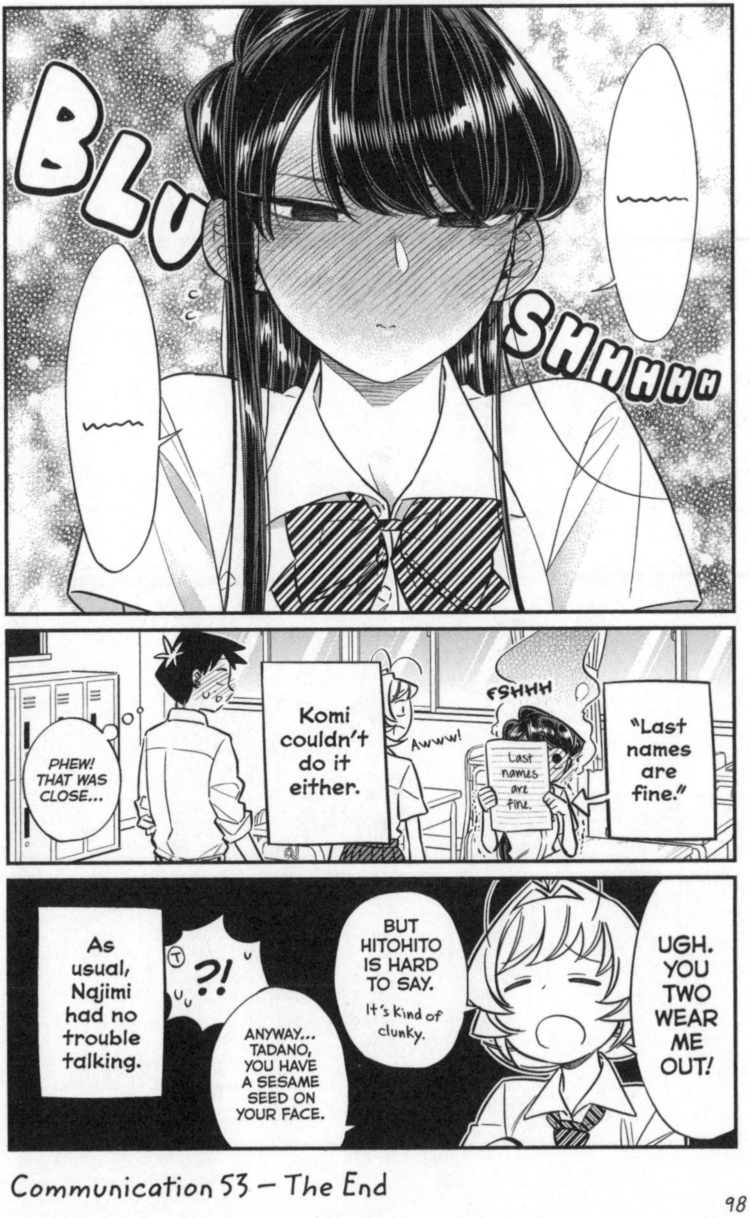
BLUSHHHHHH
"Last names are fine."
FSHHH
Last names are fine.
Awww!
Komi couldn't do it either.
PHEW! THAT WAS CLOSE...
UGH. YOU TWO WEAR ME OUT!
BUT HITOHITO IS HARD TO SAY.
It's kind of clunky.
ANYWAY... TADANO, YOU HAVE A SESAME SEED ON YOUR FACE.
?!
As usual, Najimi had no trouble talking.

Communication 53 – The End

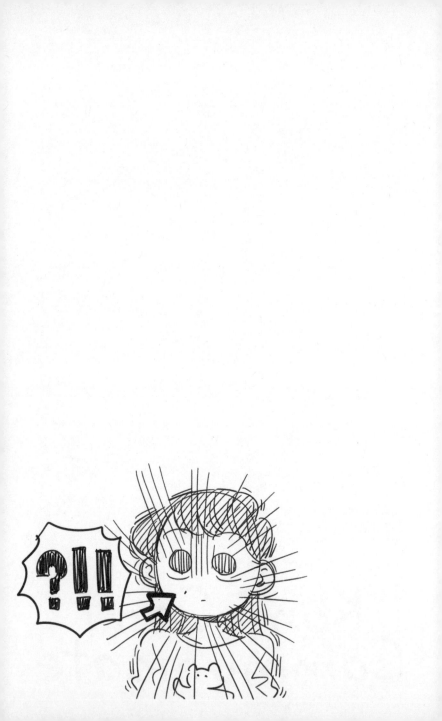

Komi Can't
Communicate

Komi Can't Communicate

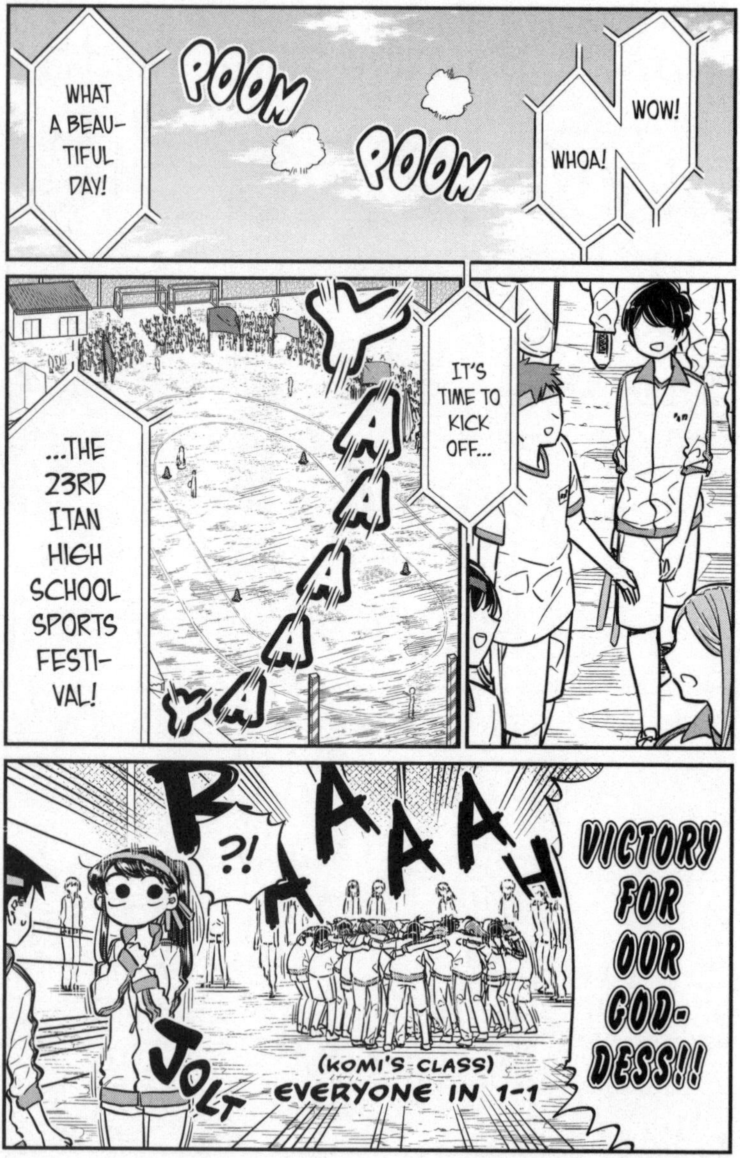

WOW!
WHOA!
POOM
POOM
WHAT A BEAU-TIFUL DAY!
IT'S TIME TO KICK OFF...
YAAAAAAA
...THE 23RD ITAN HIGH SCHOOL SPORTS FESTI-VAL!
VICTORY FOR OUR GOD-DESS!!
RAAAAH
?!
(KOMI'S CLASS) EVERYONE IN 1-1
JOLT

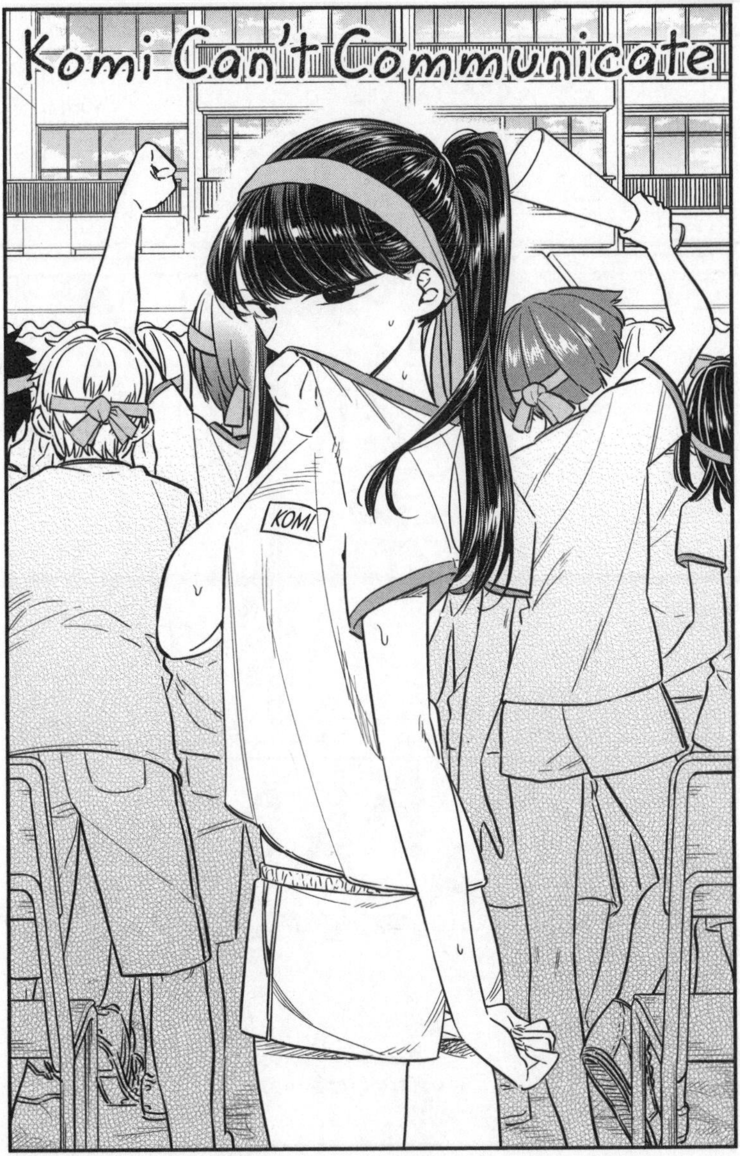
Komi Can't Communicate
KOMI

Communication 54: Sports Festival, Part 1

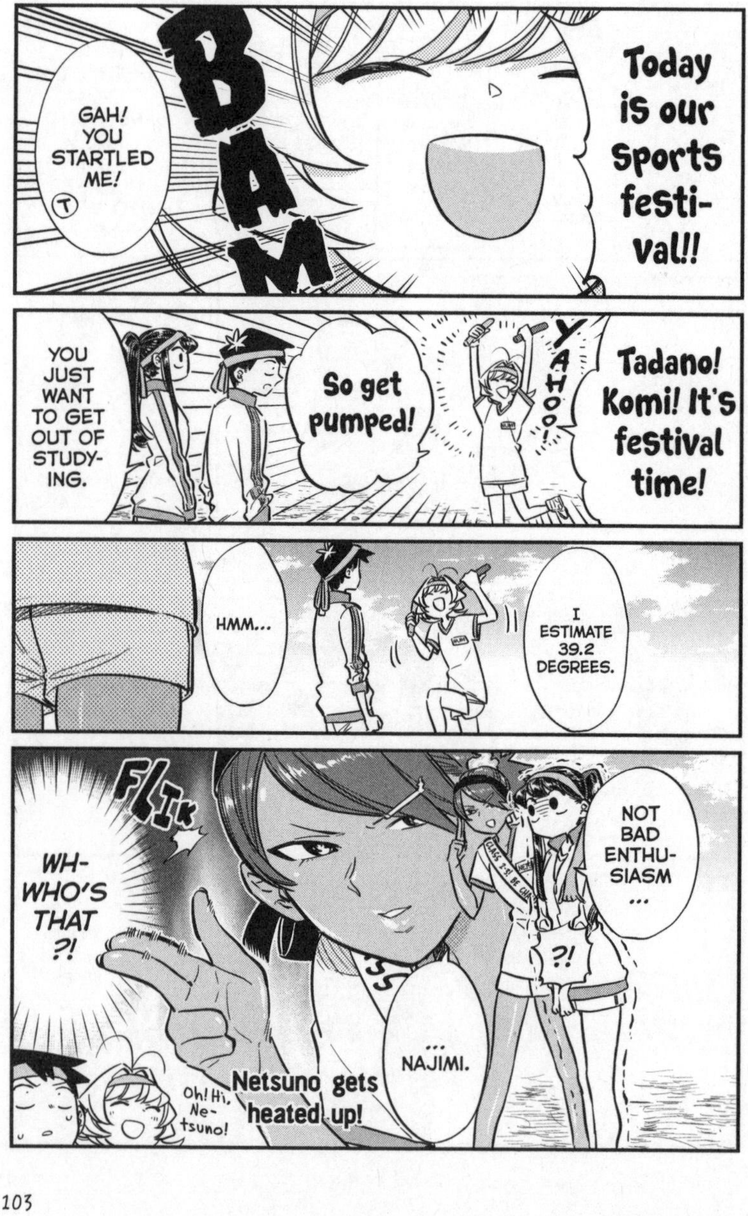
Today is our Sports festi-val!!
BAM
GAH! YOU STARTLED ME!
Tadano! Komi! It's festival time!
YAHOO!!
So get pumped!
YOU JUST WANT TO GET OUT OF STUDY-ING.
I ESTIMATE 39.2 DEGREES.
HMM...
NOT BAD ENTHU-SIASM ...
?!
... NAJIMI.
Netsuno gets heated up!
Oh! Hi, Ne-tsuno!
FLIK
WH-WHO'S THAT ?!

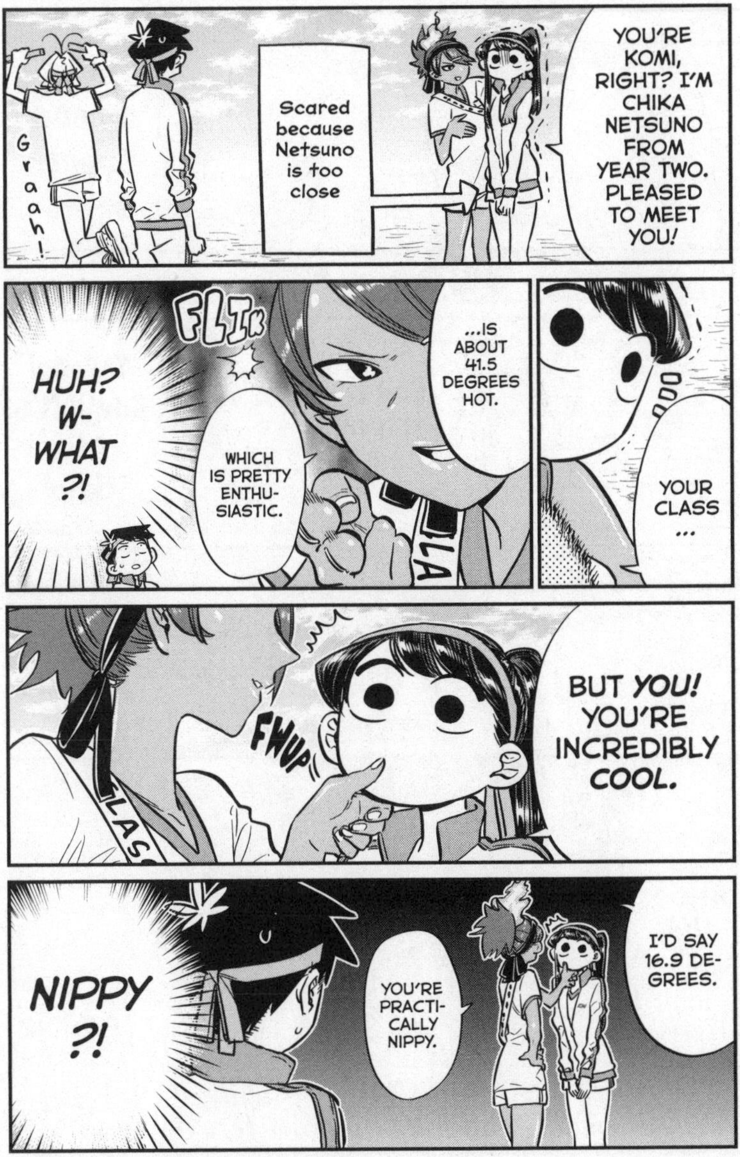
YOU'RE KOMI, RIGHT? I'M CHIKA NETSUNO FROM YEAR TWO. PLEASED TO MEET YOU!
Scared because Netsuno is too close
Graah!
YOUR CLASS ...
...IS ABOUT 41.5 DEGREES HOT.
FLIK
WHICH IS PRETTY ENTHUSIASTIC.
HUH? W-WHAT?!
BUT YOU! YOU'RE INCREDIBLY COOL.
FWUP
I'D SAY 16.9 DEGREES.
YOU'RE PRACTICALLY NIPPY.
NIPPY?!

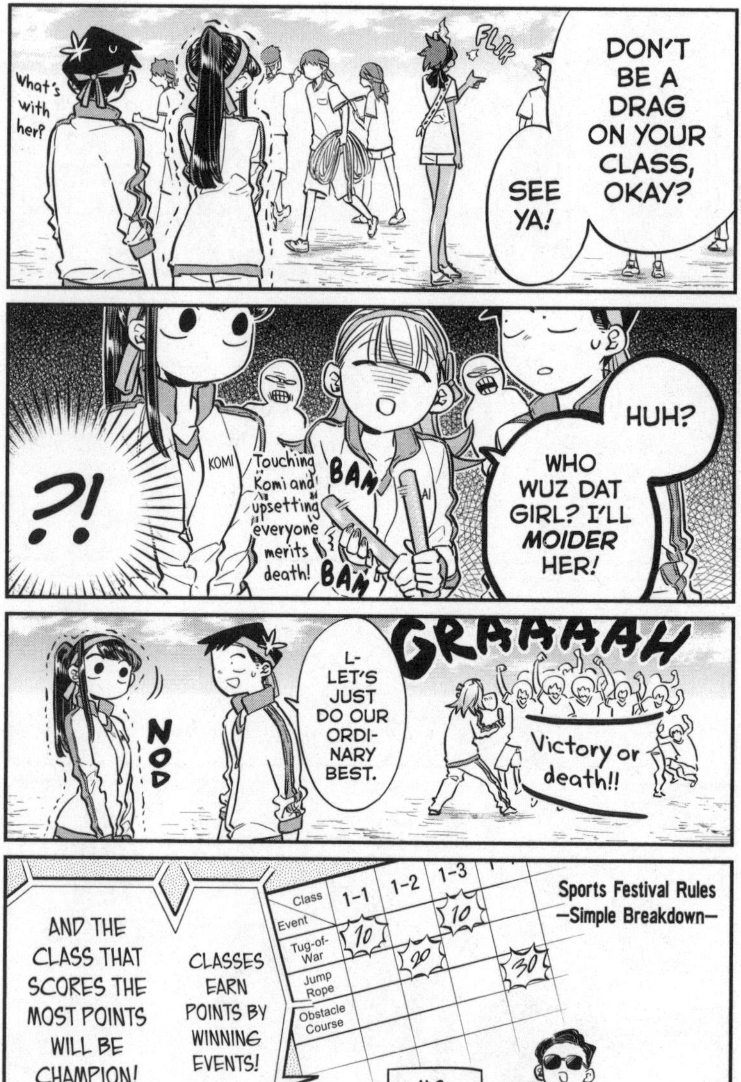
DON'T BE A DRAG ON YOUR CLASS, OKAY?
SEE YA!
FLIK
What's with her?
HUH?
WHO WUZ DAT GIRL? I'LL MOIDER HER!
AI
BAM
BAM
Touching Komi and upsetting everyone merits death!
KOMI
?!
GRAAAAH
Victory or death!!
L- LET'S JUST DO OUR ORDINARY BEST.
NOD
Sports Festival Rules
—Simple Breakdown—
Class
Event
1-1
1-2
1-3
Tug-of-War
Jump Rope
Obstacle Course
10
20
10
30
M.C.: Tsukasa Aizawa
CLASSES EARN POINTS BY WINNING EVENTS!
AND THE CLASS THAT SCORES THE MOST POINTS WILL BE CHAMPION!

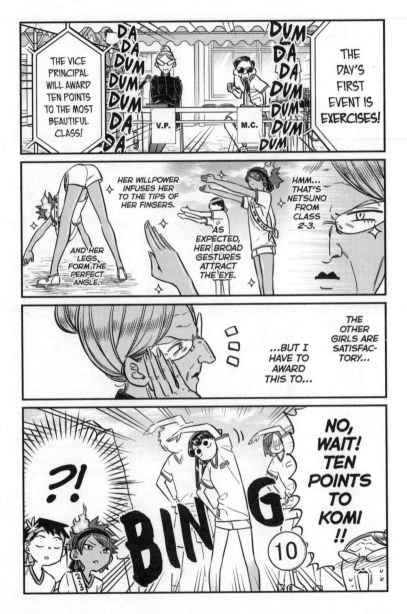

THE DAY'S FIRST EVENT IS EXERCISES!
DUM DA DA DUM DUM DUM DUM
M.C.
V.P.
DA DA DUM DUM DUM DA DA
THE VICE PRINCIPAL WILL AWARD TEN POINTS TO THE MOST BEAUTIFUL CLASS!
HMM... THAT'S NETSUNO FROM CLASS 2-3.
HER WILLPOWER INFUSES HER TO THE TIPS OF HER FINGERS.
AS EXPECTED, HER BROAD GESTURES ATTRACT THE EYE.
AND HER LEGS FORM THE PERFECT ANGLE.
THE OTHER GIRLS ARE SATISFACTORY...
...BUT I HAVE TO AWARD THIS TO...
NO, WAIT! TEN POINTS TO KOMI !!
10
BING
?!

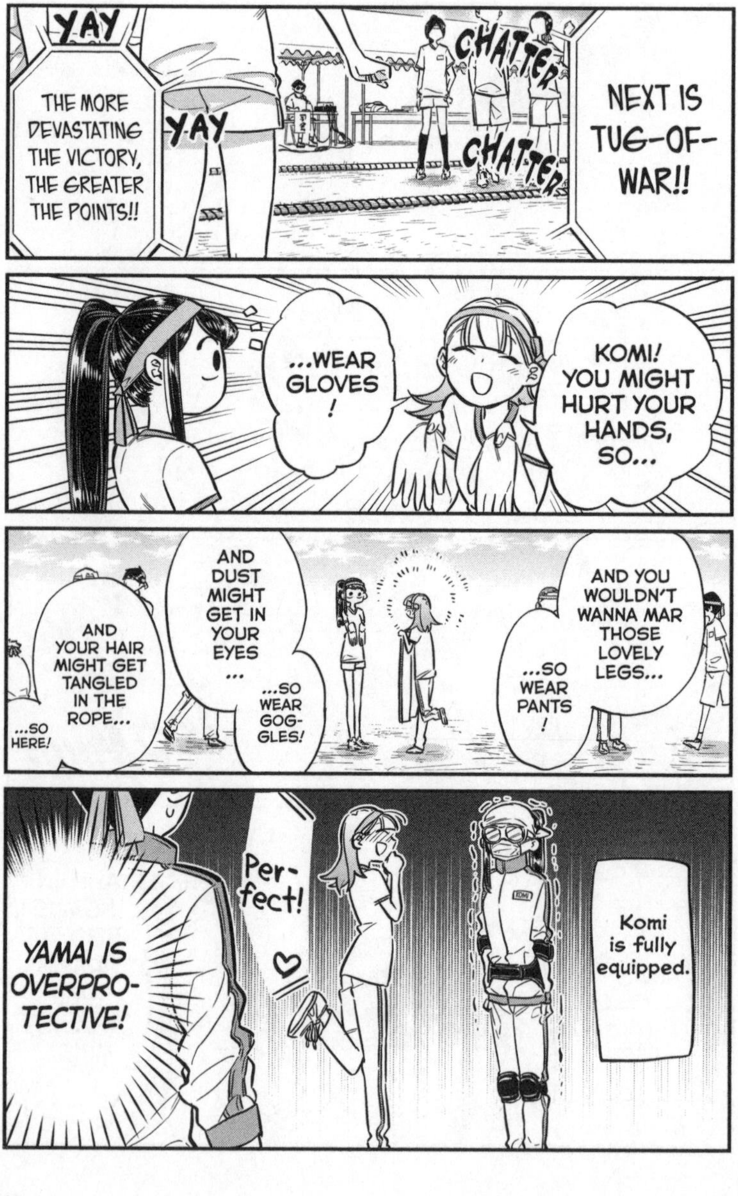
NEXT IS TUG-OF-WAR!!
CHATTER
CHATTER
YAY
YAY
THE MORE DEVASTATING THE VICTORY, THE GREATER THE POINTS!!
KOMI! YOU MIGHT HURT YOUR HANDS, SO...
...WEAR GLOVES!
AND YOU WOULDN'T WANNA MAR THOSE LOVELY LEGS...
...SO WEAR PANTS!
AND DUST MIGHT GET IN YOUR EYES...
...SO WEAR GOG-GLES!
AND YOUR HAIR MIGHT GET TANGLED IN THE ROPE...
...SO HERE!
Komi is fully equipped.
Per-fect!
YAMAI IS OVERPRO-TECTIVE!

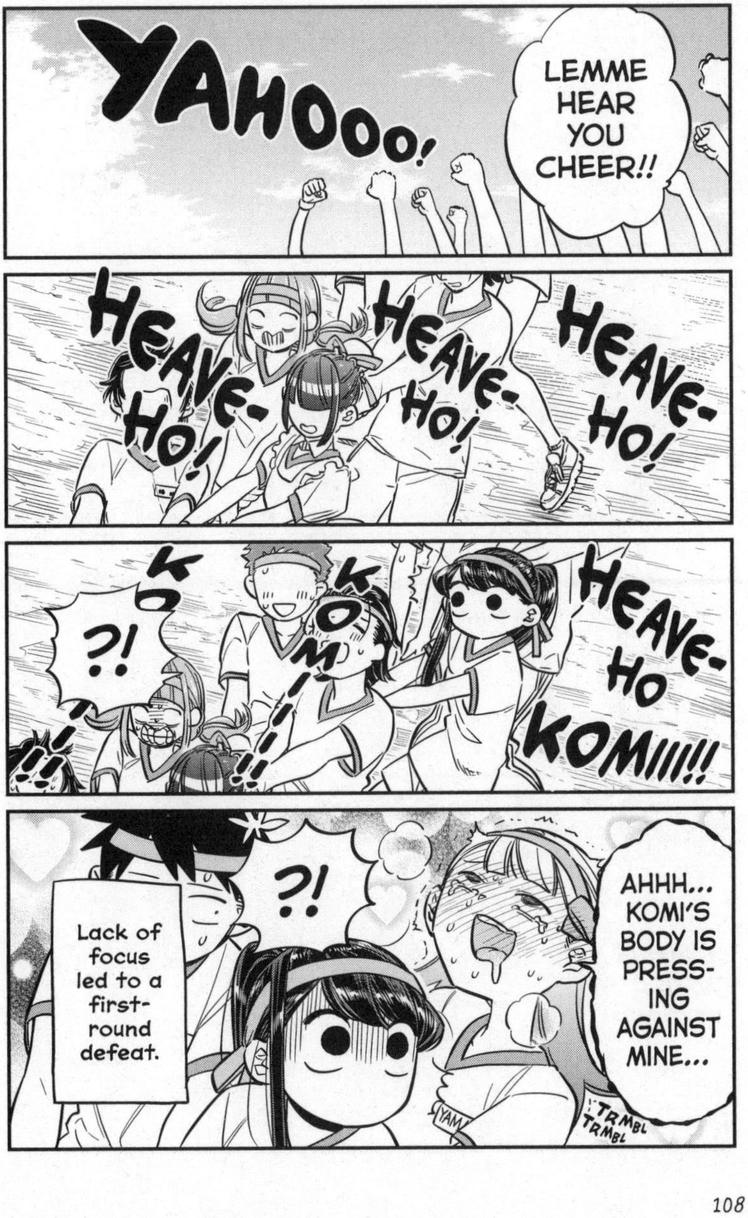
LEMME HEAR YOU CHEER!!
YAHOOO!
HEAVE-HO!
HEAVE-HO!
HEAVE-HO!
HEAVE-HO KOMIIII!!
KOMI-!!!
?!
AHHH... KOMI'S BODY IS PRESS-ING AGAINST MINE...
TRMBL TRMBL
?!
Lack of focus led to a first-round defeat.

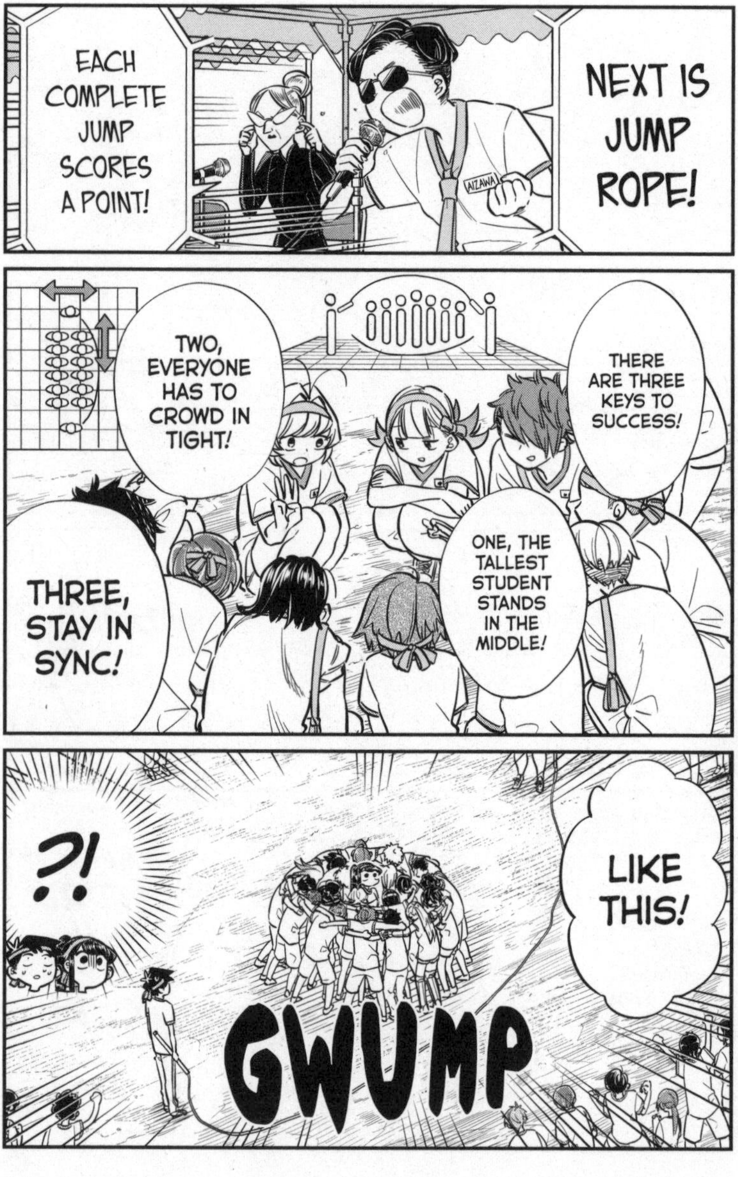
NEXT IS JUMP ROPE!
AIZAWA
EACH COMPLETE JUMP SCORES A POINT!
THERE ARE THREE KEYS TO SUCCESS!
ONE, THE TALLEST STUDENT STANDS IN THE MIDDLE!
TWO, EVERYONE HAS TO CROWD IN TIGHT!
THREE, STAY IN SYNC!
LIKE THIS!
GWUMP
?!

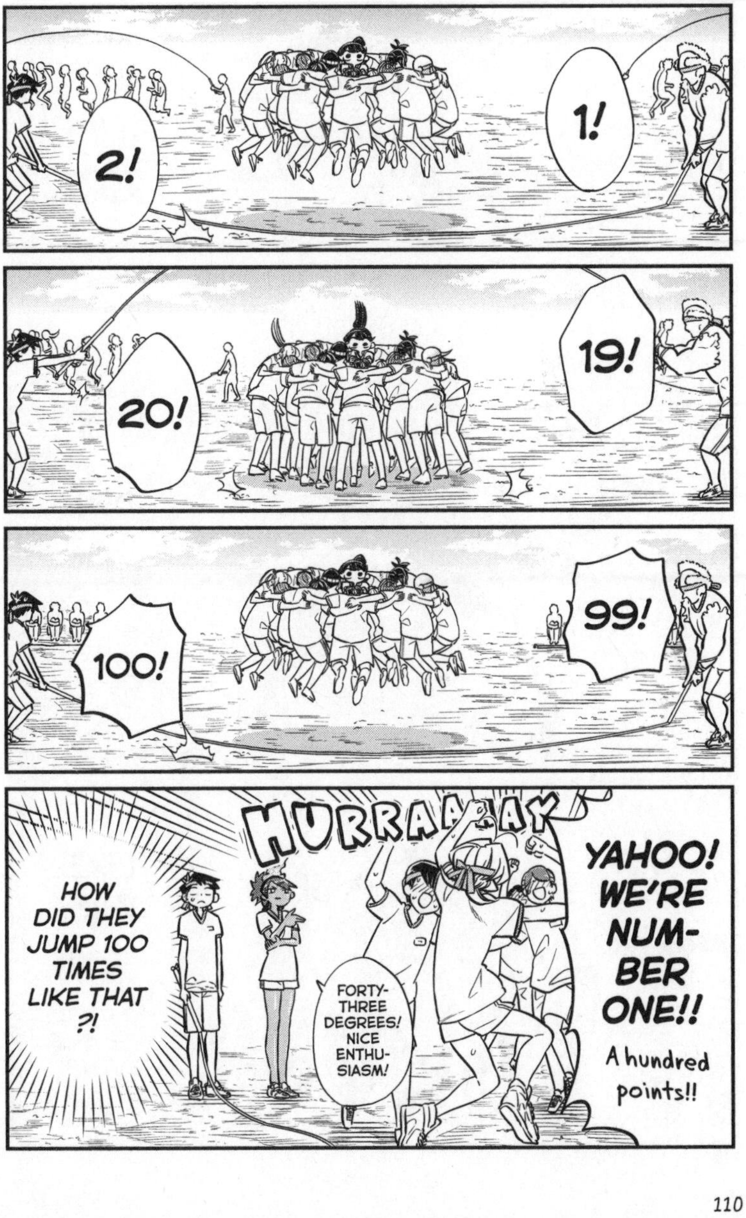

1!
2!
19!
20!
99!
100!
HURRAAAAY
YAHOO! WE'RE NUMBER ONE!!
A hundred points!!
FORTY-THREE DEGREES! NICE ENTHUSIASM!
HOW DID THEY JUMP 100 TIMES LIKE THAT?!

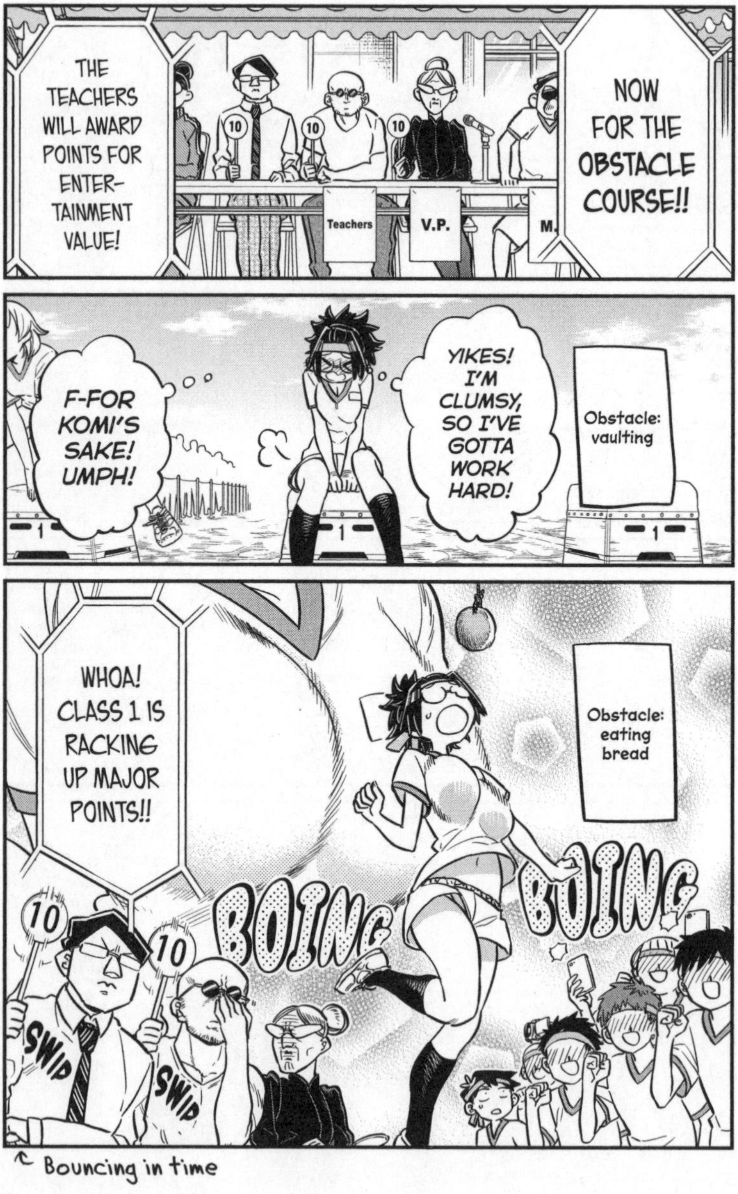
NOW FOR THE OBSTACLE COURSE!!
THE TEACHERS WILL AWARD POINTS FOR ENTER-TAINMENT VALUE!
10
10
10
Teachers
V.P.
M.
Obstacle: vaulting
YIKES! I'M CLUMSY, SO I'VE GOTTA WORK HARD!
F-FOR KOMI'S SAKE! UMPH!
1
1
1
Obstacle: eating bread
WHOA! CLASS 1 IS RACKING UP MAJOR POINTS!!
BOING
BOING
10
10
SWIP
SWIP

↖ Bouncing in time

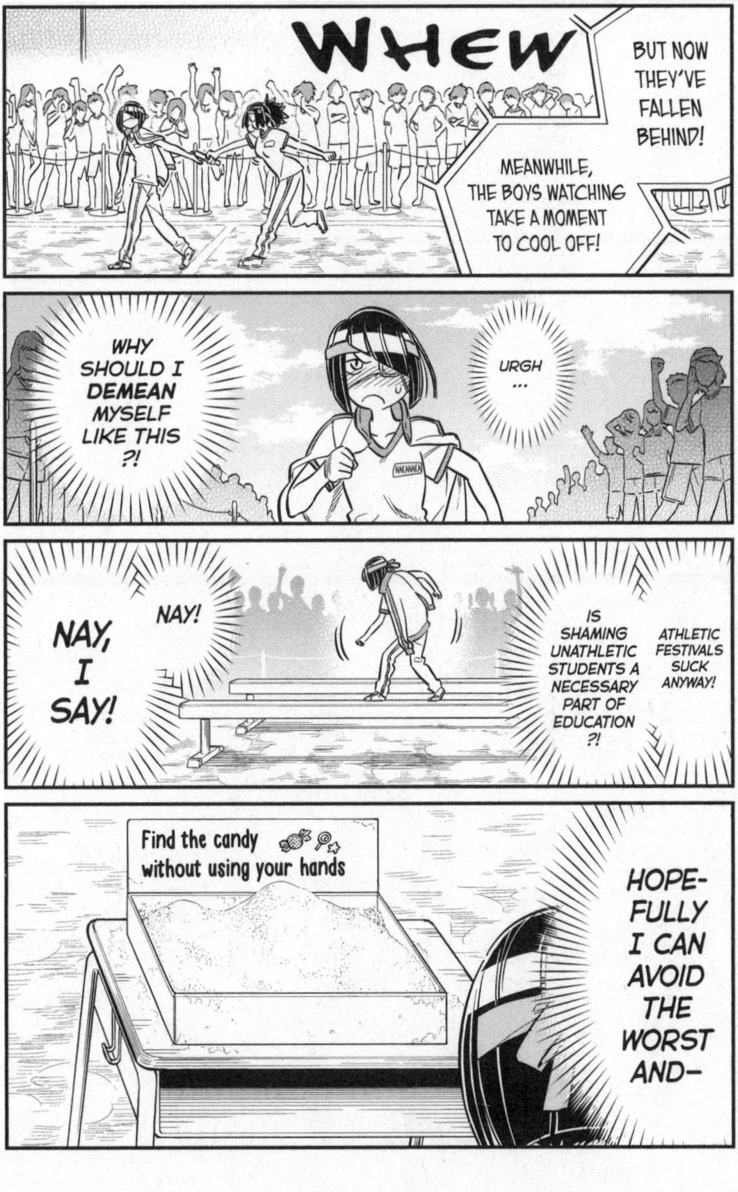
BUT NOW THEY'VE FALLEN BEHIND!
WHEW
MEANWHILE, THE BOYS WATCHING TAKE A MOMENT TO COOL OFF!
URGH...
WHY SHOULD I DEMEAN MYSELF LIKE THIS ?!
NAKANAKA
ATHLETIC FESTIVALS SUCK ANYWAY!
IS SHAMING UNATHLETIC STUDENTS A NECESSARY PART OF EDUCATION ?!
NAY!
NAY, I SAY!
HOPE-FULLY I CAN AVOID THE WORST AND—
Find the candy without using your hands

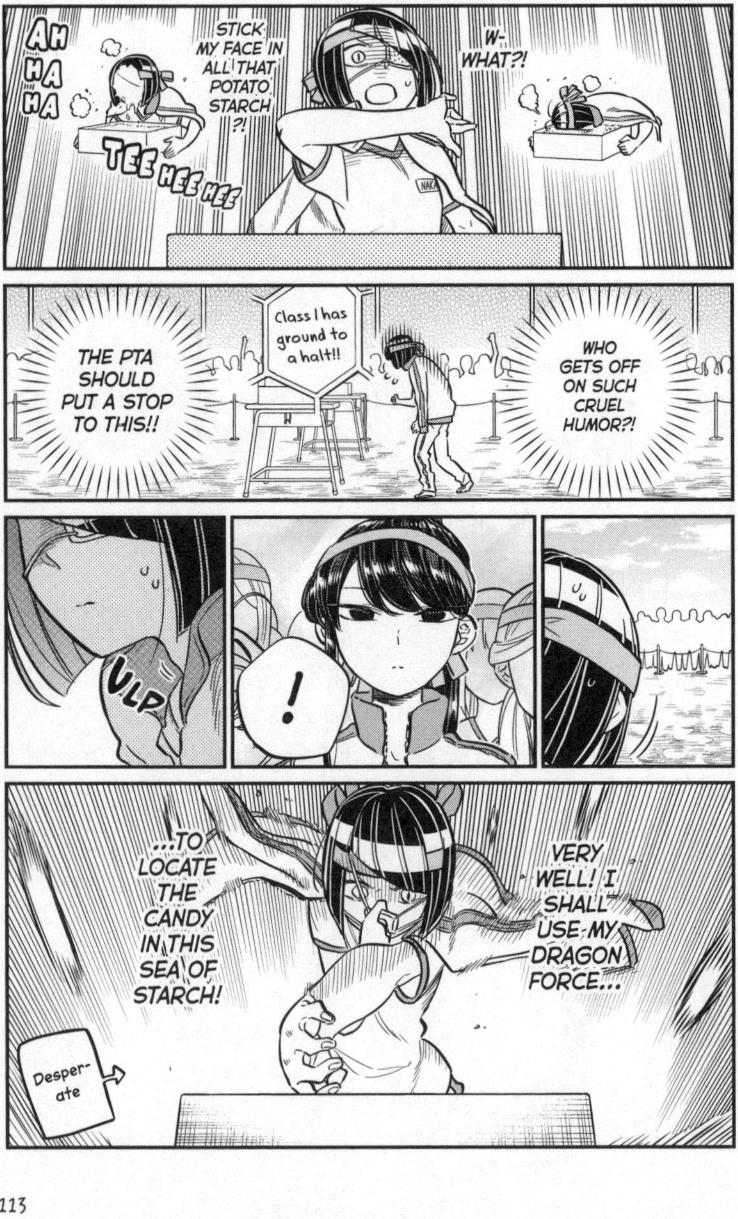
W-WHAT?!
STICK MY FACE IN ALL THAT POTATO STARCH?!
AH HA HA
TEE HEE HEE
WHO GETS OFF ON SUCH CRUEL HUMOR?!
Class 1 has ground to a halt!!
THE PTA SHOULD PUT A STOP TO THIS!!
!
ULP
VERY WELL! I SHALL USE MY DRAGON FORCE...
...TO LOCATE THE CANDY IN THIS SEA OF STARCH!
Desper-ate

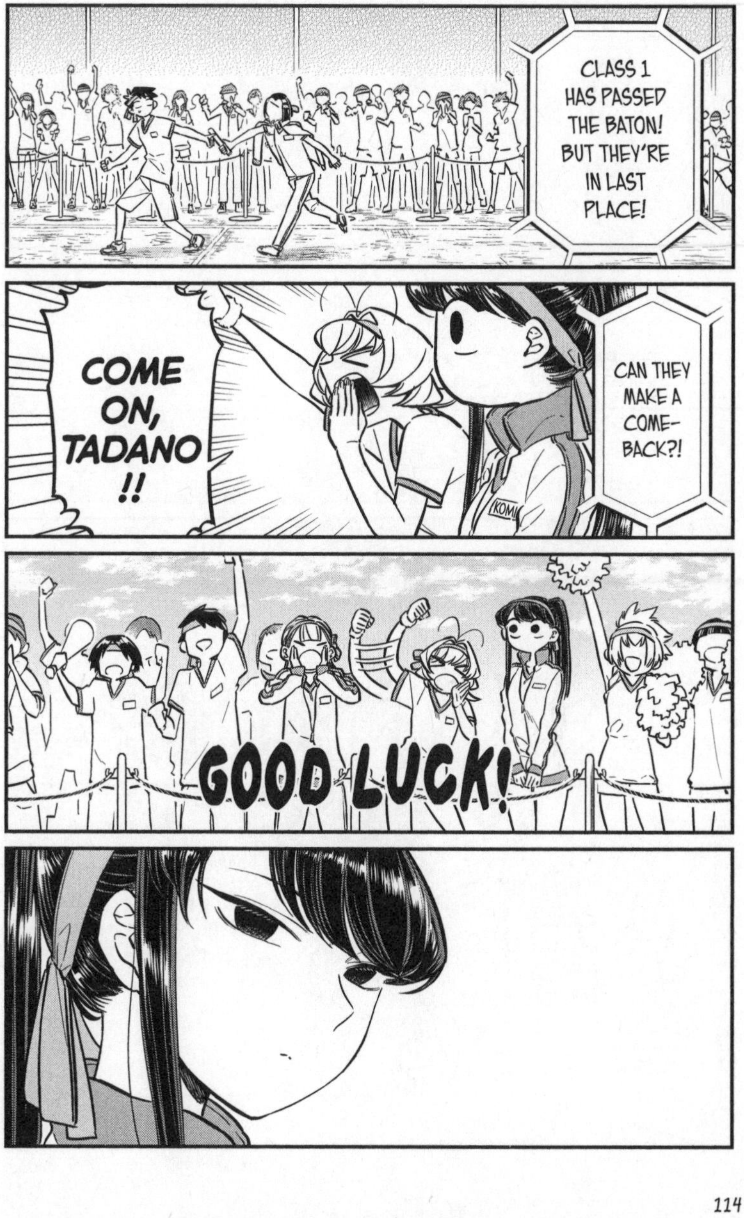
CLASS 1 HAS PASSED THE BATON! BUT THEY'RE IN LAST PLACE!
CAN THEY MAKE A COME-BACK?!
COME ON, TADANO !!
KOMI
GOOD LUCK!

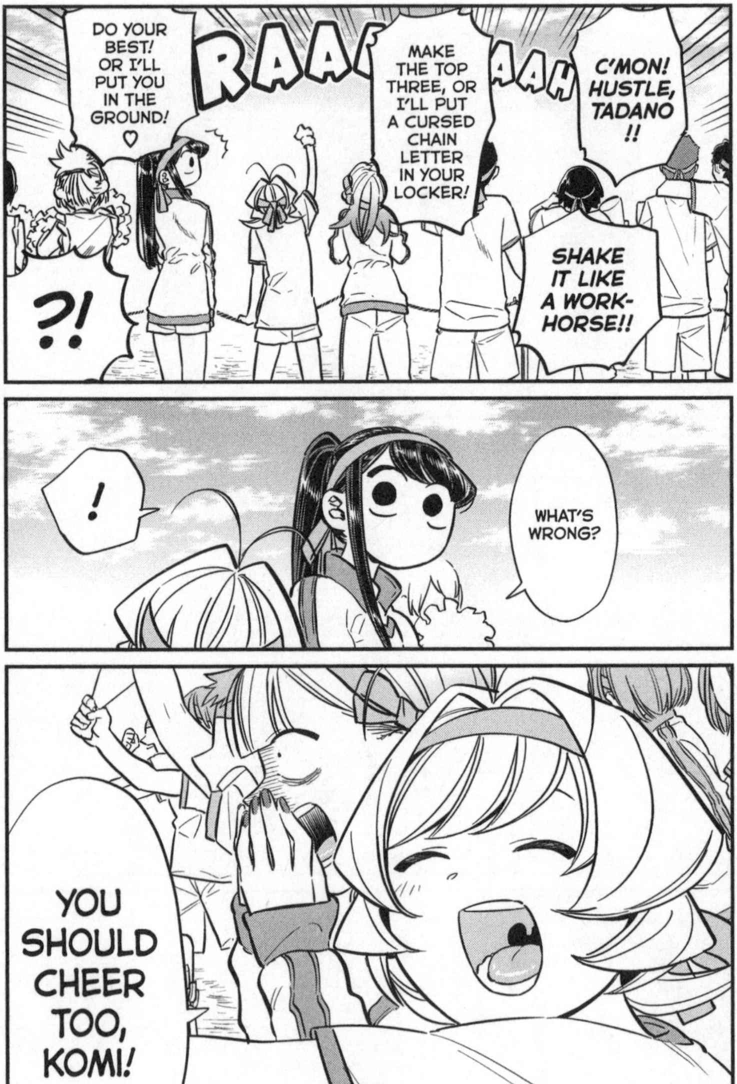
C'MON! HUSTLE, TADANO!!
SHAKE IT LIKE A WORK-HORSE!!
MAKE THE TOP THREE, OR I'LL PUT A CURSED CHAIN LETTER IN YOUR LOCKER!
RAAA AAH
DO YOUR BEST! OR I'LL PUT YOU IN THE GROUND! ♡
?!
WHAT'S WRONG?
!
YOU SHOULD CHEER TOO, KOMI!

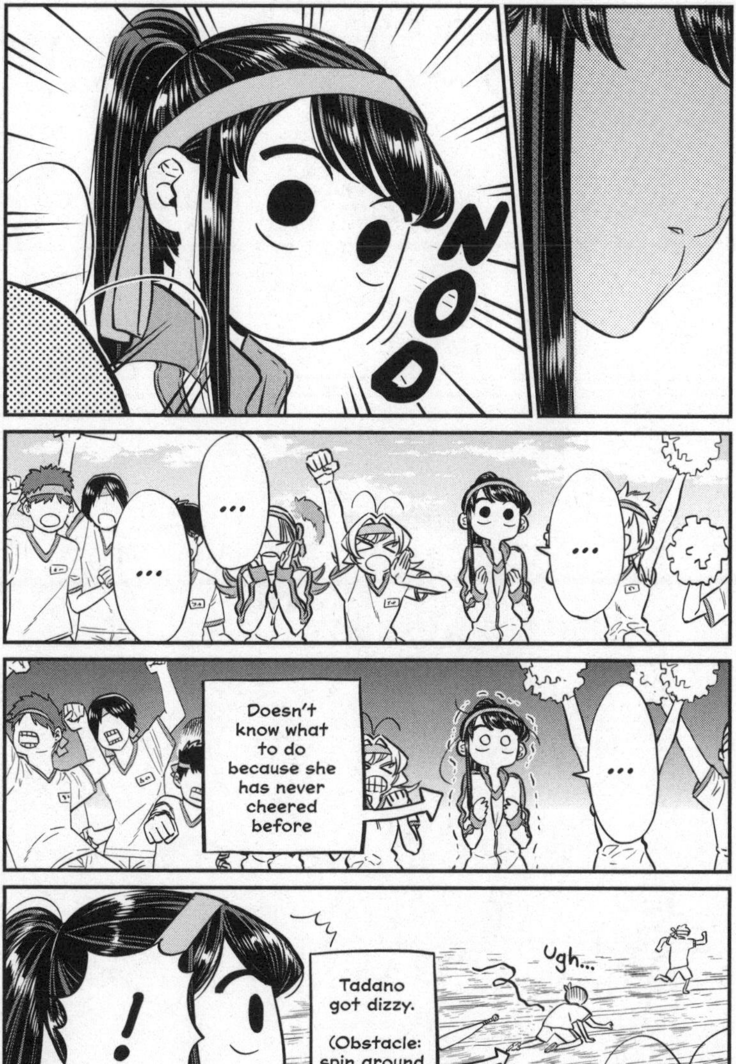
NOD
...
...
...
...
Doesn't know what to do because she has never cheered before
!
Ugh...
Tadano got dizzy.
(Obstacle: spin around a baseball bat)

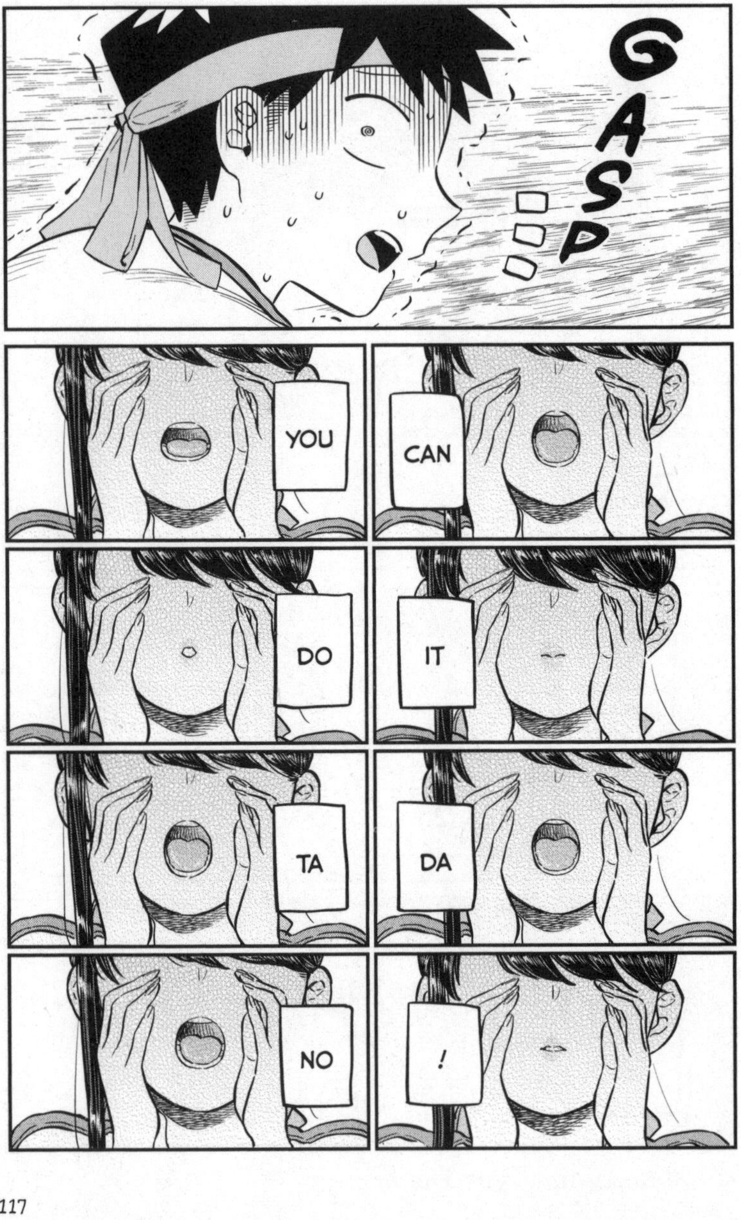
GASP
YOU
CAN
DO
IT
TA
DA
NO
!

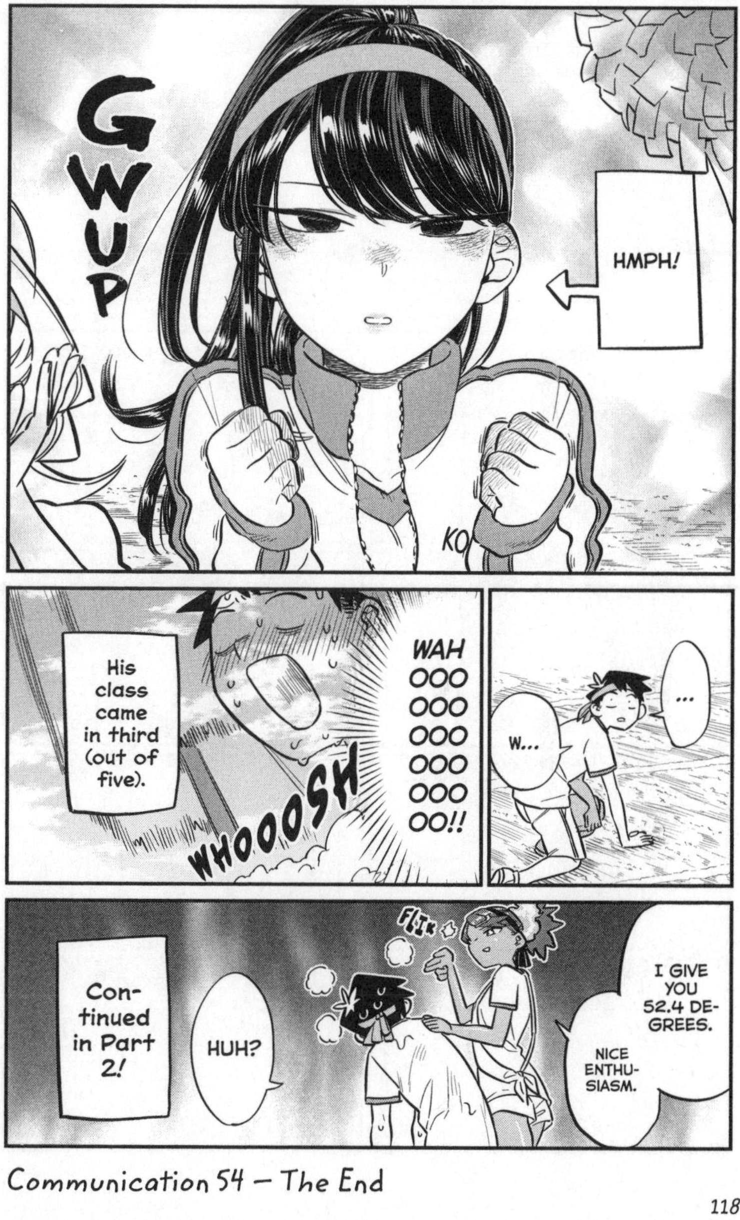
HMPH!
GWUP
KO
...
W...
WAH OOO OOO OOO OOO OOO OO!!
WHOOOSH
His class came in third (out of five).
I GIVE YOU 52.4 DE-GREES.
NICE ENTHU-SIASM.
FLIK
HUH?
Con-tinued in Part 2!

Communication 54 — The End

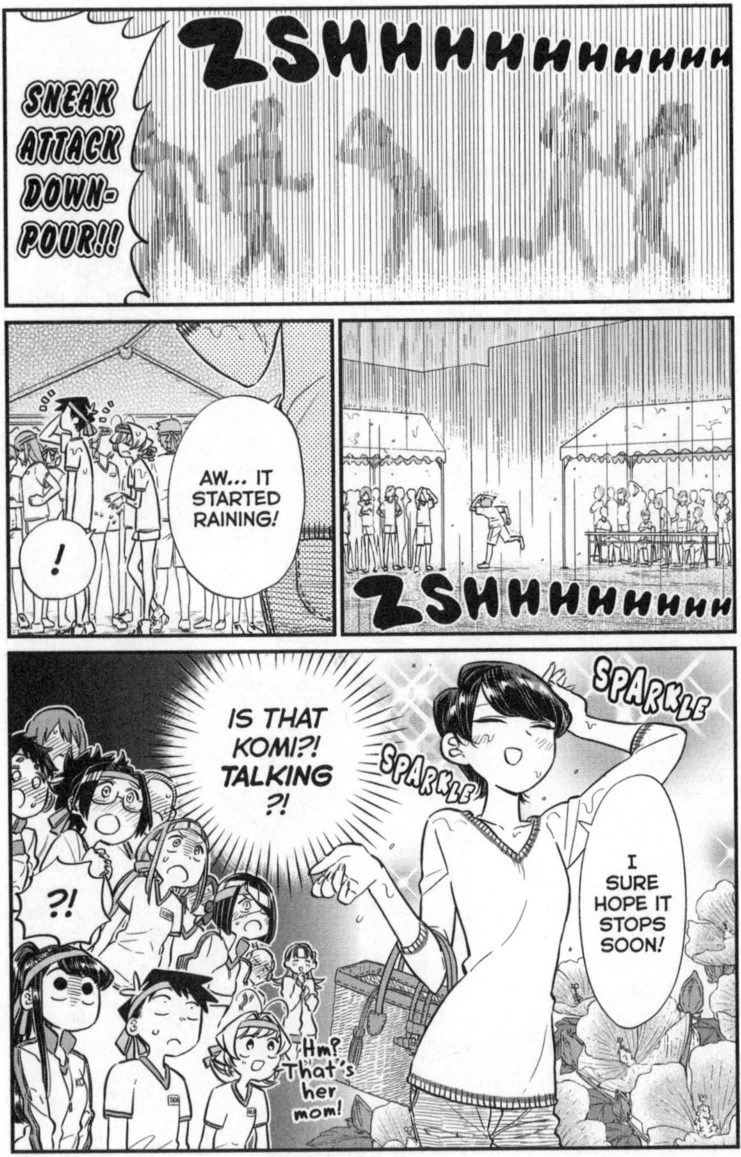
ZSHHHHHHHHHHH
SNEAK ATTACK DOWN-POUR!!
ZSHHHHHHHHHH
AW... IT STARTED RAINING!
!
SPARKLE
I SURE HOPE IT STOPS SOON!
SPARKLE
IS THAT KOMI?! TALKING?!
?!
Hm? That's her mom!

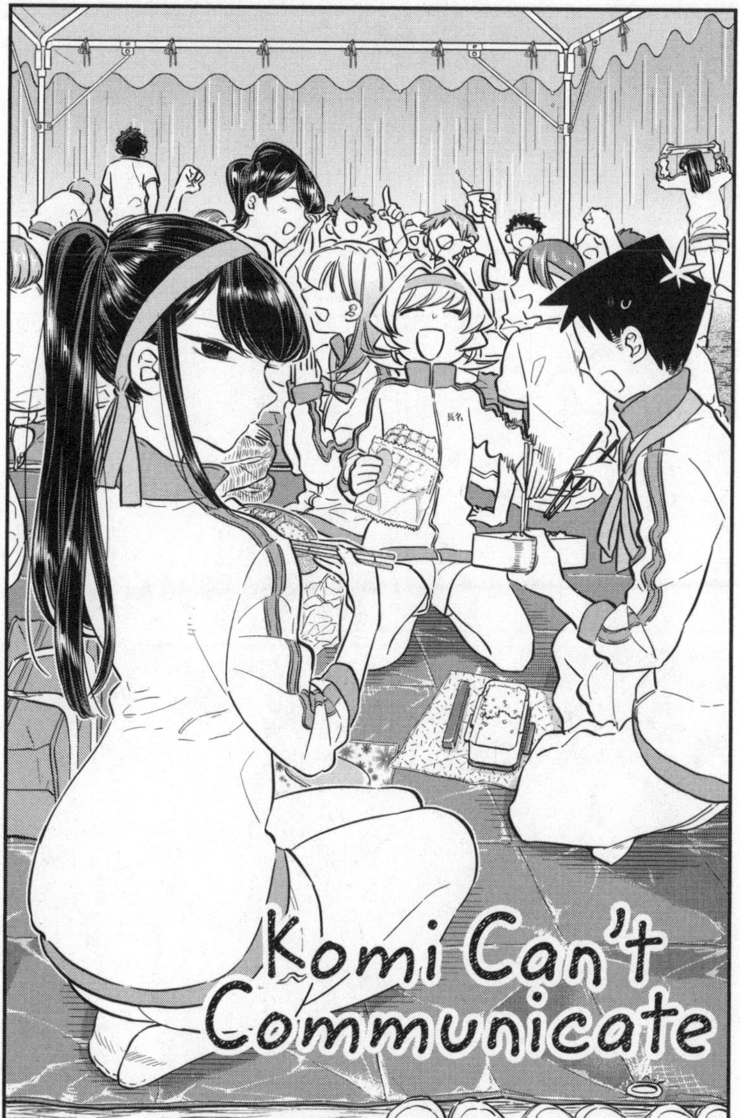
長名
Komi Can't Communicate

Communication 55: Sports Festival, Part 2

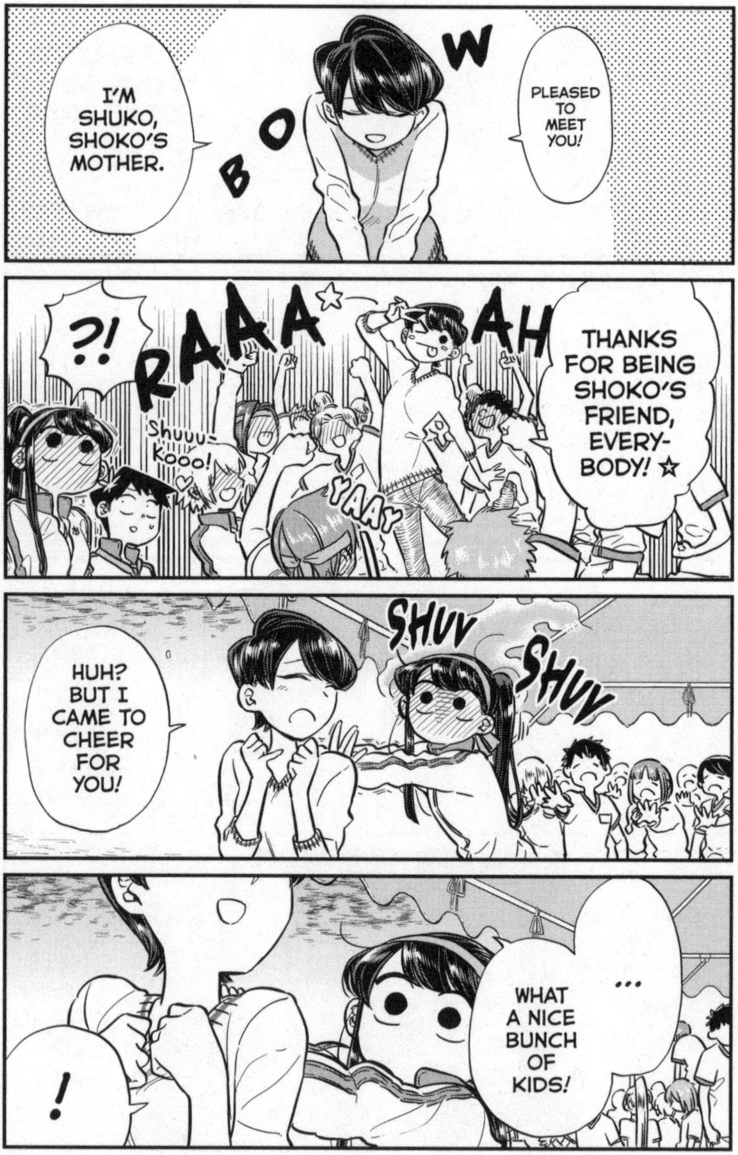
PLEASED TO MEET YOU!
BOW
I'M SHUKO, SHOKO'S MOTHER.
THANKS FOR BEING SHOKO'S FRIEND, EVERYBODY! ☆
RAAAAH
YAAY
Shuuu-kooo!
?!
SHUV SHUV
HUH? BUT I CAME TO CHEER FOR YOU!
...
WHAT A NICE BUNCH OF KIDS!
!

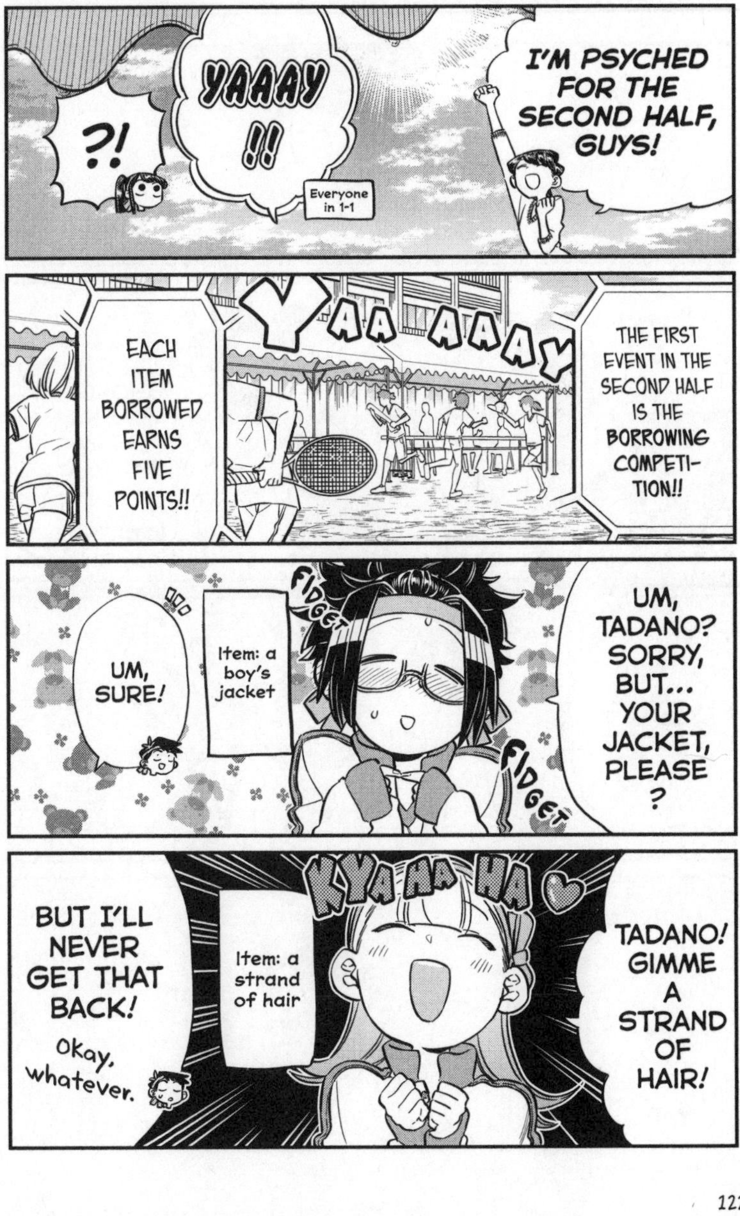
I'M PSYCHED FOR THE SECOND HALF, GUYS!
YAAAY!!
Everyone in 1-1
?!
THE FIRST EVENT IN THE SECOND HALF IS THE BORROWING COMPETITION!!
YAAAAAAY
EACH ITEM BORROWED EARNS FIVE POINTS!!
UM, TADANO? SORRY, BUT... YOUR JACKET, PLEASE?
FIDGET
FIDGET
Item: a boy's jacket
UM, SURE!
TADANO! GIMME A STRAND OF HAIR!
KYA HA HA
Item: a strand of hair
BUT I'LL NEVER GET THAT BACK!
Okay, whatever.

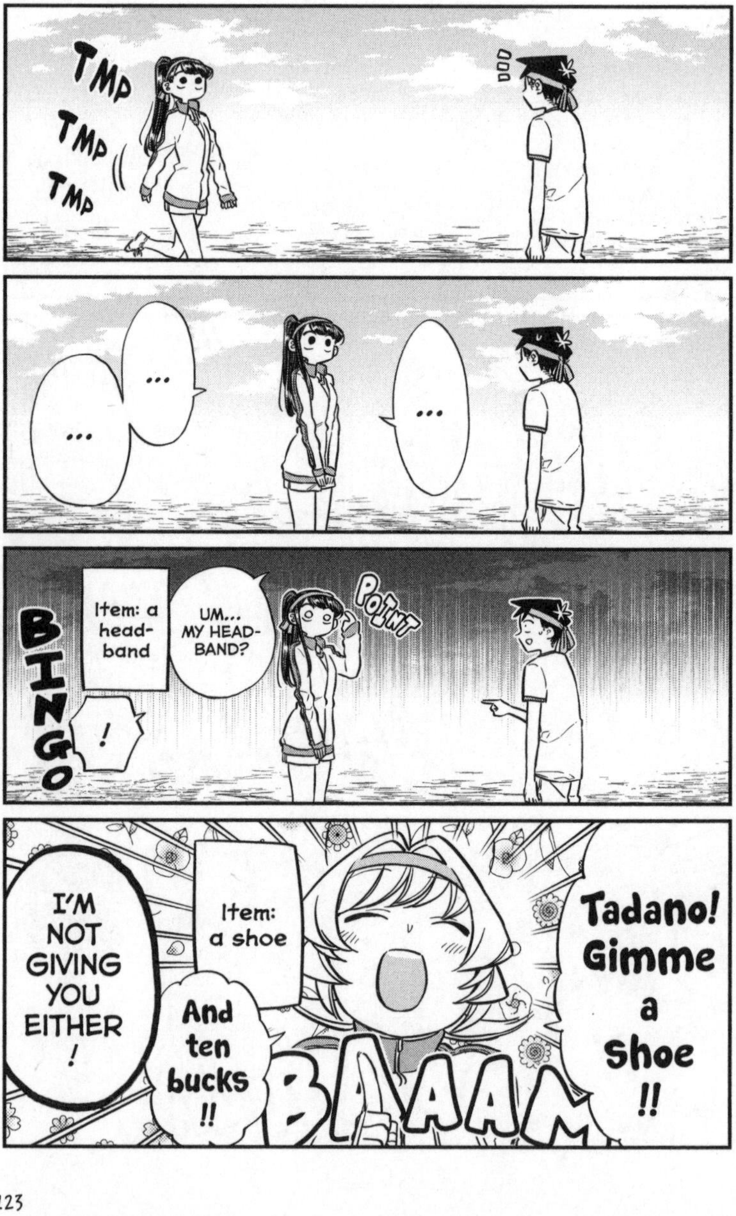
TMP TMP TMP
...
...
...
POINT
UM... MY HEAD-BAND?
Item: a head-band
!
BINGO
Tadano! Gimme a Shoe!!
BAAAM
Item: a shoe
And ten bucks!!
I'M NOT GIVING YOU EITHER!

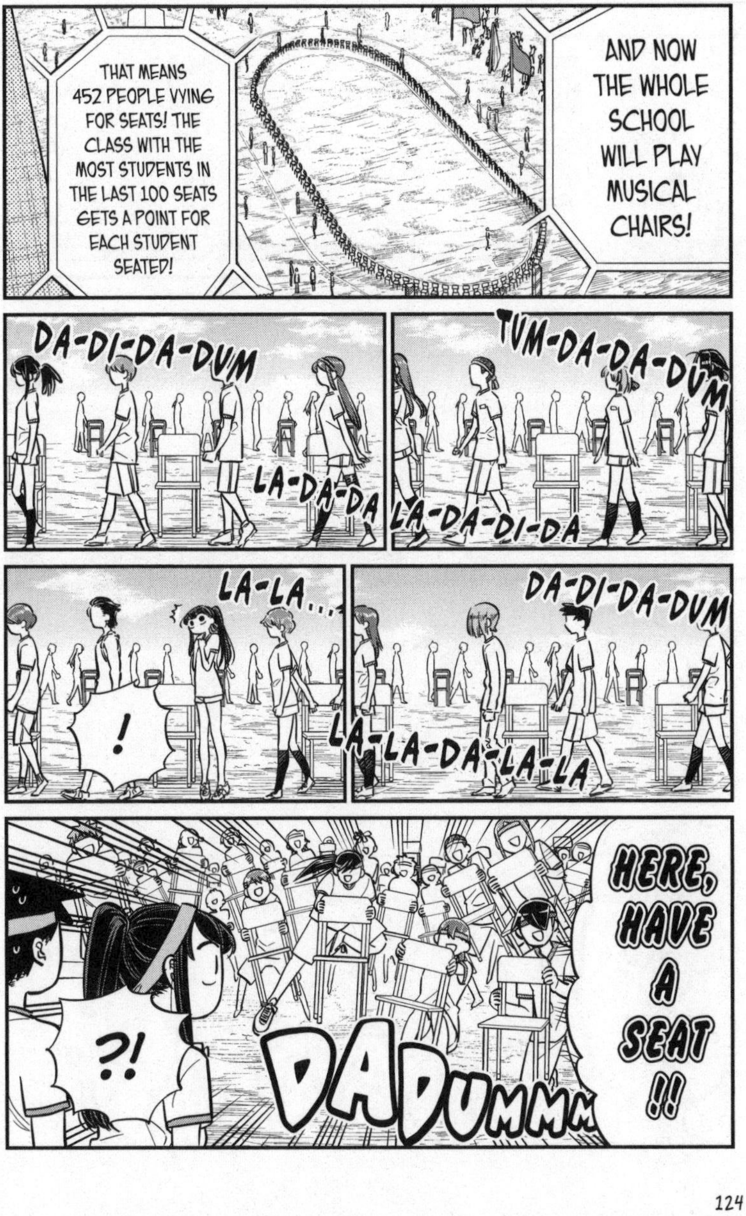
AND NOW THE WHOLE SCHOOL WILL PLAY MUSICAL CHAIRS!
THAT MEANS 452 PEOPLE VYING FOR SEATS! THE CLASS WITH THE MOST STUDENTS IN THE LAST 100 SEATS GETS A POINT FOR EACH STUDENT SEATED!
TUM-DA-DA-DUM
LA-DA-DI-DA
DA-DI-DA-DUM
LA-DA-DA
DA-DI-DA-DUM
LA-LA-DA-LA-LA
LA-LA...
!
HERE, HAVE A SEAT!!
DADUMMM
?!

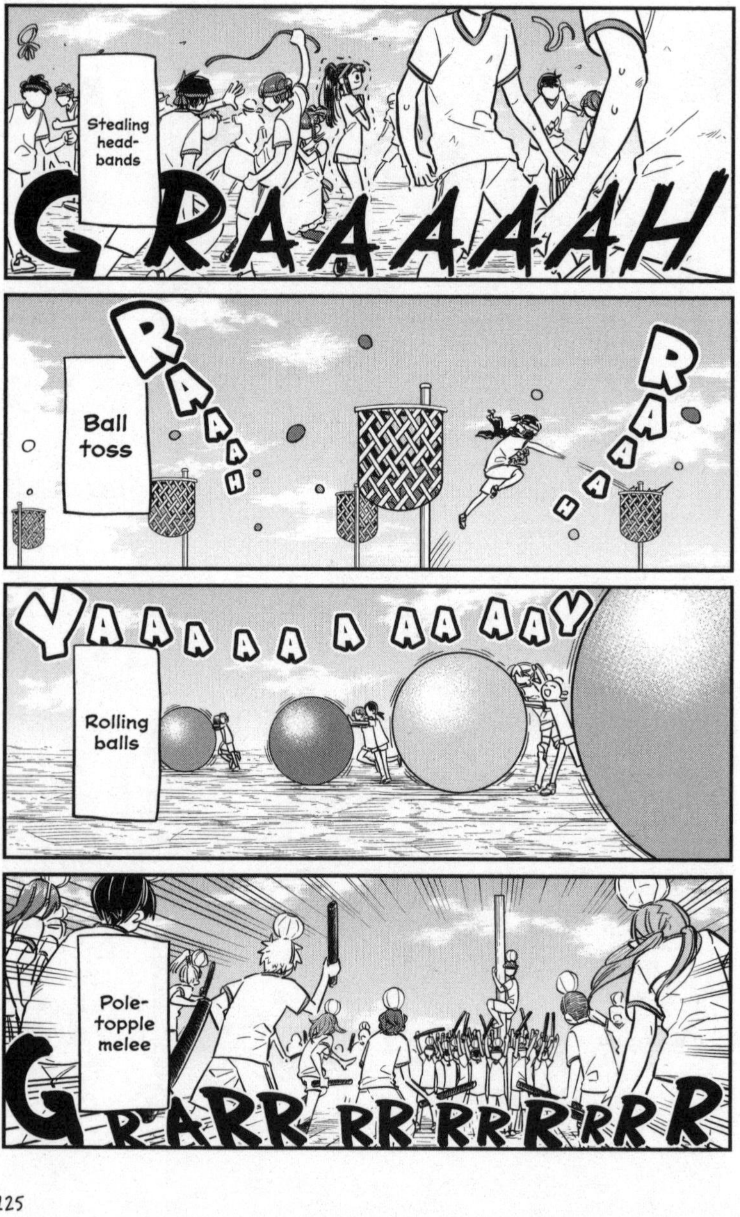
Stealing head-bands
GRAAAAAH
Ball toss
RAAAAH
RAAAAH
Rolling balls
YAAAAAAAAAAY
Pole-topple melee
GRARRRRRRRRRR

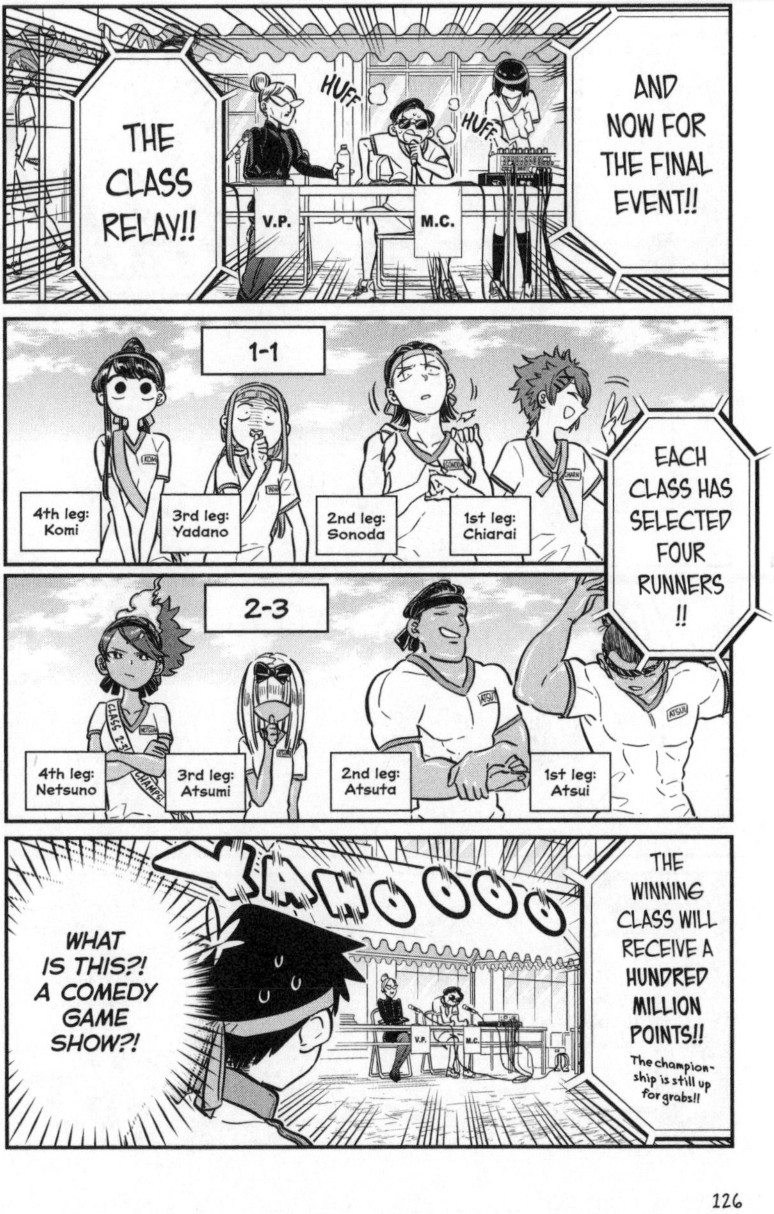
AND NOW FOR THE FINAL EVENT!!
HUFF
HUFF
THE CLASS RELAY!!
M.C.
V.P.
EACH CLASS HAS SELECTED FOUR RUNNERS!!
1-1
1st leg: Chiarai
2nd leg: Sonoda
3rd leg: Yadano
4th leg: Komi
2-3
1st leg: Atsui
2nd leg: Atsuta
3rd leg: Atsumi
4th leg: Netsuno
THE WINNING CLASS WILL RECEIVE A HUNDRED MILLION POINTS!!
The championship is still up for grabs!!
YAHOOOOO
WHAT IS THIS?! A COMEDY GAME SHOW?!

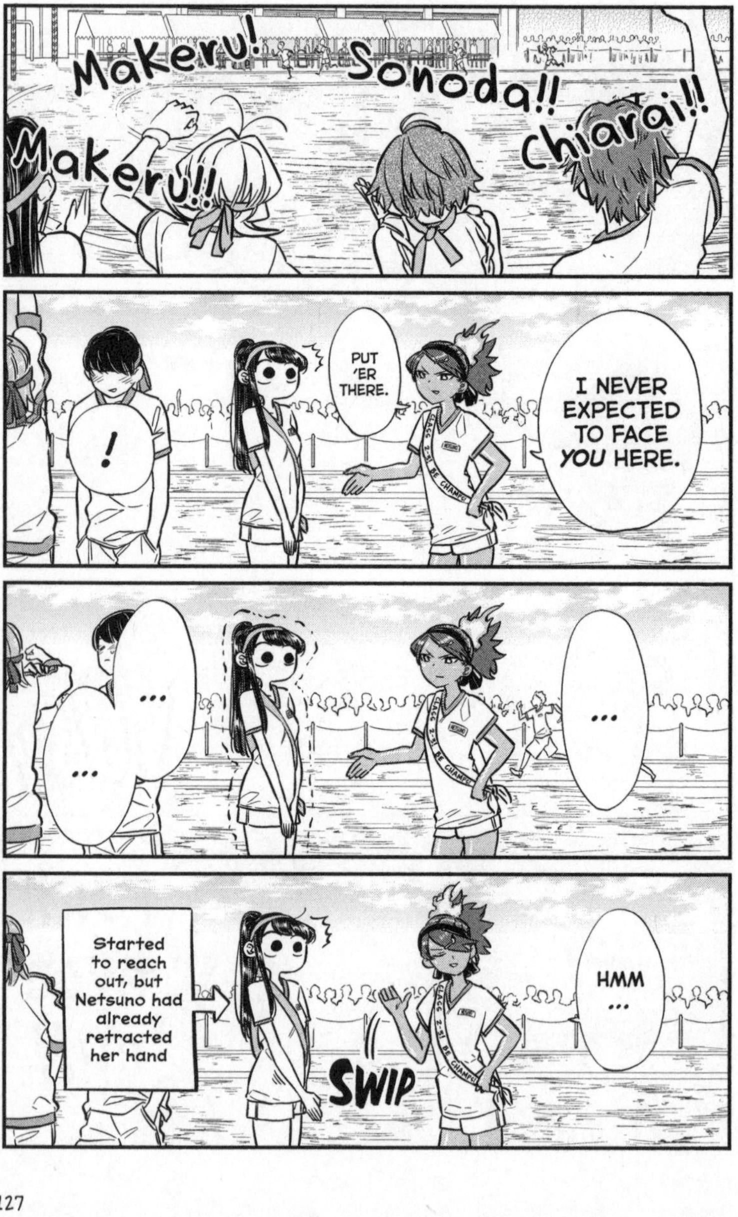
Chiarai!!
Sonoda!!
Makeru!
Makeru!!
I NEVER EXPECTED TO FACE *YOU* HERE.
PUT 'ER THERE.
!
...
...
...
HMM ...
SWIP
Started to reach out, but Netsuno had already retracted her hand

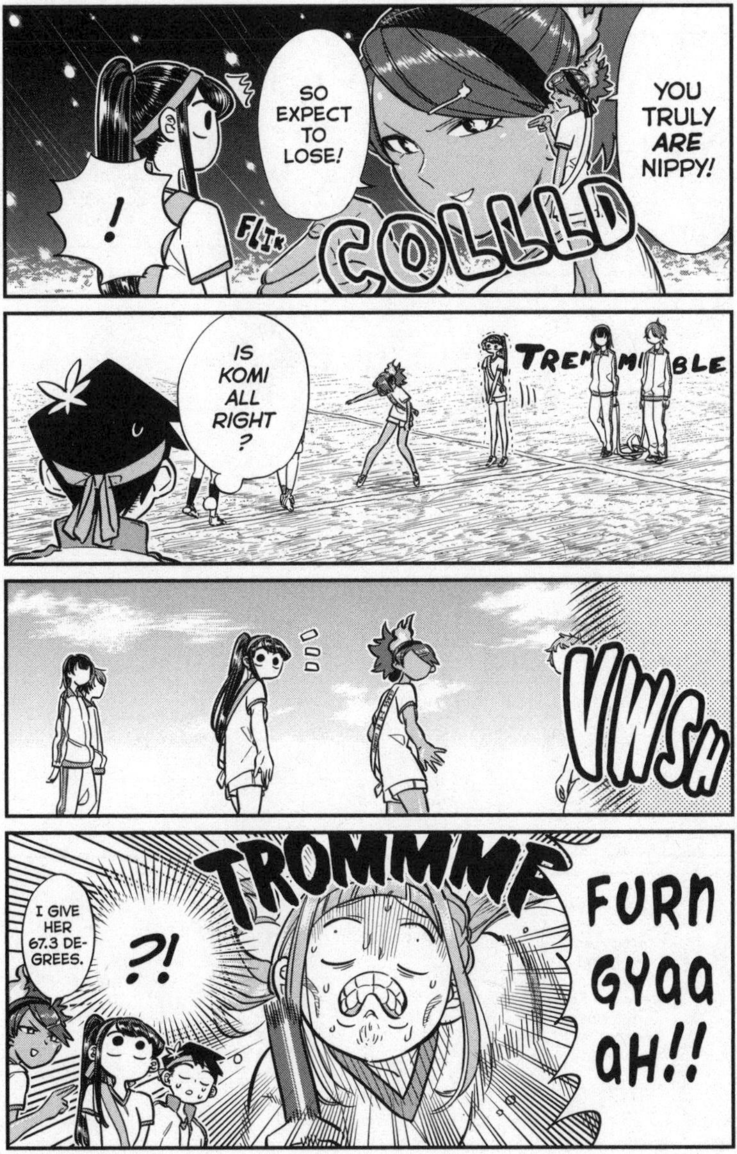
YOU TRULY ARE NIPPY!
COLLLD
SO EXPECT TO LOSE!
FLIK
!
TREM MBLE
IS KOMI ALL RIGHT?
VWSH
FURN GYAA AH!!
TROMMMF
?!
I GIVE HER 67.3 DEGREES.

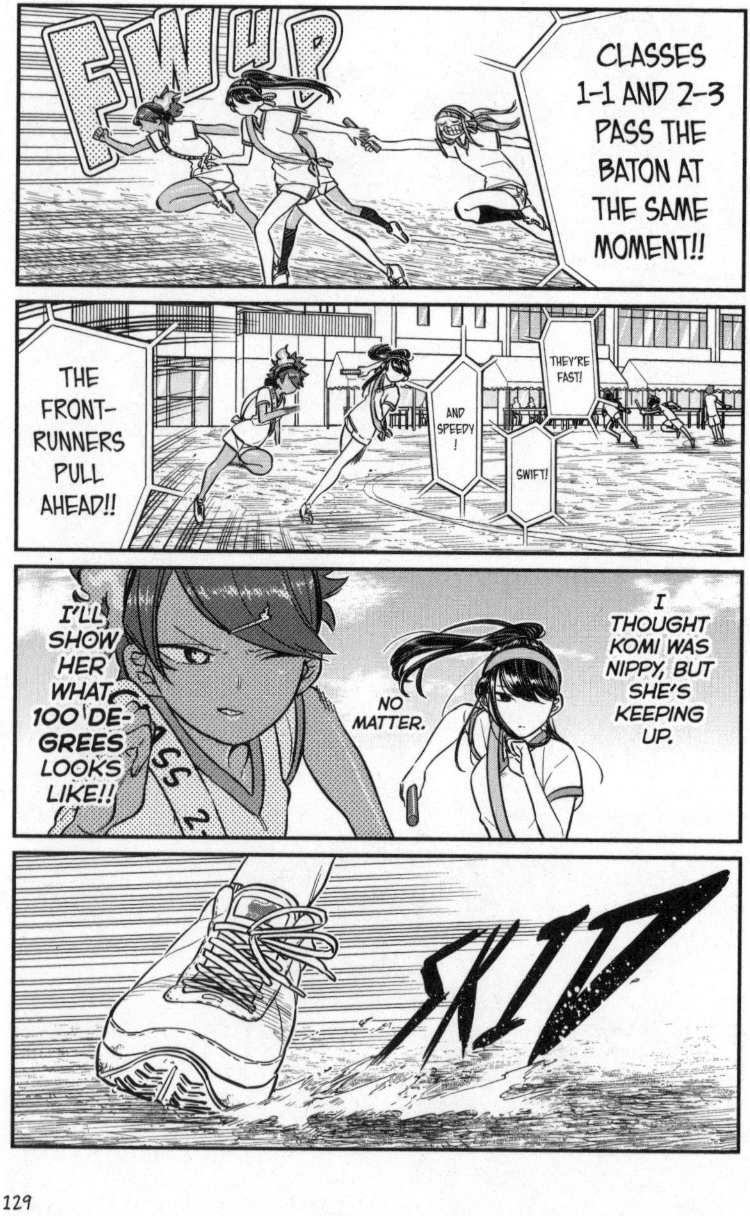
CLASSES 1-1 AND 2-3 PASS THE BATON AT THE SAME MOMENT!!
FWUP
THEY'RE FAST!
SWIFT!
AND SPEEDY!
THE FRONT-RUNNERS PULL AHEAD!!
I THOUGHT KOMI WAS NIPPY, BUT SHE'S KEEPING UP.
NO MATTER.
I'LL SHOW HER WHAT 100 DE-GREES LOOKS LIKE!!
SKID

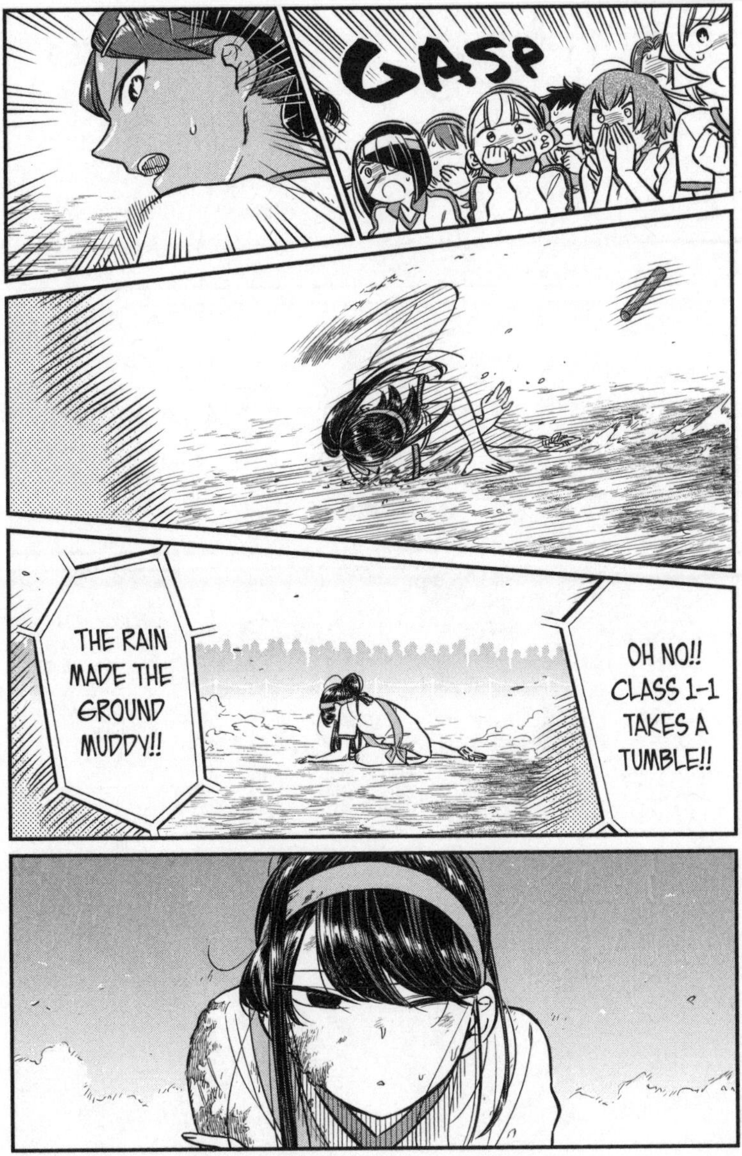
GASP
OH NO!! CLASS 1-1 TAKES A TUMBLE!!
THE RAIN MADE THE GROUND MUDDY!!

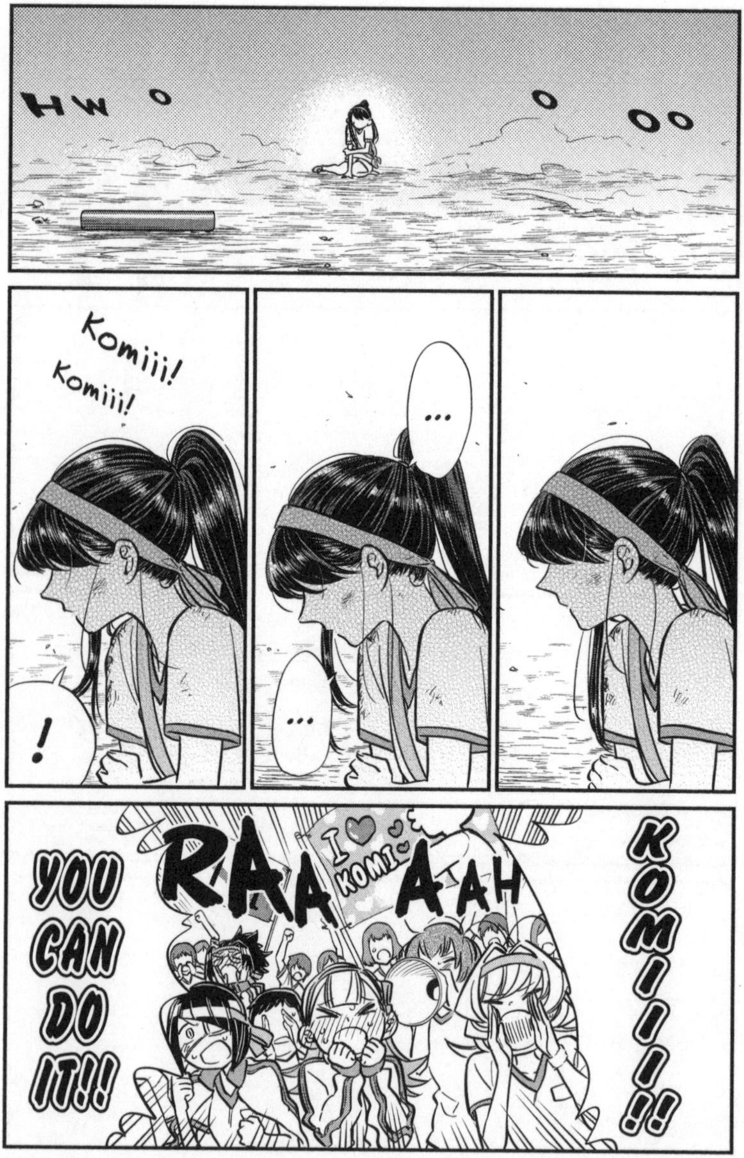
HWOOOOO
...
...
Komiii!
Komiii!
!
KOMIIII!!
RAAAAH
I ♥ KOMI
YOU CAN DO IT!!

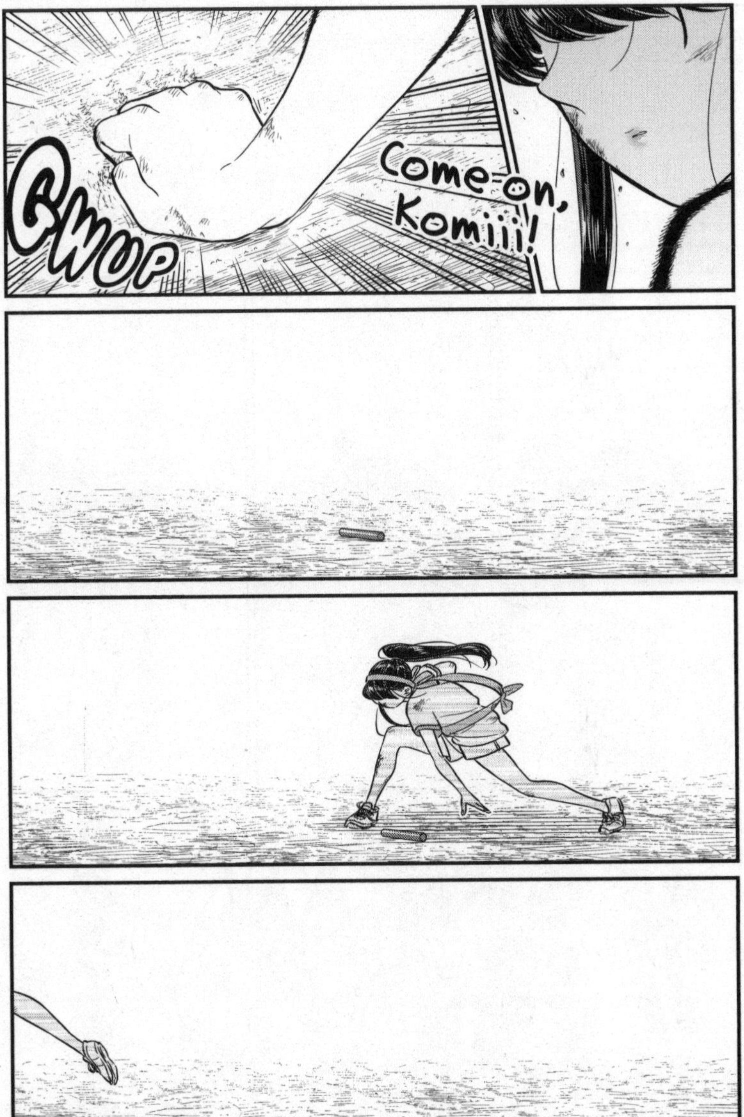
Come on, Komiii!
GWUP

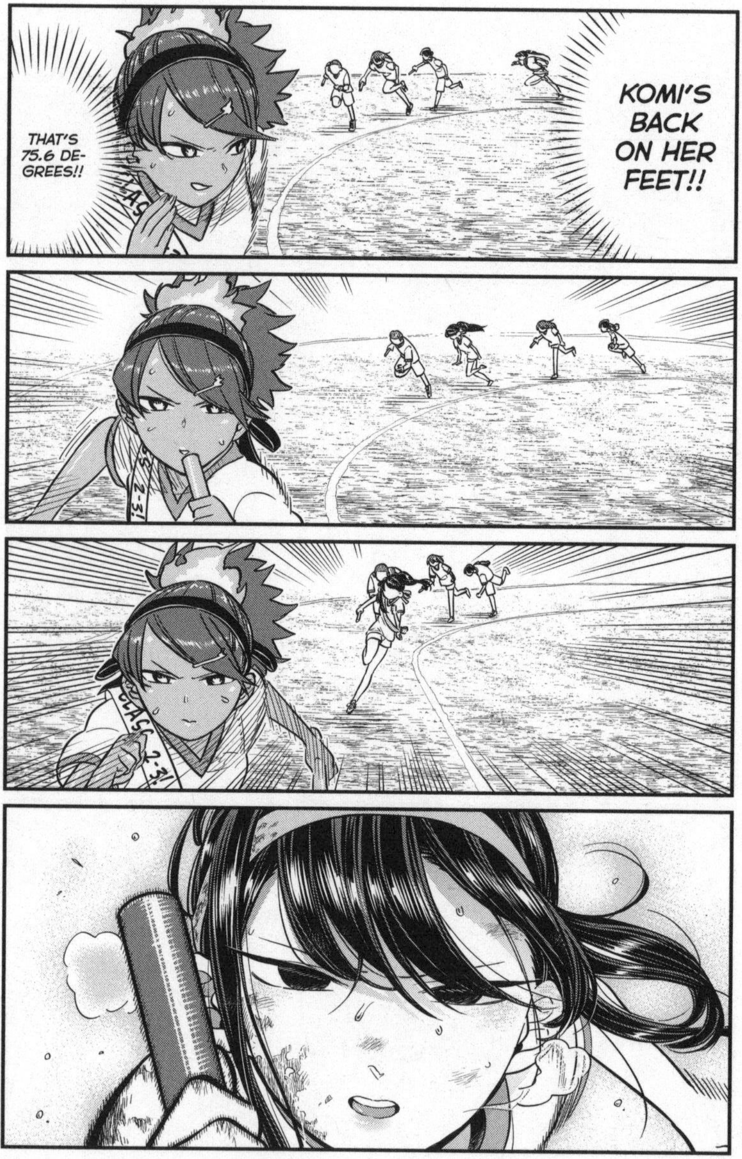
KOMI'S BACK ON HER FEET!!
THAT'S 75.6 DE-GREES!!

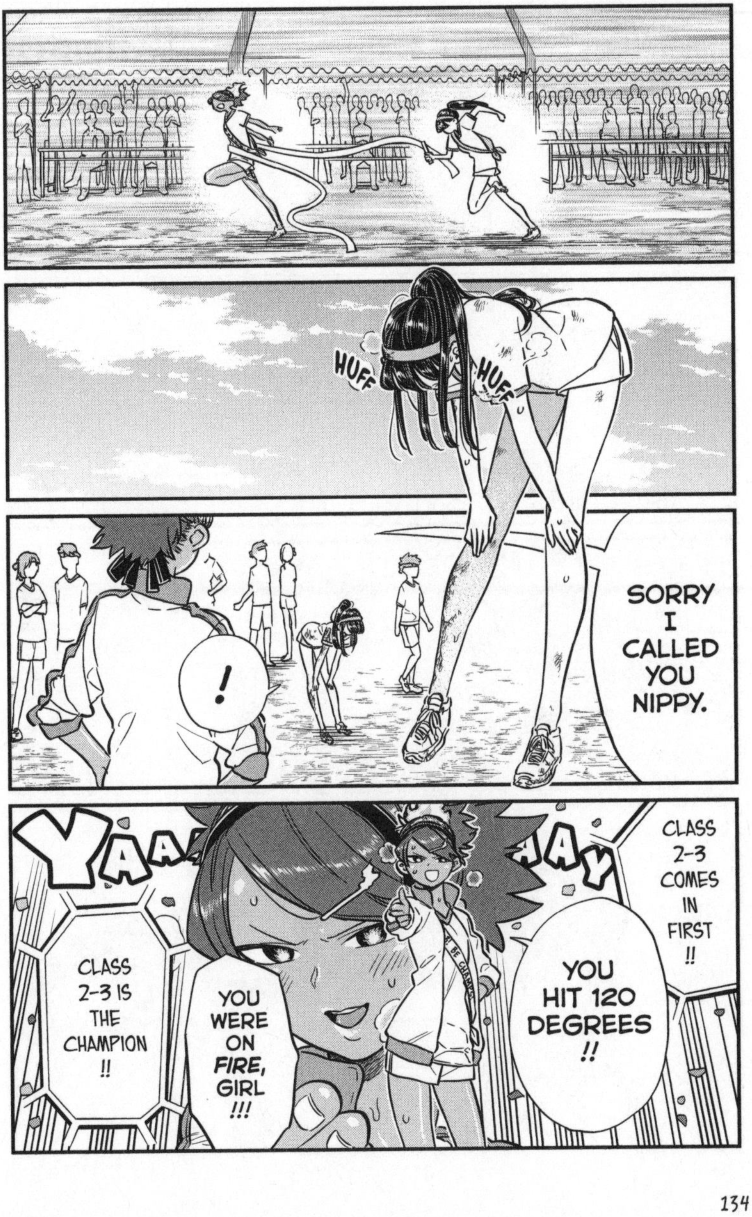
HUFF
HUFF
SORRY I CALLED YOU NIPPY.
!
YAA
AAY
CLASS 2-3 COMES IN FIRST !!
YOU HIT 120 DEGREES !!
YOU WERE ON *FIRE*, GIRL !!!
CLASS 2-3 IS THE CHAMPION !!

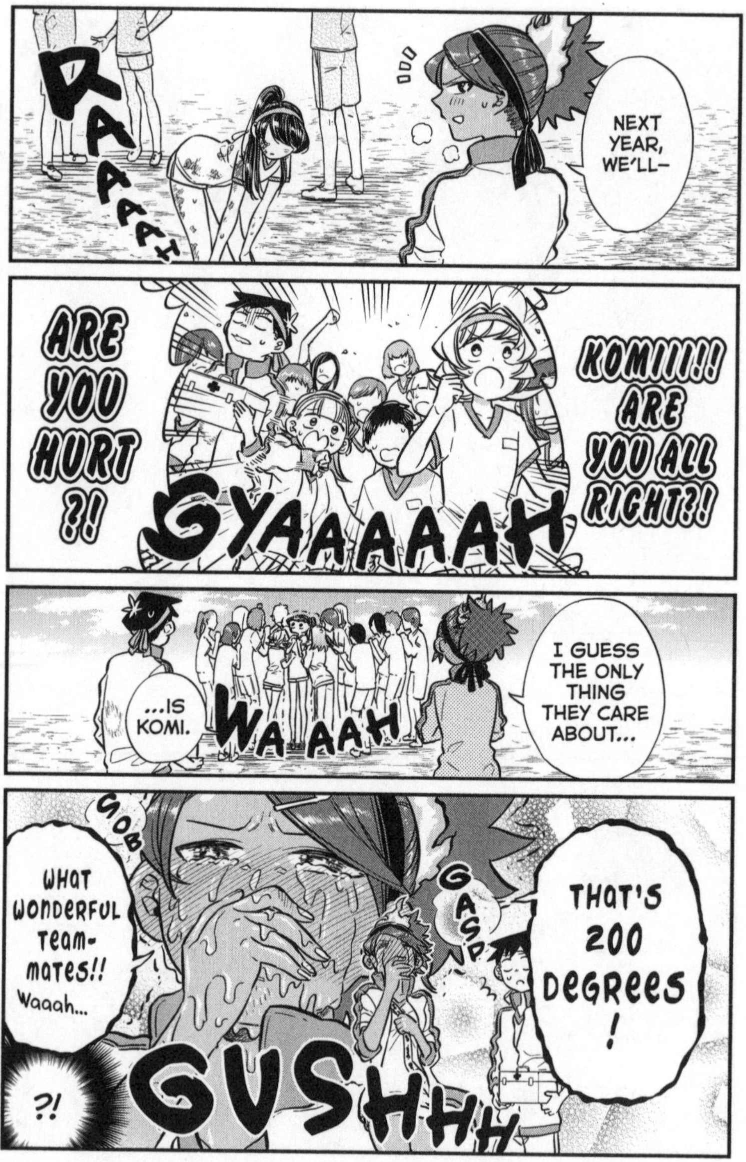
NEXT YEAR, WE'LL–
RAAAAH
KOMIIII!! ARE YOU ALL RIGHT?!
GYAAAAAH
ARE YOU HURT?!
I GUESS THE ONLY THING THEY CARE ABOUT...
WA AAH
...IS KOMI.
THAT'S 200 DEGREES!
GASP
SOB
WHAT WONDERFUL TEAM-MATES!! Waaah...
GUSHHH
?!

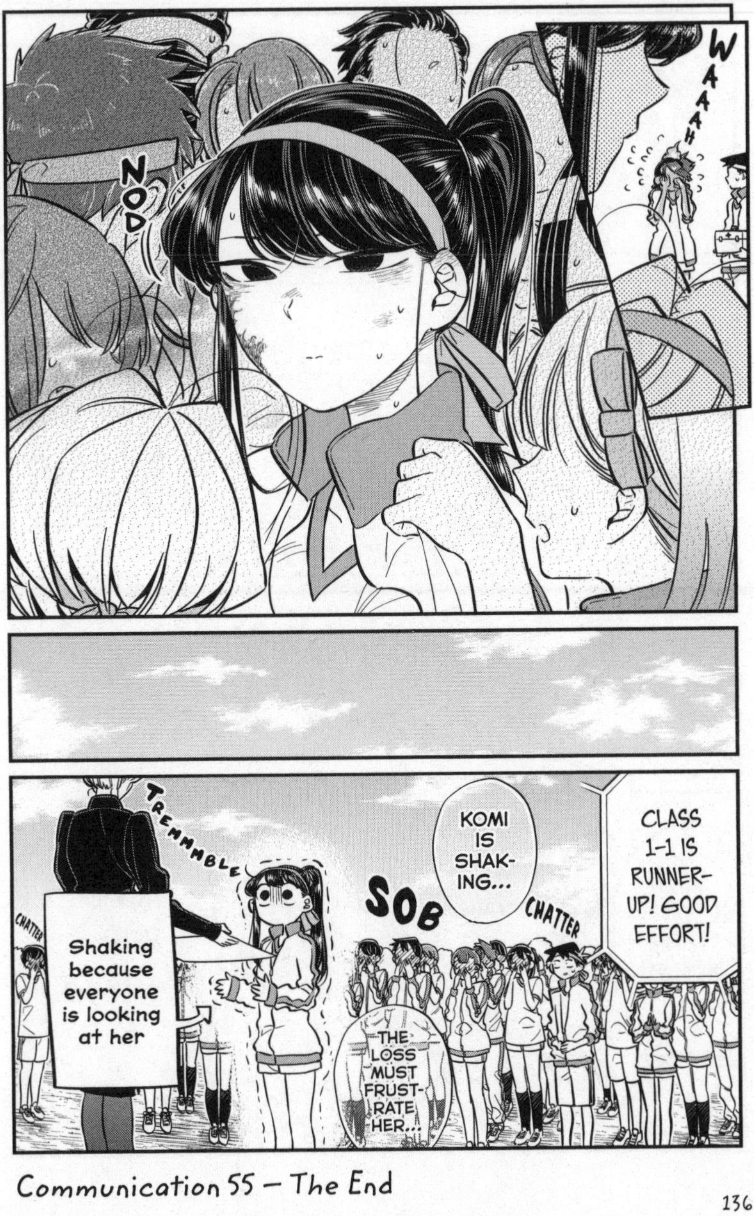
WAAAAH
NOD
CLASS 1-1 IS RUNNER-UP! GOOD EFFORT!
KOMI IS SHAK-ING...
CHATTER
SOB
TREMMMBLE
THE LOSS MUST FRUST-RATE HER...
Shaking because everyone is looking at her
CHATTER

Communication 55 – The End

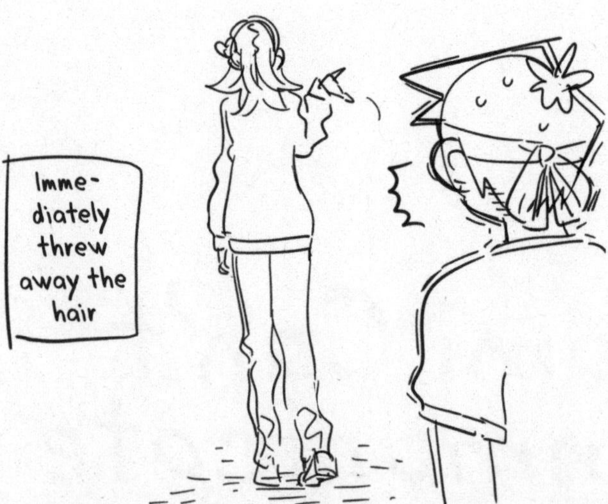
Imme-
diately
threw
away the
hair

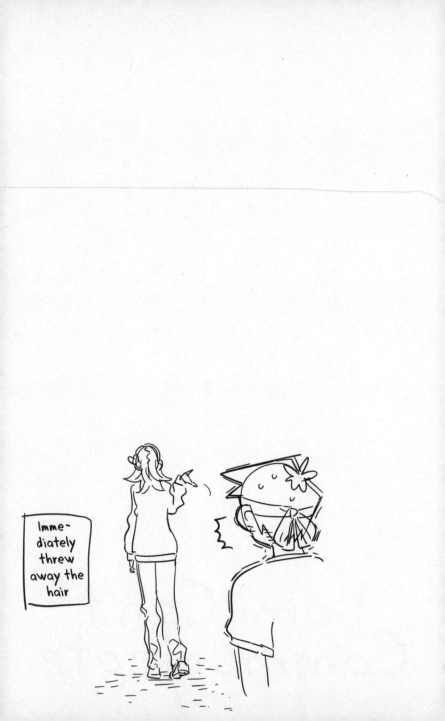

Komi Can't
Communicate

Komi Can't Communicate

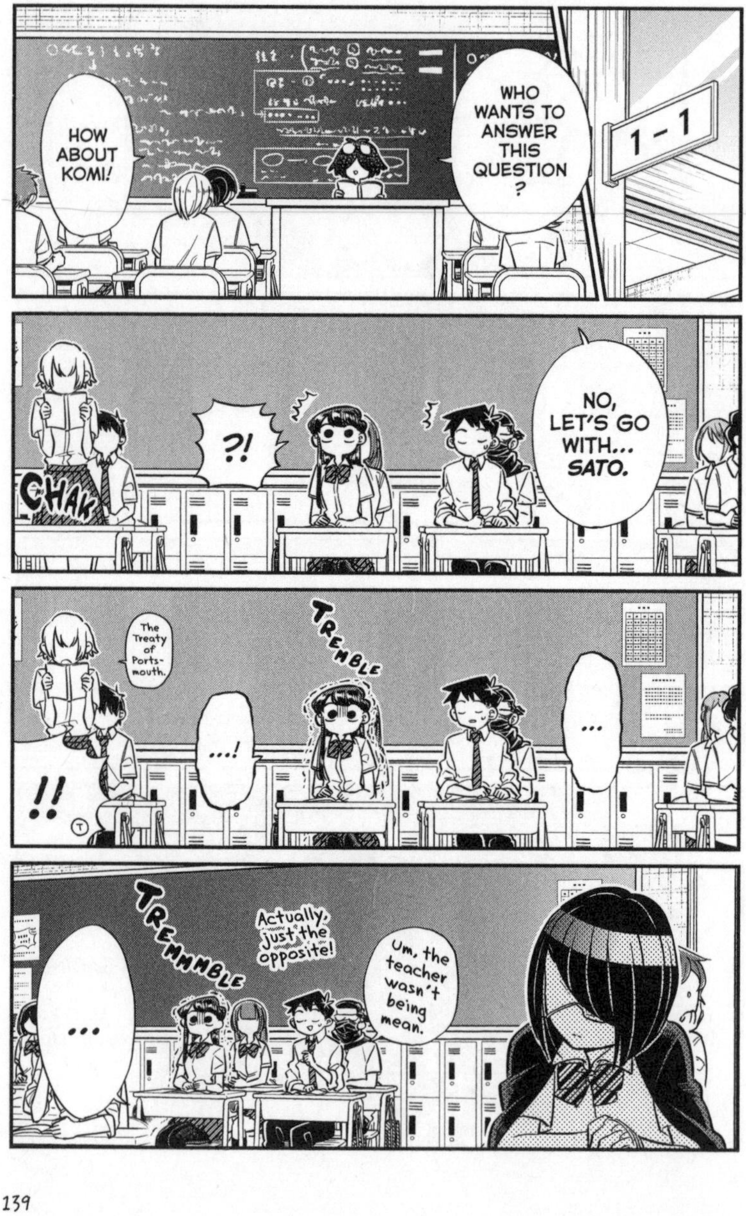
1-1
WHO WANTS TO ANSWER THIS QUESTION?
HOW ABOUT KOMI!
NO, LET'S GO WITH... SATO.
?!
CHAK
...
TREMBLE
...!
The Treaty of Portsmouth.
!!
Um, the teacher wasn't being mean.
Actually, just the opposite!
TREMMMBLE
...

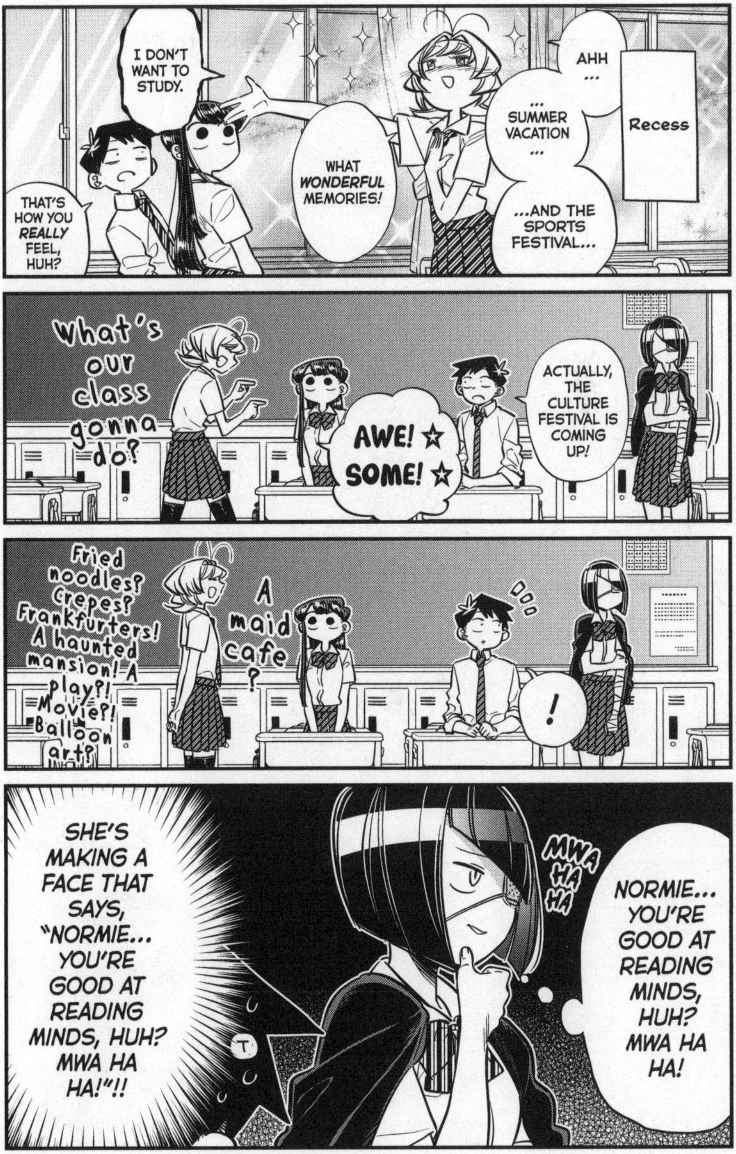
Recess
AHH... ...SUMMER VACATION... ...AND THE SPORTS FESTIVAL...
WHAT WONDERFUL MEMORIES!
I DON'T WANT TO STUDY.
THAT'S HOW YOU REALLY FEEL, HUH?
ACTUALLY, THE CULTURE FESTIVAL IS COMING UP!
AWE! ☆ SOME! ☆
What's our class gonna do?
!
A maid cafe?
Fried noodles? Crepes? Frankfurters! A haunted mansion! A play?! Movie?! Balloon art?!
NORMIE... YOU'RE GOOD AT READING MINDS, HUH? MWA HA HA!
MWA HA HA
SHE'S MAKING A FACE THAT SAYS, "NORMIE... YOU'RE GOOD AT READING MINDS, HUH? MWA HA HA!"!!

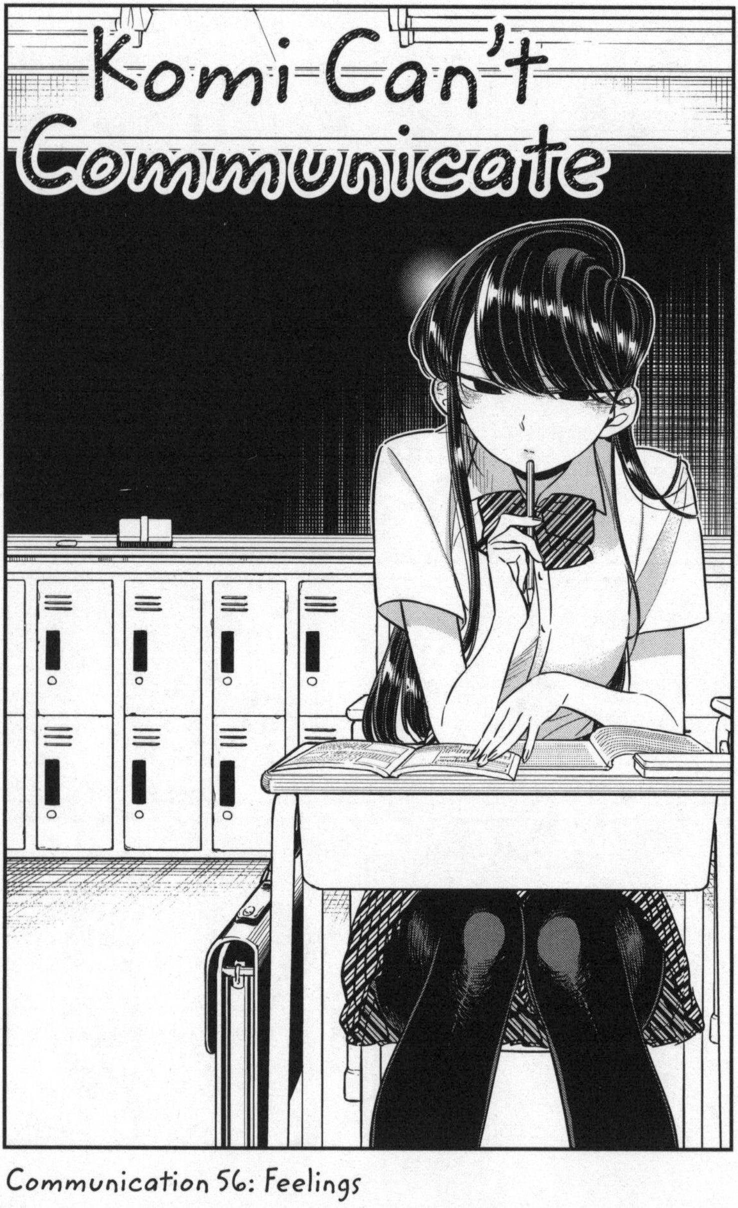
Komi Can't Communicate

Communication 56: Feelings

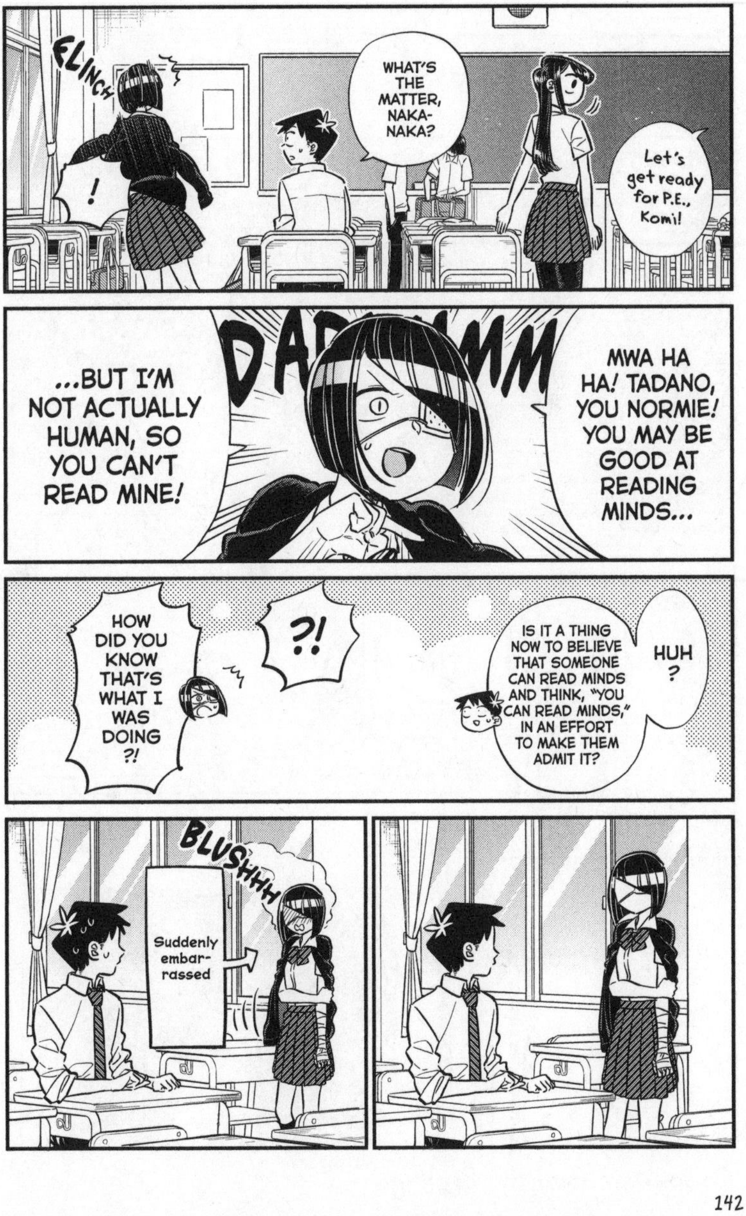
Let's get ready for P.E., Komi!
WHAT'S THE MATTER, NAKA-NAKA?
FLINCH
!
MWA HA HA! TADANO, YOU NORMIE! YOU MAY BE GOOD AT READING MINDS...
...BUT I'M NOT ACTUALLY HUMAN, SO YOU CAN'T READ MINE!
HUH ?
IS IT A THING NOW TO BELIEVE THAT SOMEONE CAN READ MINDS AND THINK, "YOU CAN READ MINDS," IN AN EFFORT TO MAKE THEM ADMIT IT?
?!
HOW DID YOU KNOW THAT'S WHAT I WAS DOING ?!
BLUSHHH
Suddenly embar-rassed

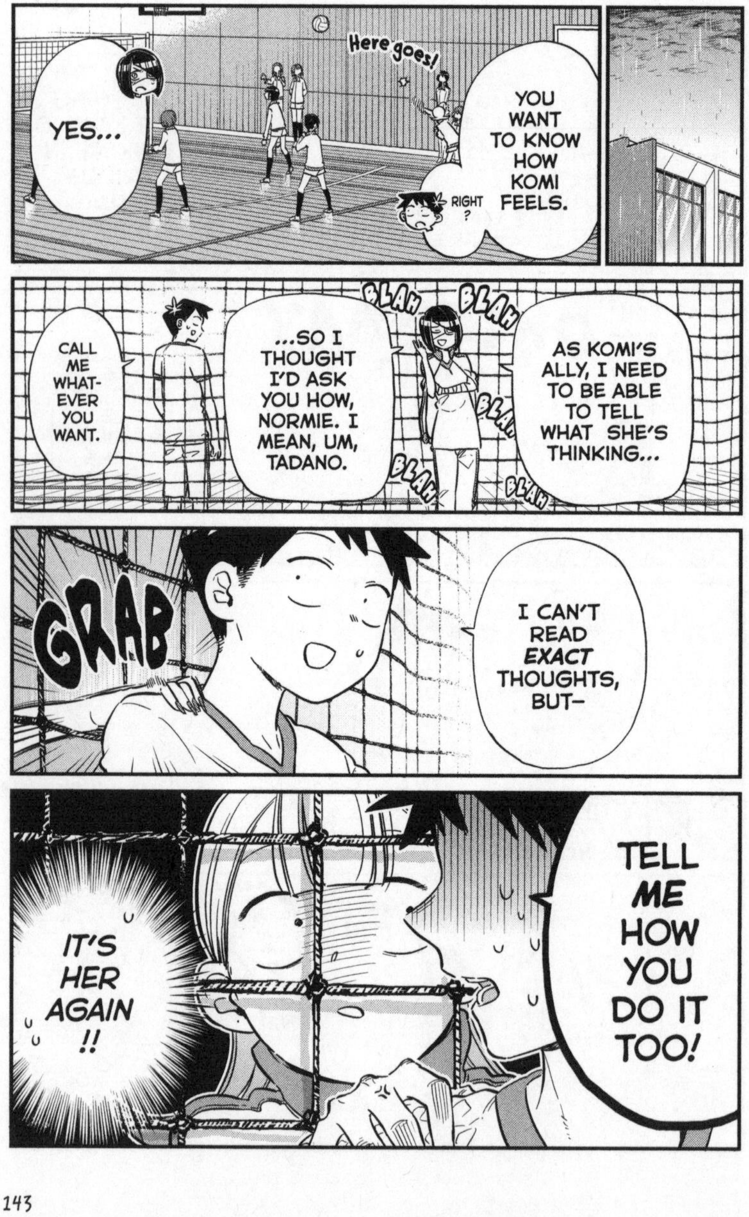
YOU WANT TO KNOW HOW KOMI FEELS.
RIGHT?
Here goes!
YES...
BLAH BLAH BLAH BLAH BLAH
AS KOMI'S ALLY, I NEED TO BE ABLE TO TELL WHAT SHE'S THINKING...
...SO I THOUGHT I'D ASK YOU HOW, NORMIE. I MEAN, UM, TADANO.
CALL ME WHATEVER YOU WANT.
I CAN'T READ *EXACT* THOUGHTS, BUT–
GRAB
TELL *ME* HOW YOU DO IT TOO!
IT'S HER AGAIN!!

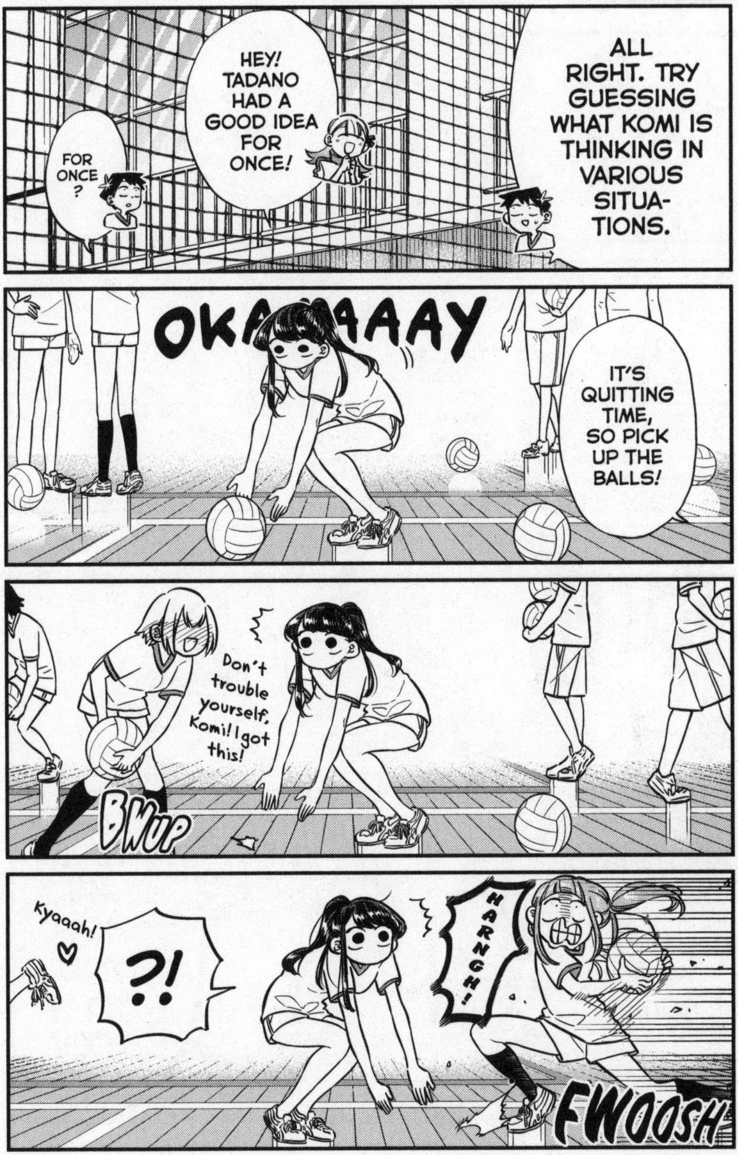
ALL RIGHT. TRY GUESSING WHAT KOMI IS THINKING IN VARIOUS SITUATIONS.
HEY! TADANO HAD A GOOD IDEA FOR ONCE!
FOR ONCE?
IT'S QUITTING TIME, SO PICK UP THE BALLS!
OKA AAAY
Don't trouble yourself, Komi! I got this!
BWUP
HARNGH!
Kyaaah! ♥
?!
FWOOSH

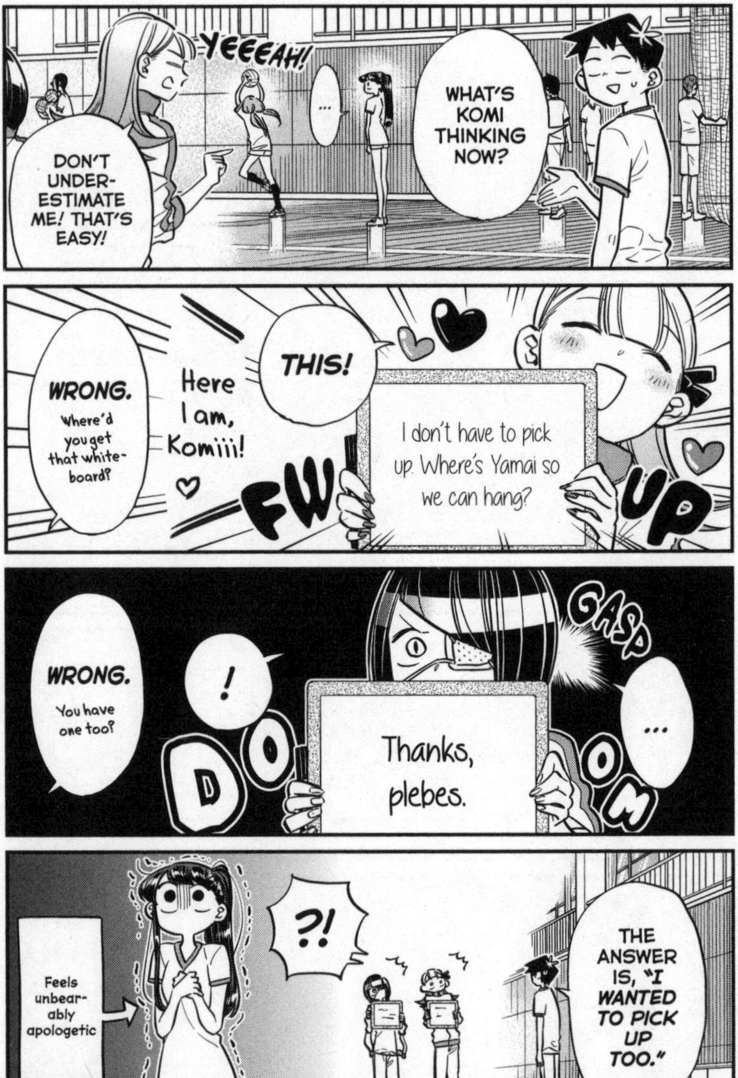
WHAT'S KOMI THINKING NOW?
YEEEAH!
...
DON'T UNDER-ESTIMATE ME! THAT'S EASY!
UP
I don't have to pick up. Where's Yamai so we can hang?
THIS!
FW
Here I am, Komiii! ♡
WRONG.
Where'd you get that white-board?
GASP
...
OM
Thanks, plebes.
!
DO
D
WRONG.
You have one too?
THE ANSWER IS, "I WANTED TO PICK UP TOO."
?!
Feels unbear-ably apologetic

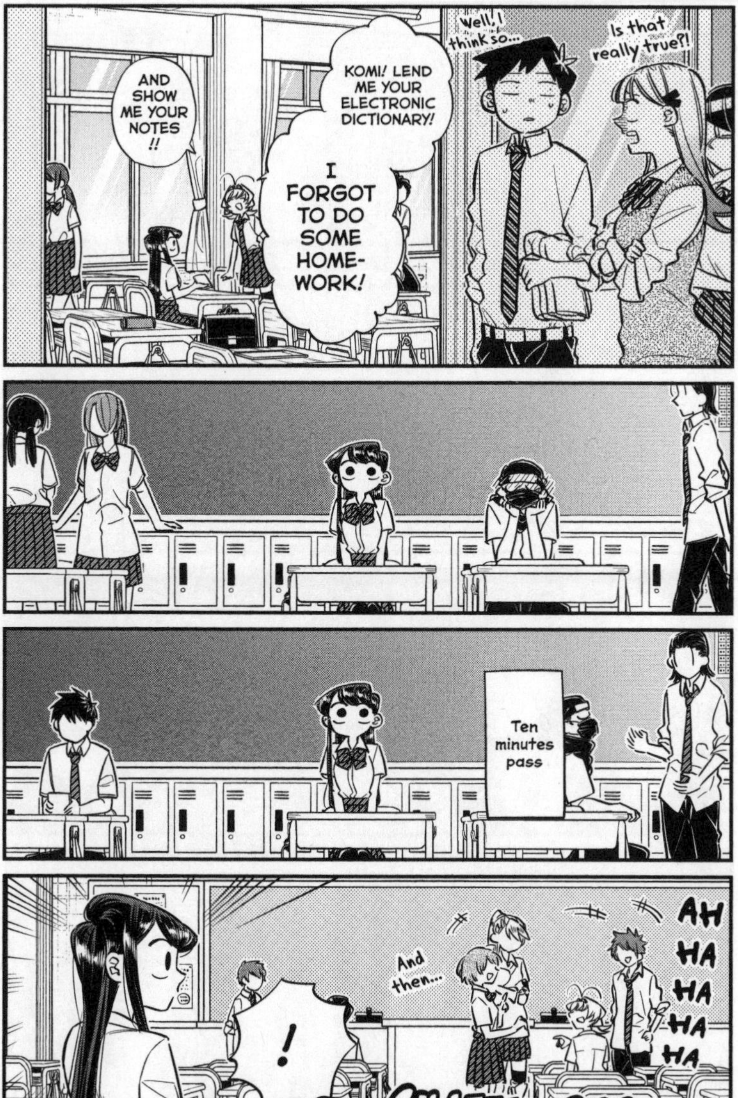
Is that really true?!
Well, I think so...
KOMI! LEND ME YOUR ELECTRONIC DICTIONARY!
I FORGOT TO DO SOME HOMEWORK!
AND SHOW ME YOUR NOTES!!
Ten minutes pass
AH HA HA HA HA
And then...
!
CHATTER CHATTER

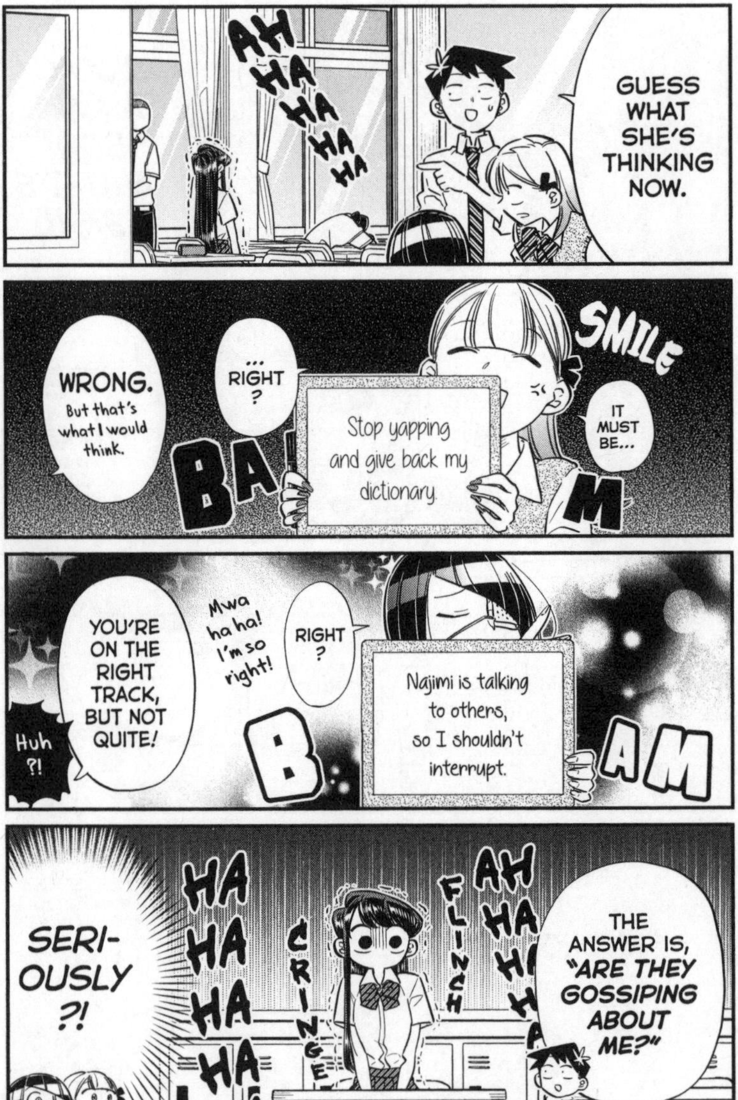
GUESS WHAT SHE'S THINKING NOW.
AH HA HA HA HA HA
SMILE
IT MUST BE...
Stop yapping and give back my dictionary.
BAM
...RIGHT?
WRONG.
But that's what I would think.
BAM
Najimi is talking to others, so I shouldn't interrupt.
RIGHT?
Mwa ha ha! I'm so right!
YOU'RE ON THE RIGHT TRACK, BUT NOT QUITE!
Huh?!
THE ANSWER IS, "ARE THEY GOSSIPING ABOUT ME?"
AH HA HA HA HA
FLINCH
CRINGE
HA HA HA HA HA HA HA
!
SERI-OUSLY?!

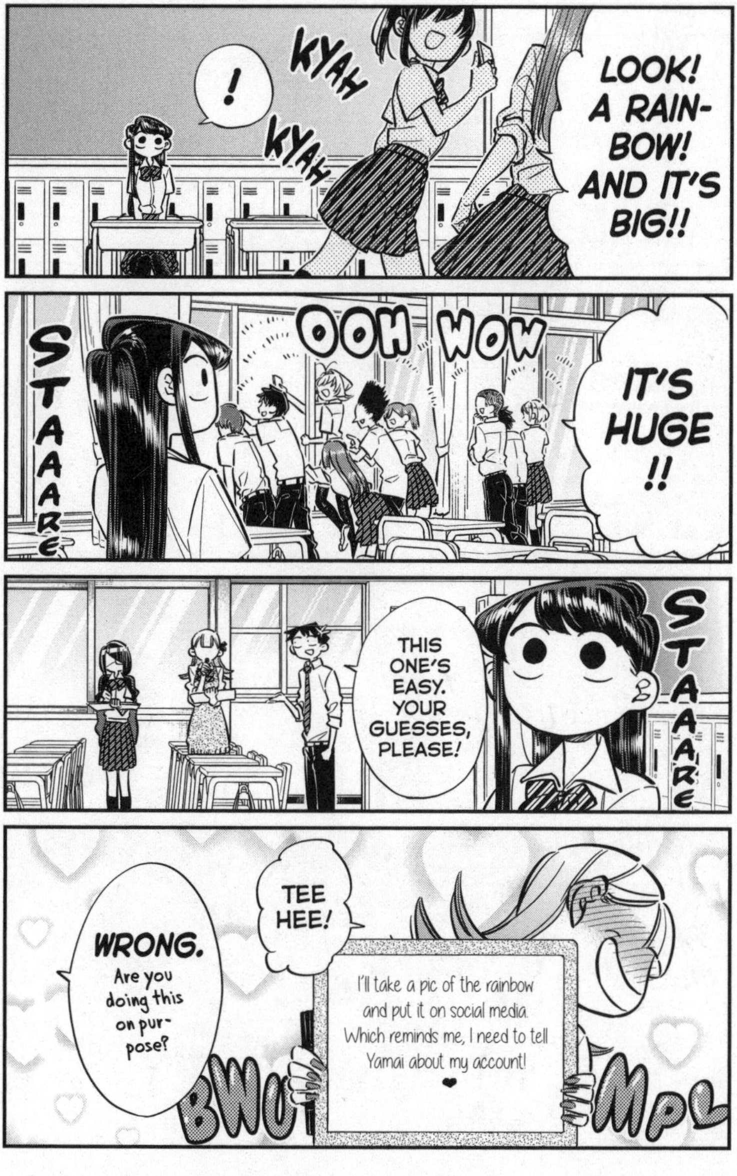
LOOK! A RAIN-BOW! AND IT'S BIG!!
KYAH KYAH
!
IT'S HUGE!!
OOH WOW
STAAAARE
STAAARE
THIS ONE'S EASY. YOUR GUESSES, PLEASE!
TEE HEE!
I'll take a pic of the rainbow and put it on social media. Which reminds me, I need to tell Yamai about my account! ❤
WRONG. Are you doing this on pur-pose?
BWOMPL

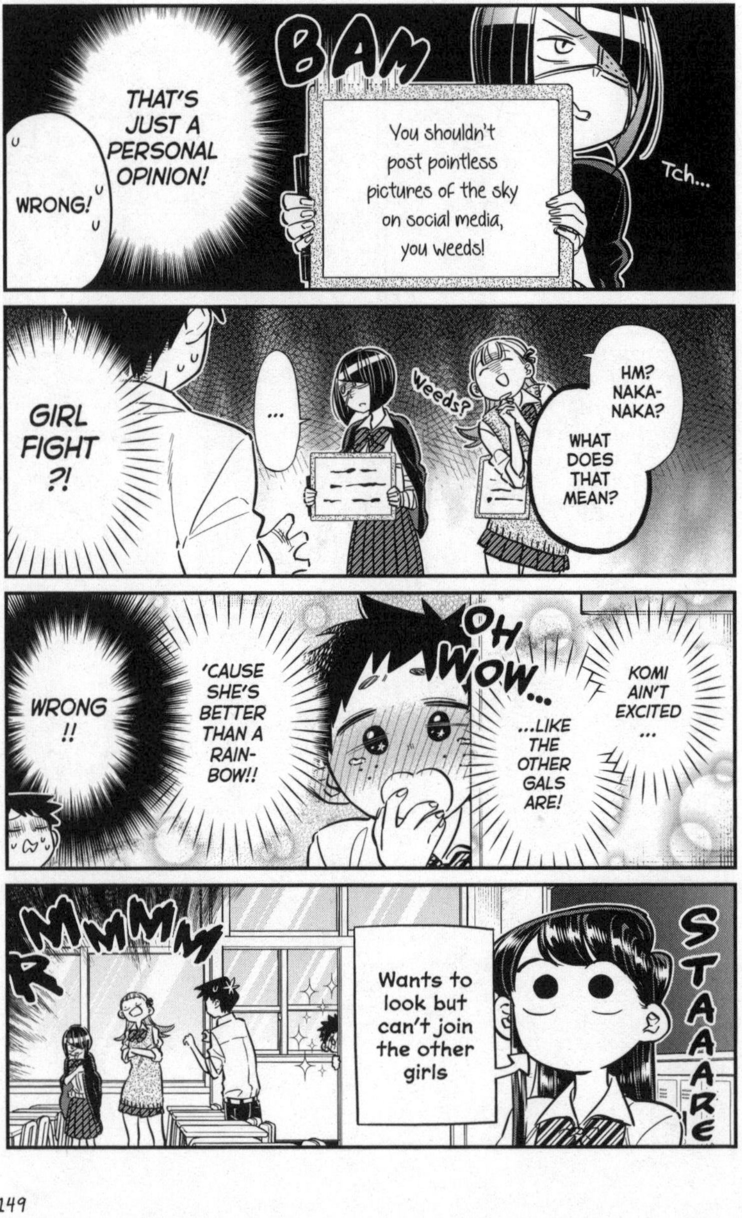
Tch...
BAM
You shouldn't post pointless pictures of the sky on social media, you weeds!
THAT'S JUST A PERSONAL OPINION!
WRONG!
HM? NAKA-NAKA? WHAT DOES THAT MEAN?
Weeds?
...
GIRL FIGHT?!
KOMI AIN'T EXCITED...
...LIKE THE OTHER GALS ARE!
OH WOW...
'CAUSE SHE'S BETTER THAN A RAINBOW!!
WRONG!!
STAAARE
Wants to look but can't join the other girls
RMMMM

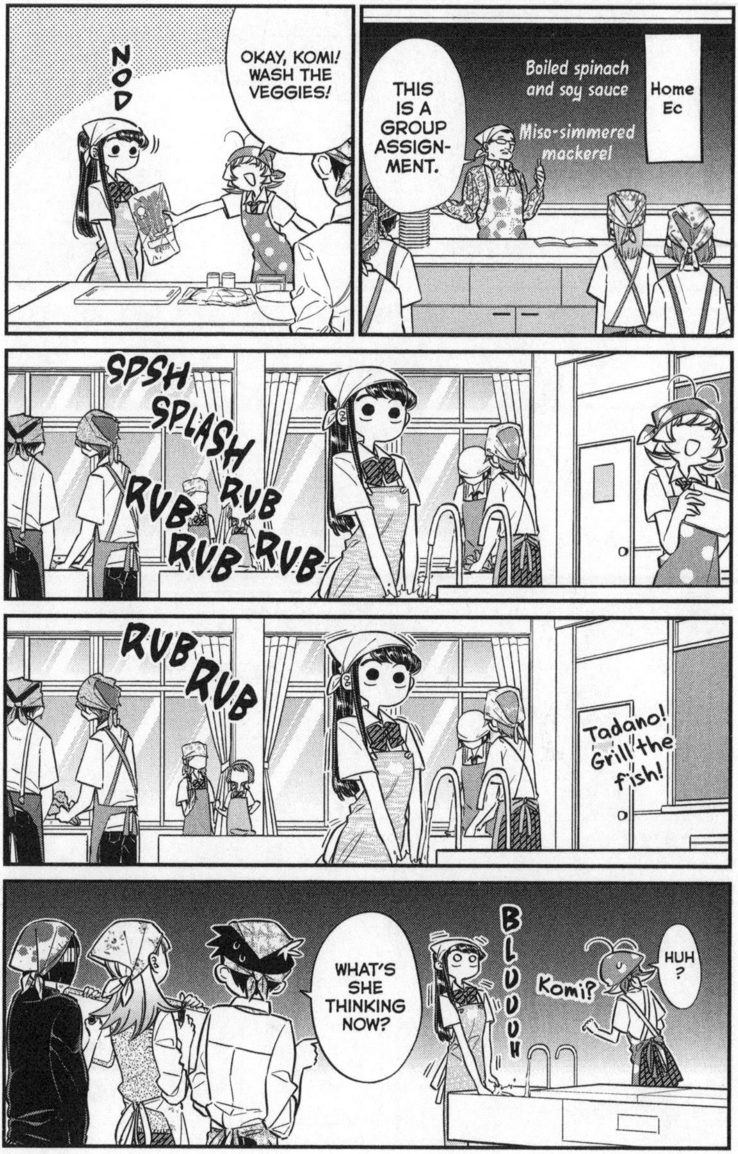
Home Ec
Boiled spinach and soy sauce
Miso-simmered mackerel
THIS IS A GROUP ASSIGNMENT.
OKAY, KOMI! WASH THE VEGGIES!
NOD
SPSH
SPLASH
RUB
RUB
RUB
RUB
Tadano! Grill the fish!
RUB
RUB
HUH?
Komi?
BLUUUH
WHAT'S SHE THINKING NOW?

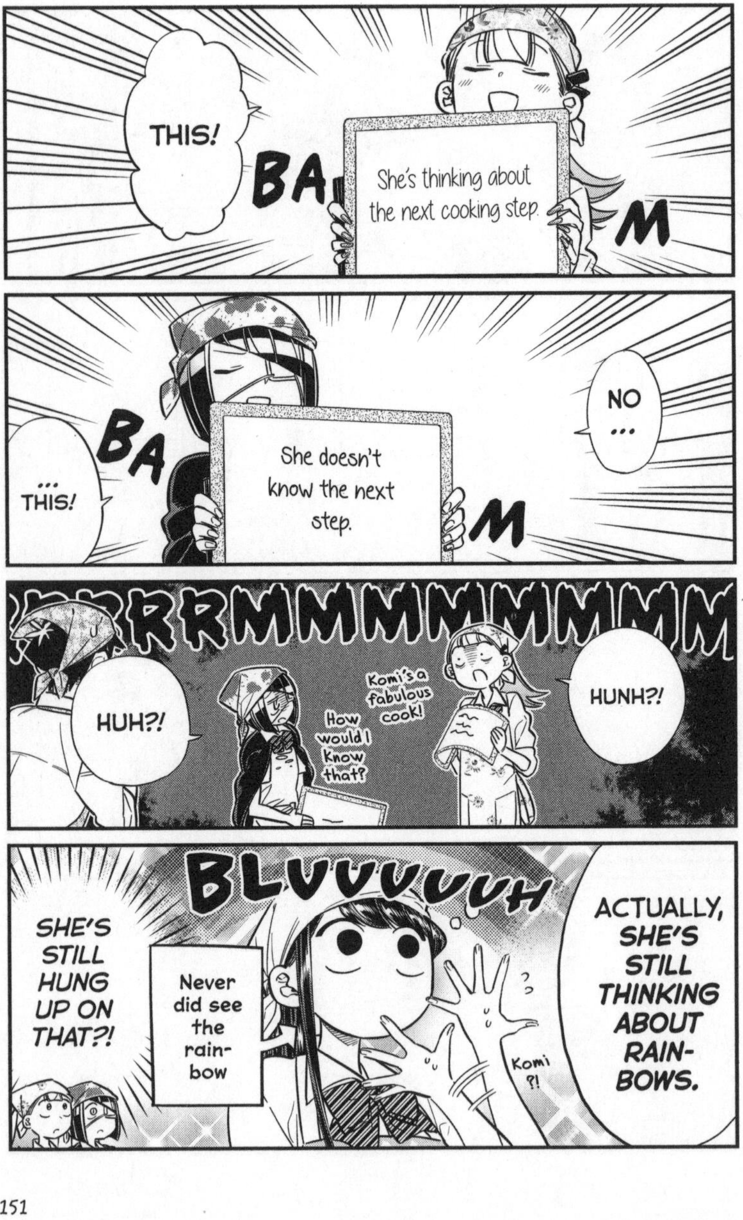

She's thinking about the next cooking step.
BAM
THIS!
NO...
She doesn't know the next step.
BAM
...THIS!
RRMMMMMMMMMMM
HUNH?!
Komi's a fabulous cook!
How would I know that?
HUH?!
BLUUUUUH
ACTUALLY, SHE'S STILL THINKING ABOUT RAIN-BOWS.
Komi?!
Never did see the rain-bow
SHE'S STILL HUNG UP ON THAT?!

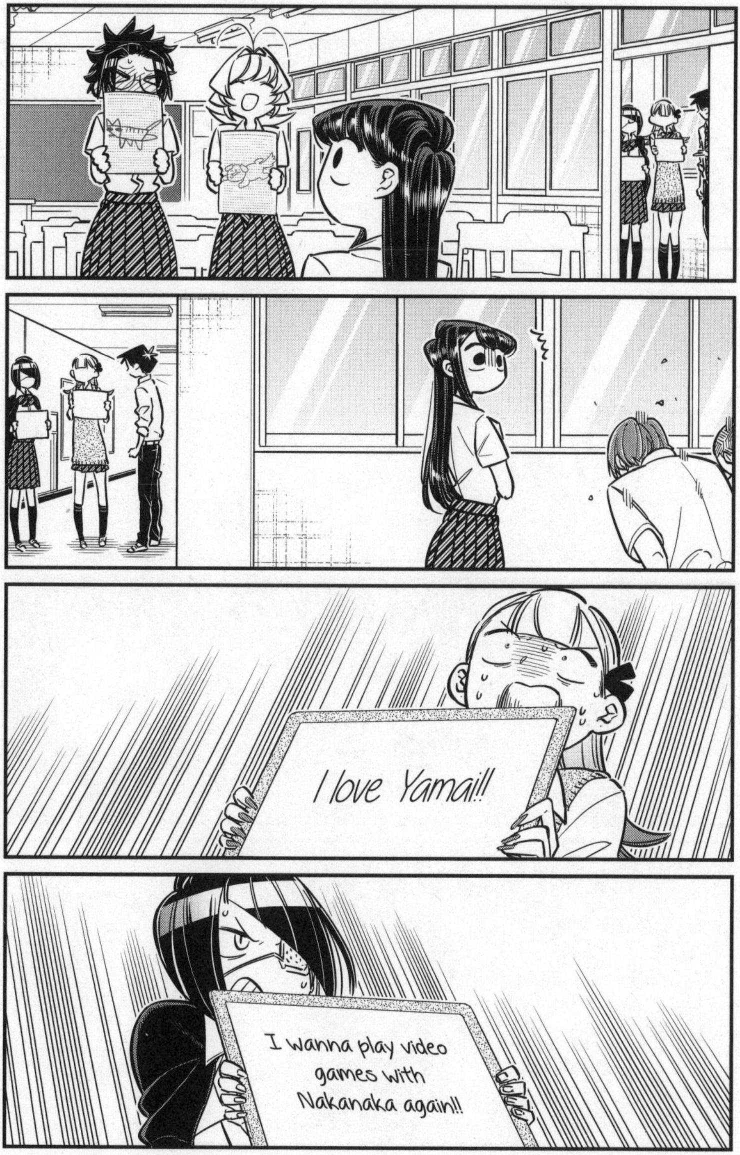
I love Yamai!!
I wanna play video games with Nakanaka again!!

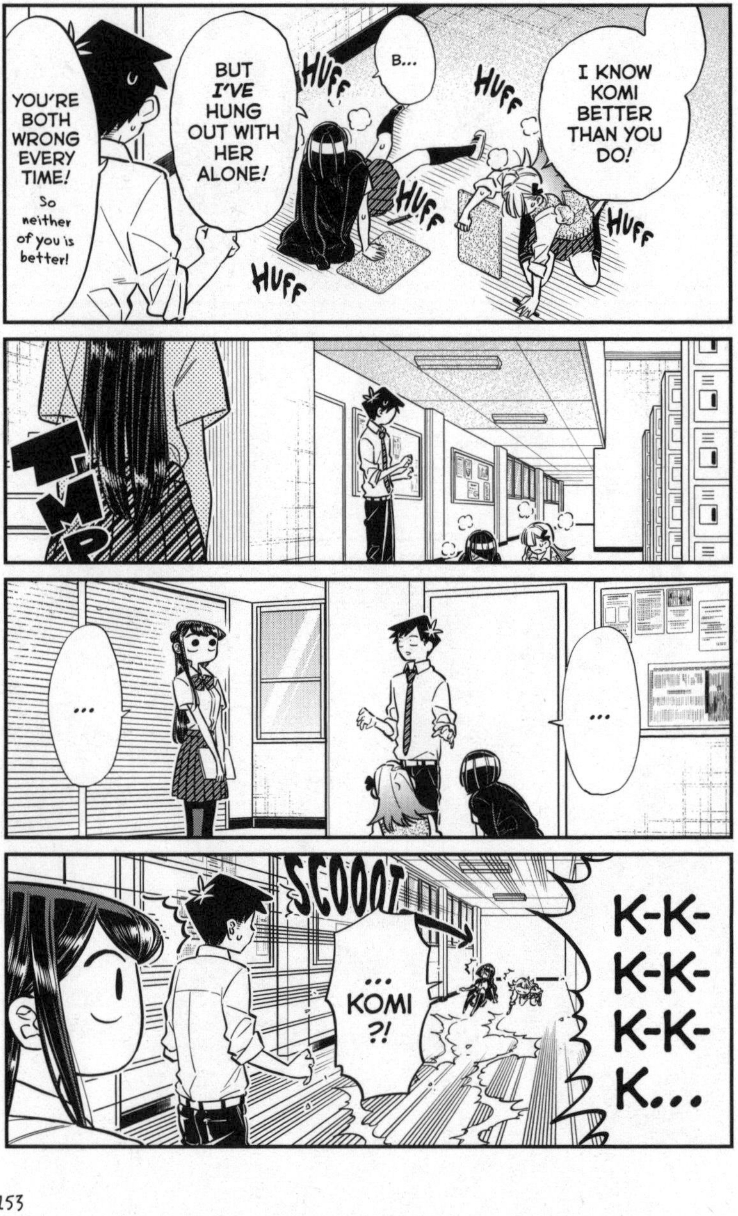
I KNOW KOMI BETTER THAN YOU DO!
HUFF
HUFF
B...
HUFF
HUFF
HUFF
BUT I'VE HUNG OUT WITH HER ALONE!
YOU'RE BOTH WRONG EVERY TIME!
So neither of you is better!
TMP
...
...
K-K-K-K-K-K-K...
SCOOOT
... KOMI ?!

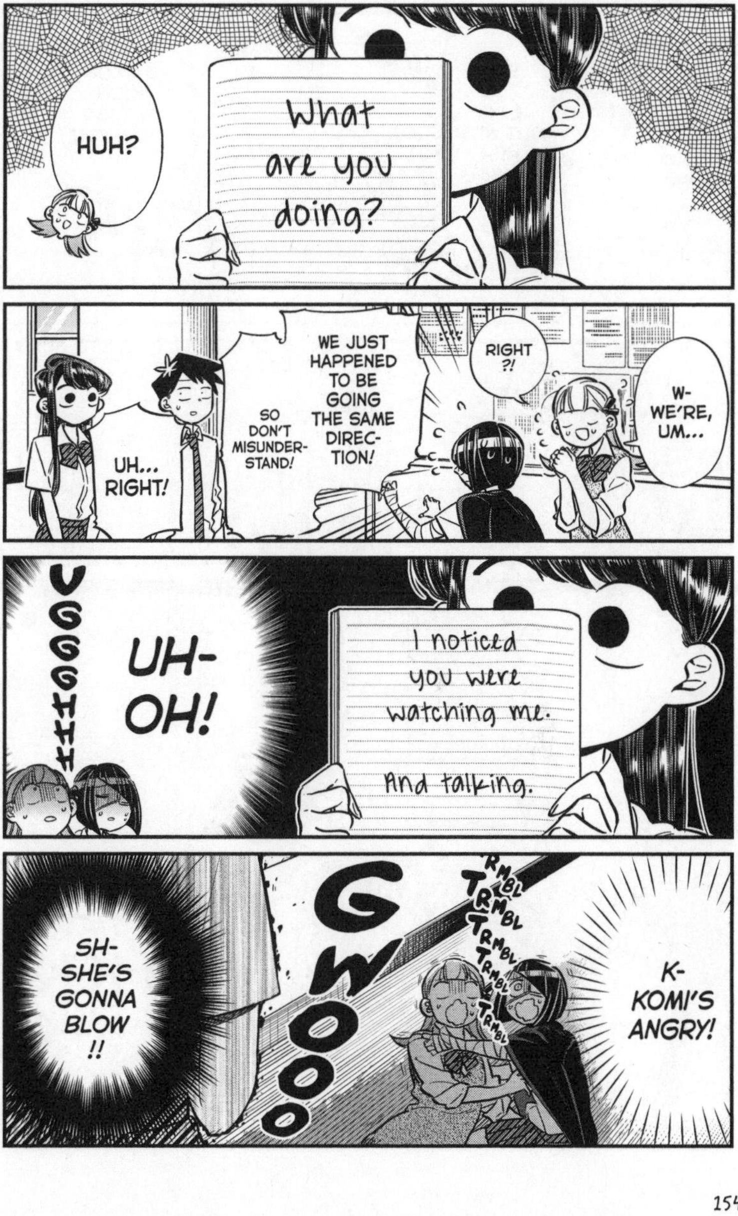
What are you doing?
HUH?
W-WE'RE, UM...
RIGHT?!
WE JUST HAPPENED TO BE GOING THE SAME DIRECTION!
SO DON'T MISUNDERSTAND!
UH... RIGHT!
I noticed you were watching me.
And talking.
UH-OH!
VGGGHHH
K-KOMI'S ANGRY!
TRMBL TRMBL TRMBL TRMBL TRMBL TRMBL
GWOOO
SH-SHE'S GONNA BLOW!!

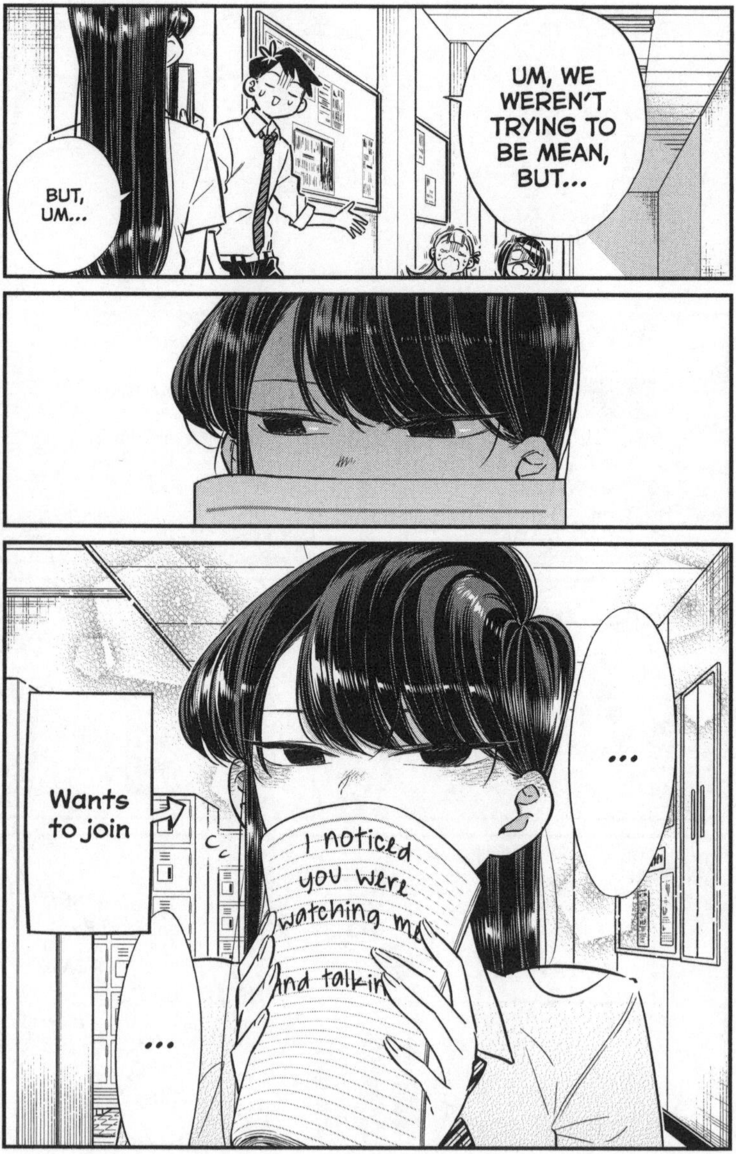
UM, WE WEREN'T TRYING TO BE MEAN, BUT...
BUT, UM...
...
I noticed you were watching m
And talkin
Wants to join
...

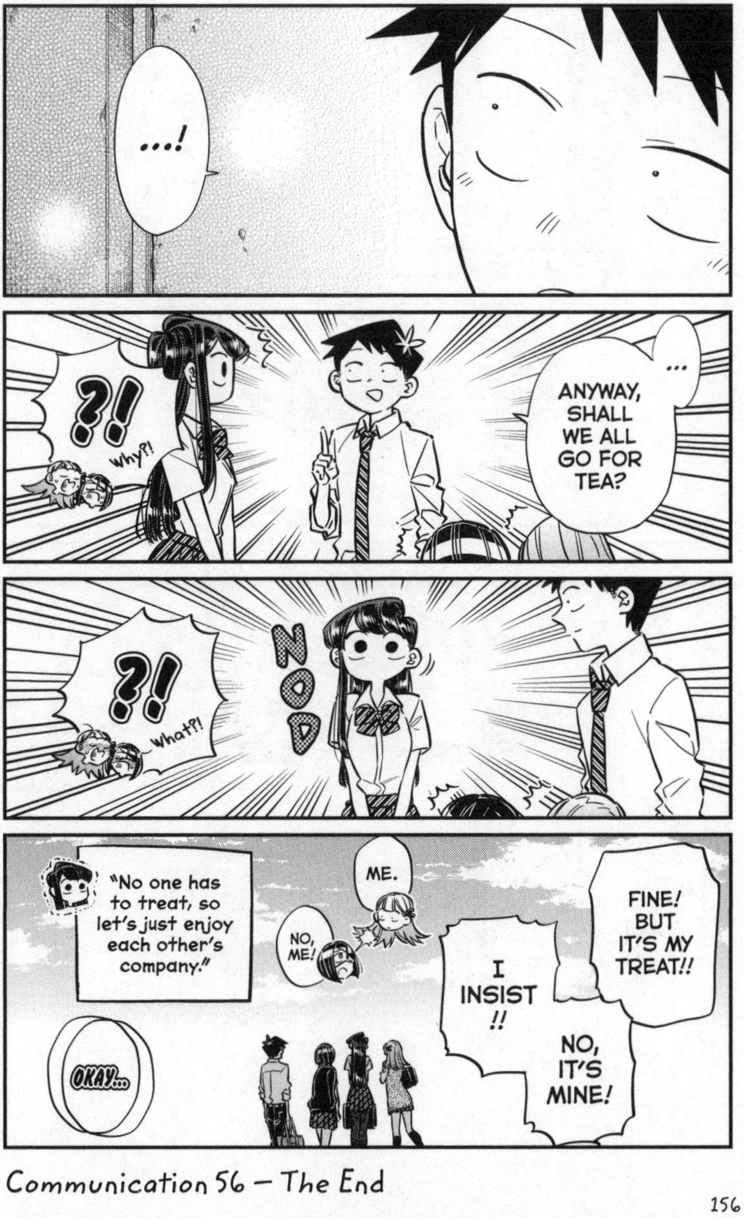
...!
...
ANYWAY, SHALL WE ALL GO FOR TEA?
?!
Why?!
NOD
?!
What?!
FINE! BUT IT'S MY TREAT!!
NO, IT'S MINE!
I INSIST!!
ME.
NO, ME!
"No one has to treat, so let's just enjoy each other's company."
OKAY...

Communication 56 – The End

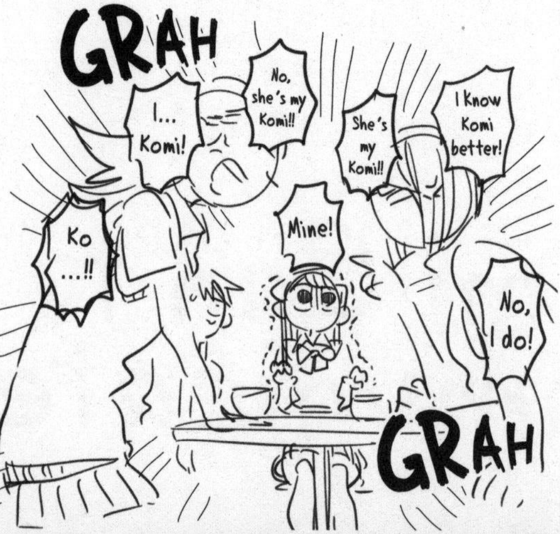
I know Komi better!
She's my Komi!!
No, she's my Komi!!
I... Komi!
GRAH
No, I do!
Mine!
Ko ...!!
GRAH

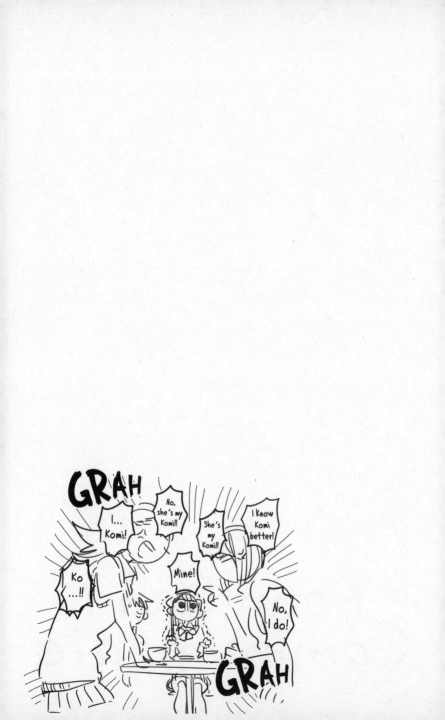

Komi Can't
Communicate

Komi Can't Communicate

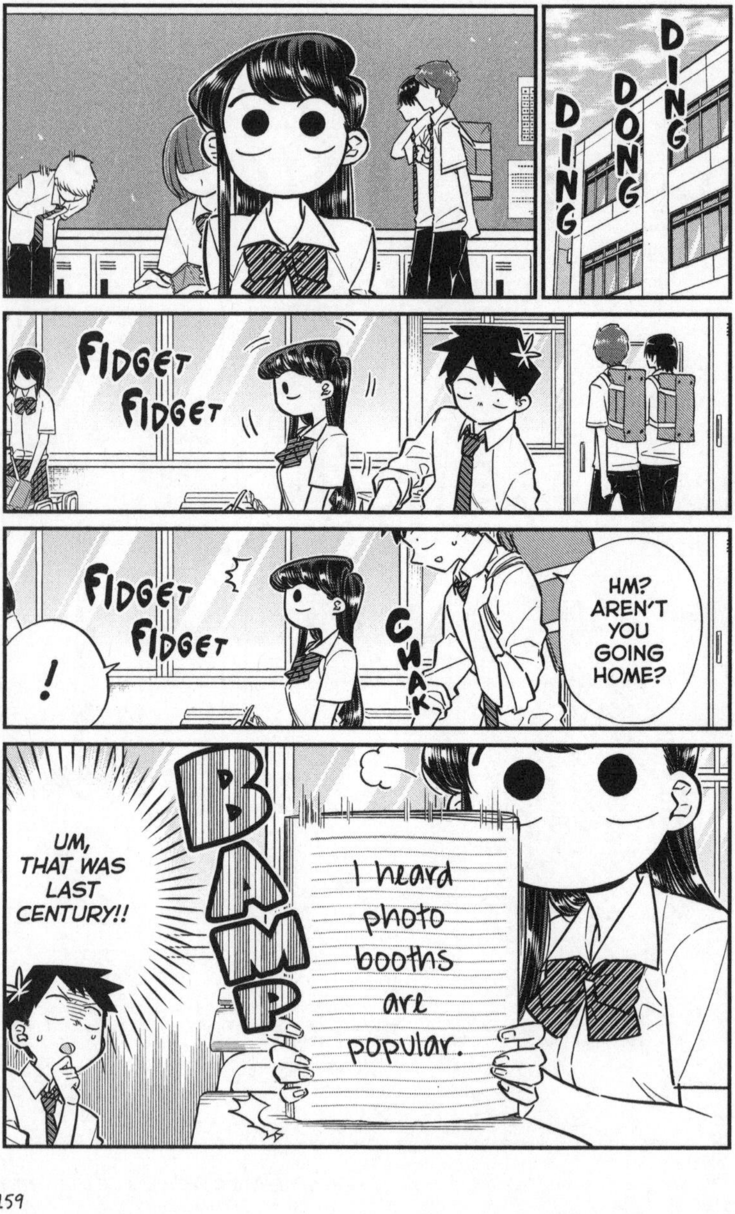
DING DONG DING
FIDGET FIDGET
HM? AREN'T YOU GOING HOME?
CHAK
FIDGET FIDGET
!
I heard photo booths are popular.
BAMP
UM, THAT WAS LAST CENTURY!!

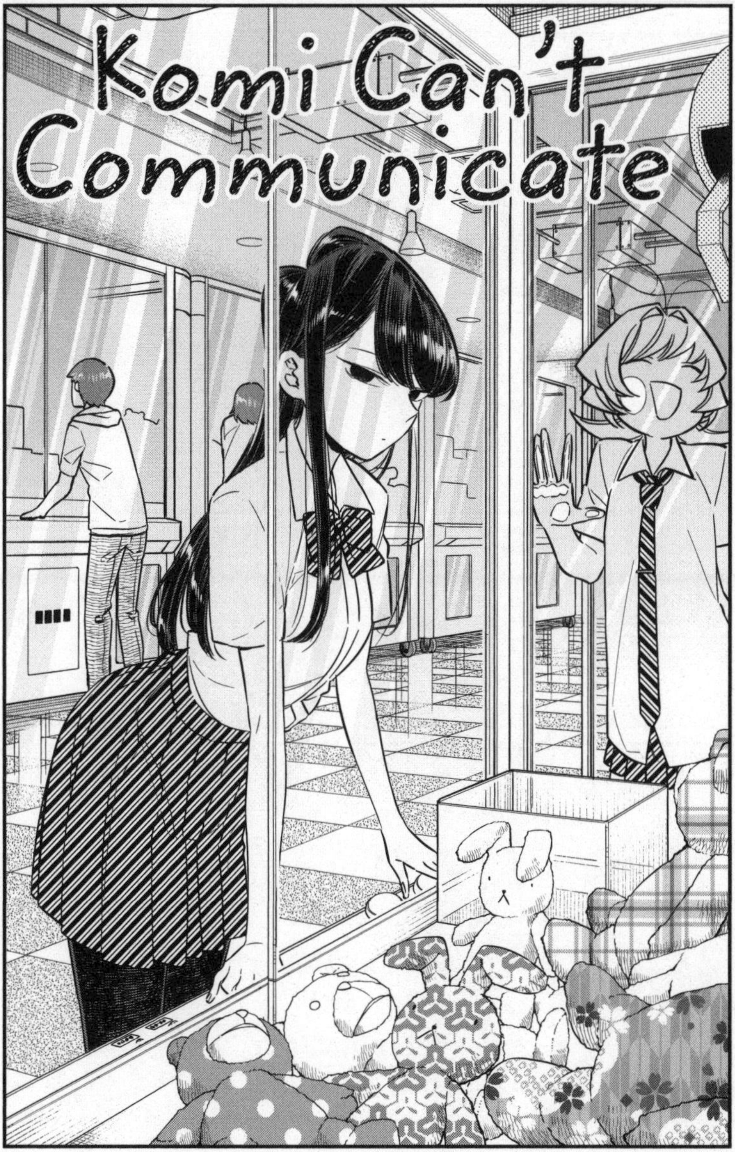
Komi Can't Communicate

Communication 57: Purikura

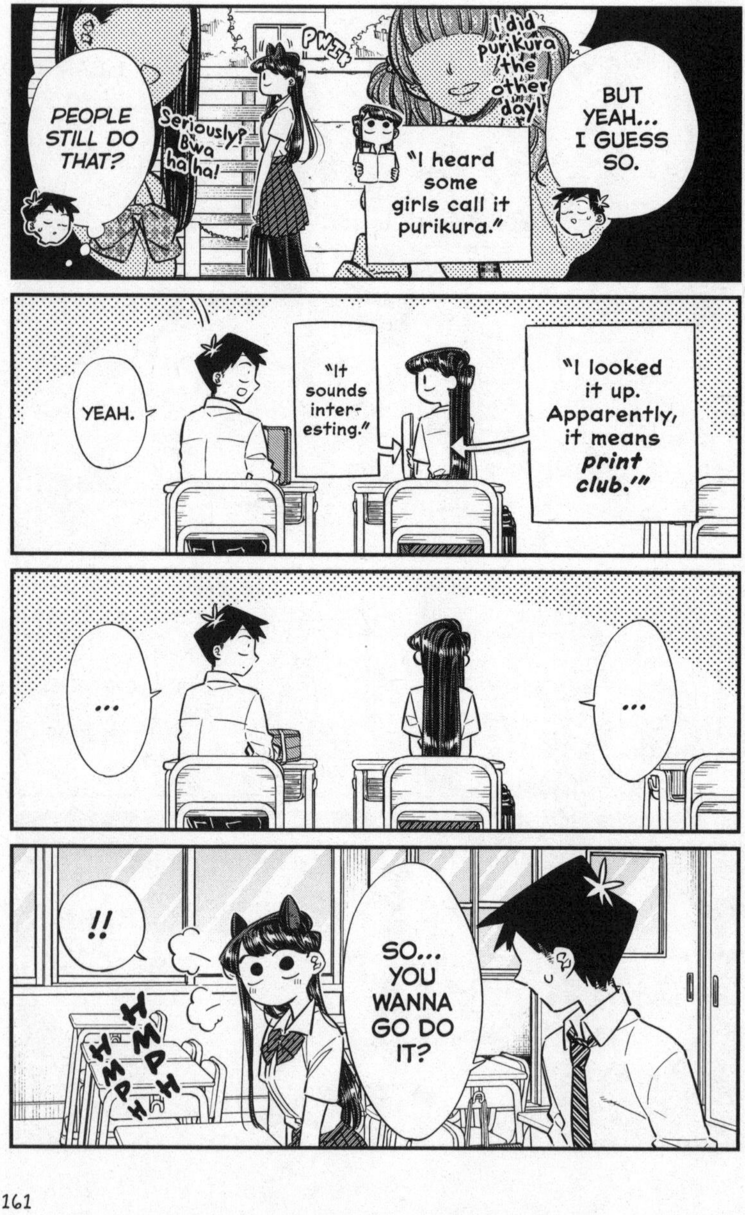
I did purikura the other day!
BUT YEAH... I GUESS SO.
"I heard some girls call it purikura."
PWIT
Seriously? Bwa ha ha!
PEOPLE STILL DO THAT?
"I looked it up. Apparently, it means **print club**."
"It sounds interesting."
YEAH.
...
...
SO... YOU WANNA GO DO IT?
!!
HMPH HMPH

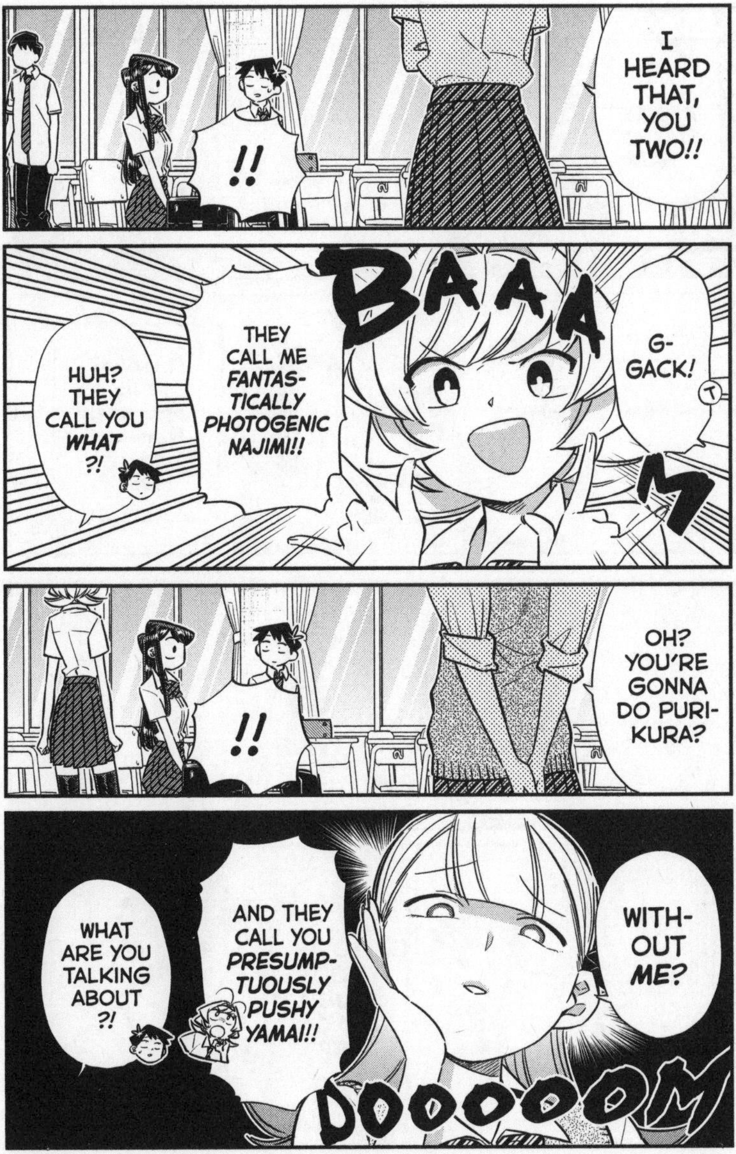

I HEARD THAT, YOU TWO!!
!!
G-GACK!
BAAAM
THEY CALL ME FANTASTICALLY PHOTOGENIC NAJIMI!!
HUH? THEY CALL YOU WHAT?!
OH? YOU'RE GONNA DO PURIKURA?
!!
WITHOUT ME?
DOOOOOM
AND THEY CALL YOU PRESUMPTUOUSLY PUSHY YAMAI!!
WHAT ARE YOU TALKING ABOUT?!

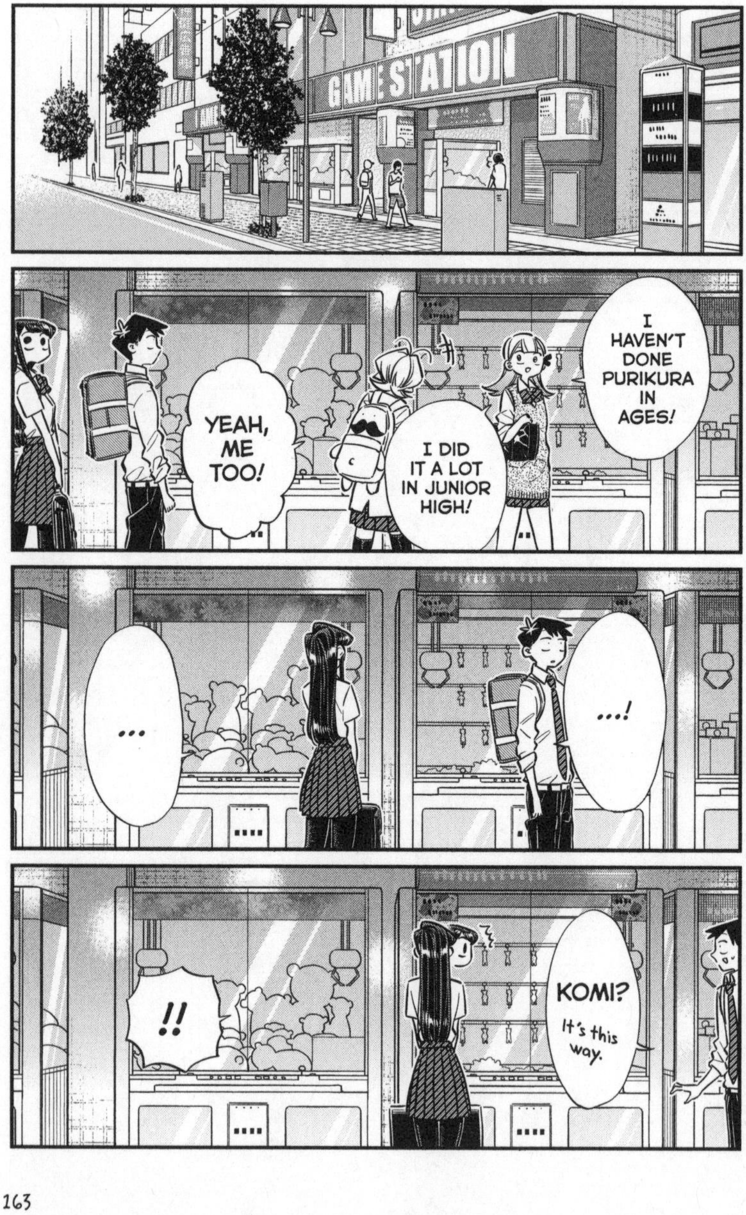
GAME STATION
I HAVEN'T DONE PURIKURA IN AGES!
I DID IT A LOT IN JUNIOR HIGH!
YEAH, ME TOO!
...!
...
KOMI? It's this way.
!!

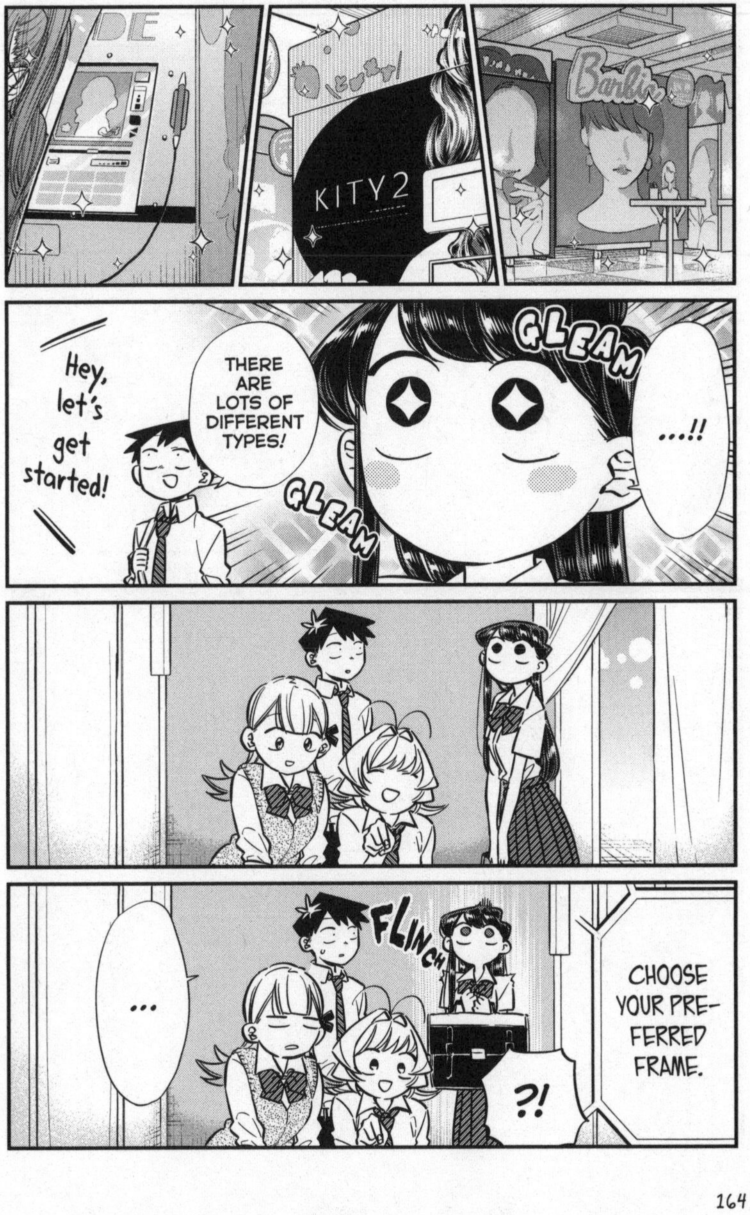
KITY 2
DE
...!!
GLEAM
GLEAM
THERE ARE LOTS OF DIFFERENT TYPES!
Hey, let's get started!
CHOOSE YOUR PRE-FERRED FRAME.
?!
FLINCH
...

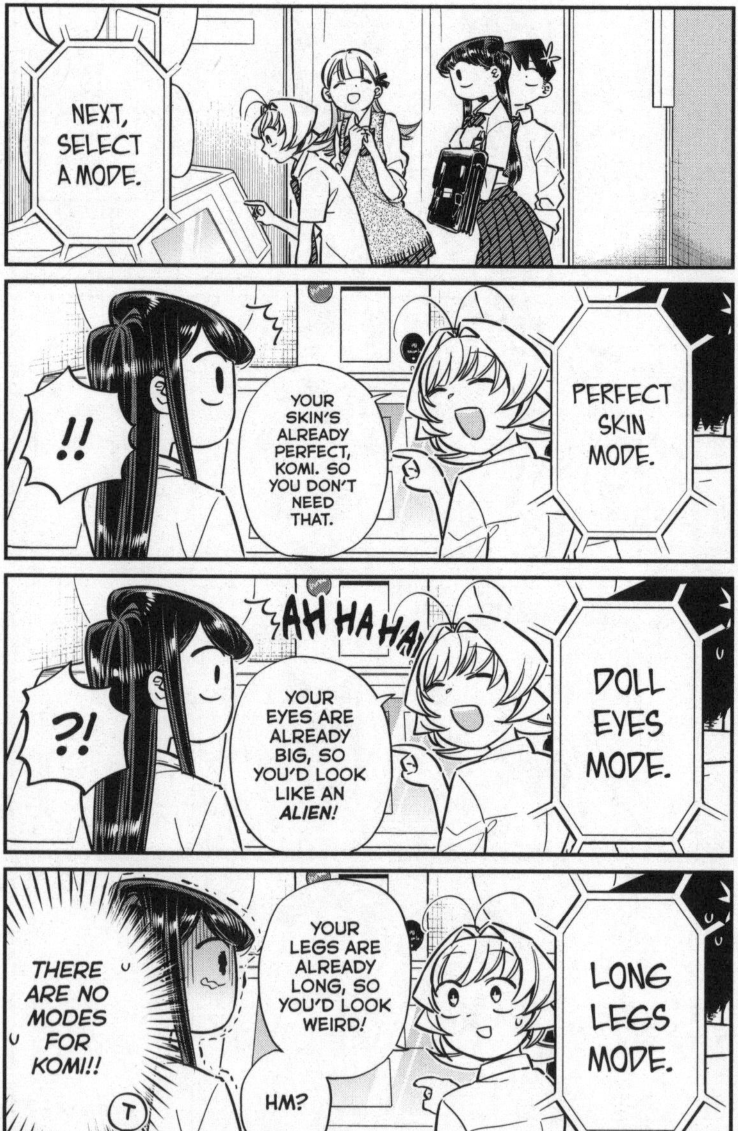
NEXT, SELECT A MODE.
PERFECT SKIN MODE.
YOUR SKIN'S ALREADY PERFECT, KOMI. SO YOU DON'T NEED THAT.
!!
DOLL EYES MODE.
AH HA HA
YOUR EYES ARE ALREADY BIG, SO YOU'D LOOK LIKE AN *ALIEN!*
?!
LONG LEGS MODE.
YOUR LEGS ARE ALREADY LONG, SO YOU'D LOOK WEIRD!
HM?
THERE ARE NO MODES FOR KOMI!!

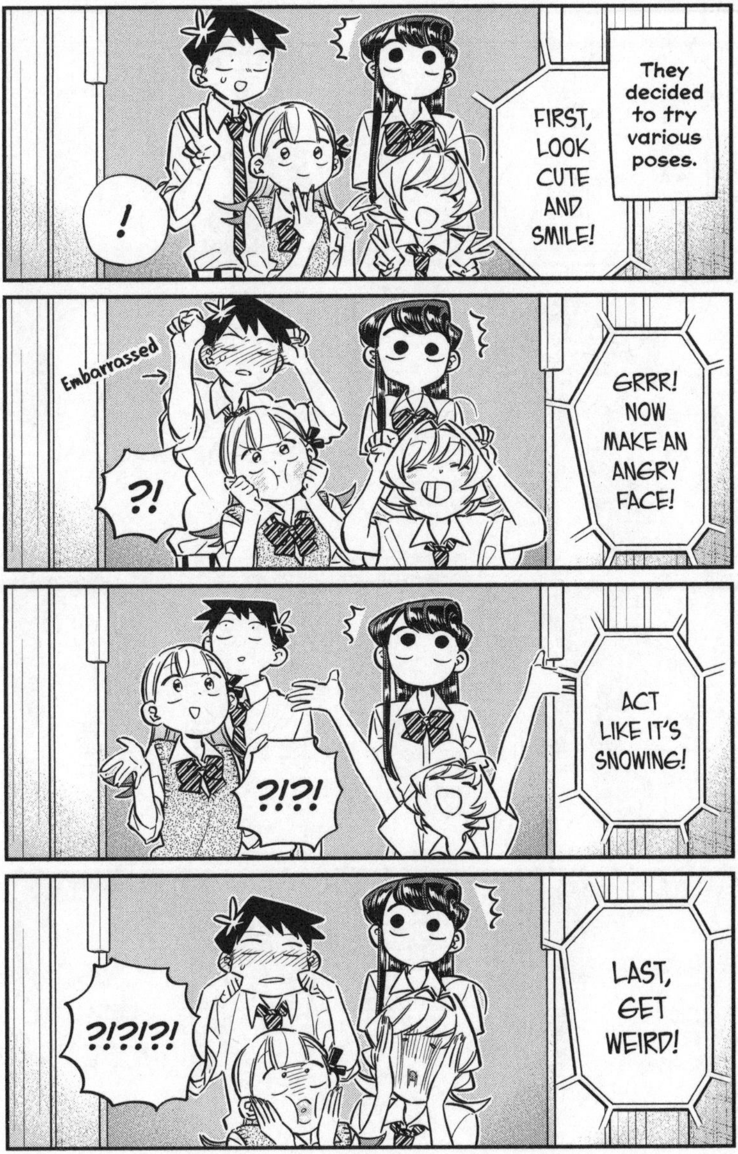
They decided to try various poses.
FIRST, LOOK CUTE AND SMILE!
!
GRRR! NOW MAKE AN ANGRY FACE!
Embarrassed
?!
ACT LIKE IT'S SNOWING!
?!?!
LAST, GET WEIRD!
?!?!?!

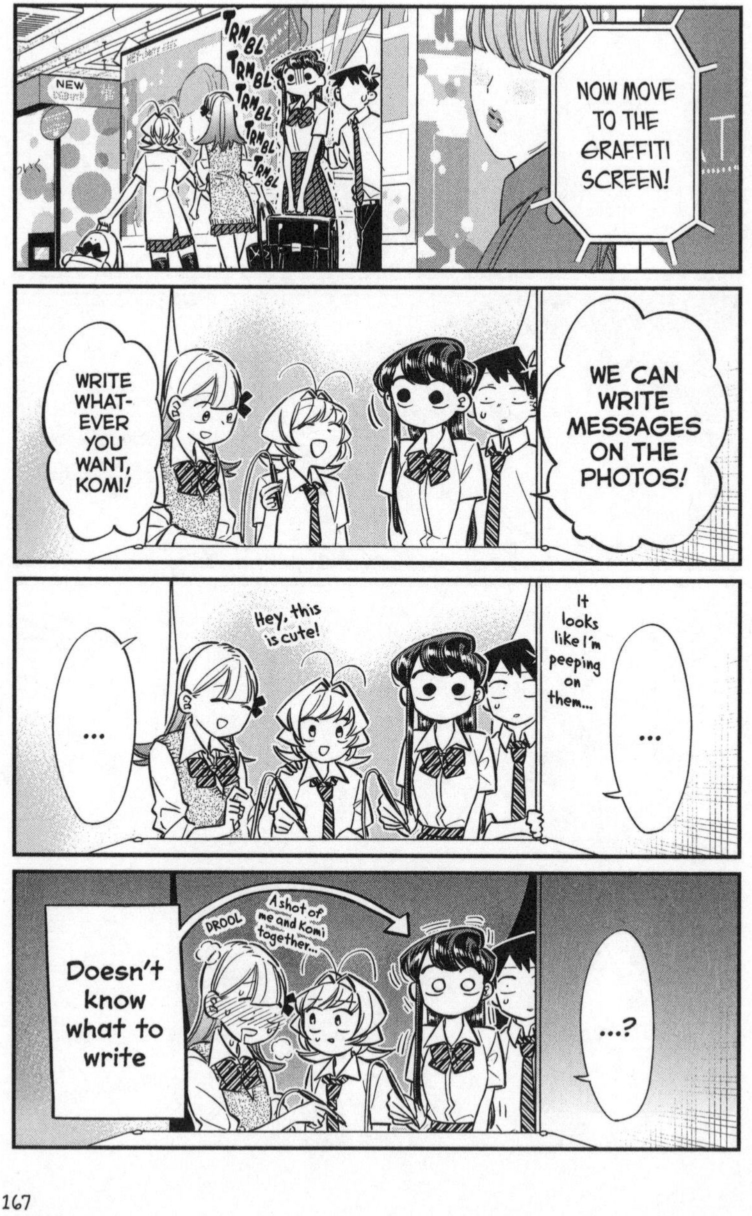
NOW MOVE TO THE GRAFFITI SCREEN!
TRMBL TRMBL TRMBL TRMBL TRMBL TRMBL
NEW
WE CAN WRITE MESSAGES ON THE PHOTOS!
WRITE WHATEVER YOU WANT, KOMI!
...
It looks like I'm peeping on them...
Hey, this is cute!
...
...?
A shot of me and Komi together...
DROOL
Doesn't know what to write

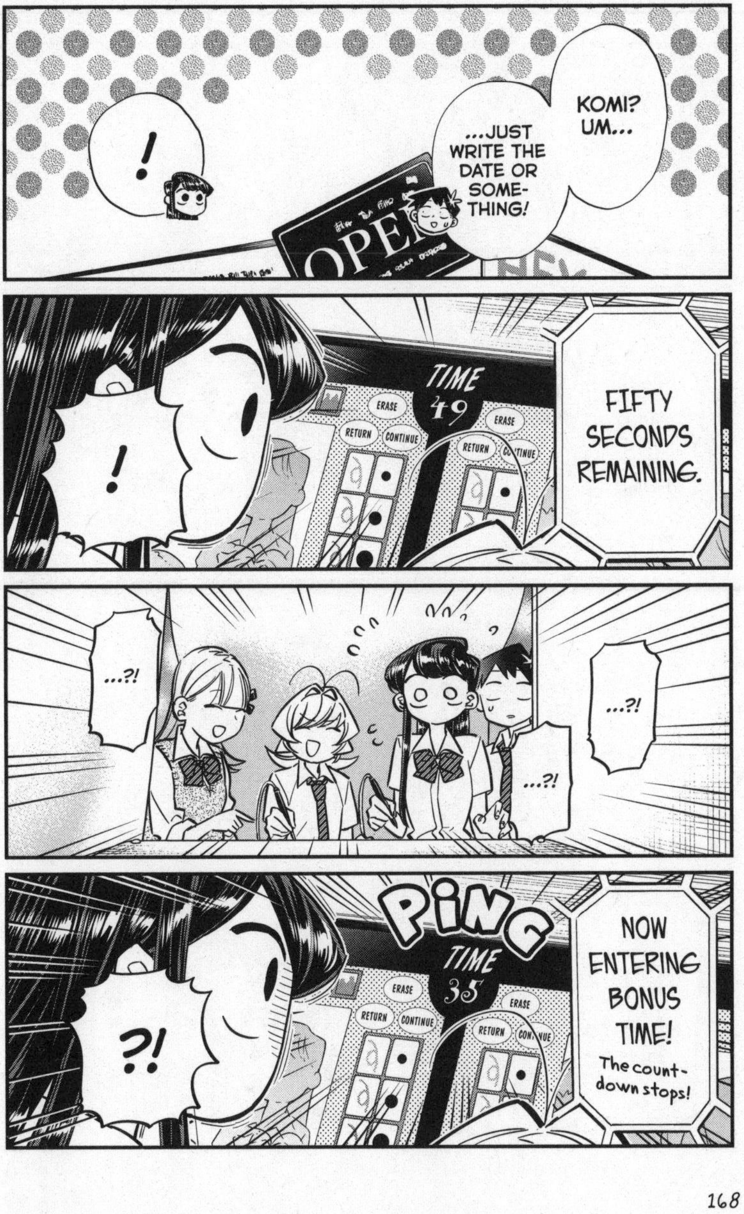
KOMI? UM...
...JUST WRITE THE DATE OR SOME-THING!
!
FIFTY SECONDS REMAINING.
TIME 49
!
...?!
...?!
...?!
NOW ENTERING BONUS TIME!
The count-down stops!
PING
TIME 35
?!

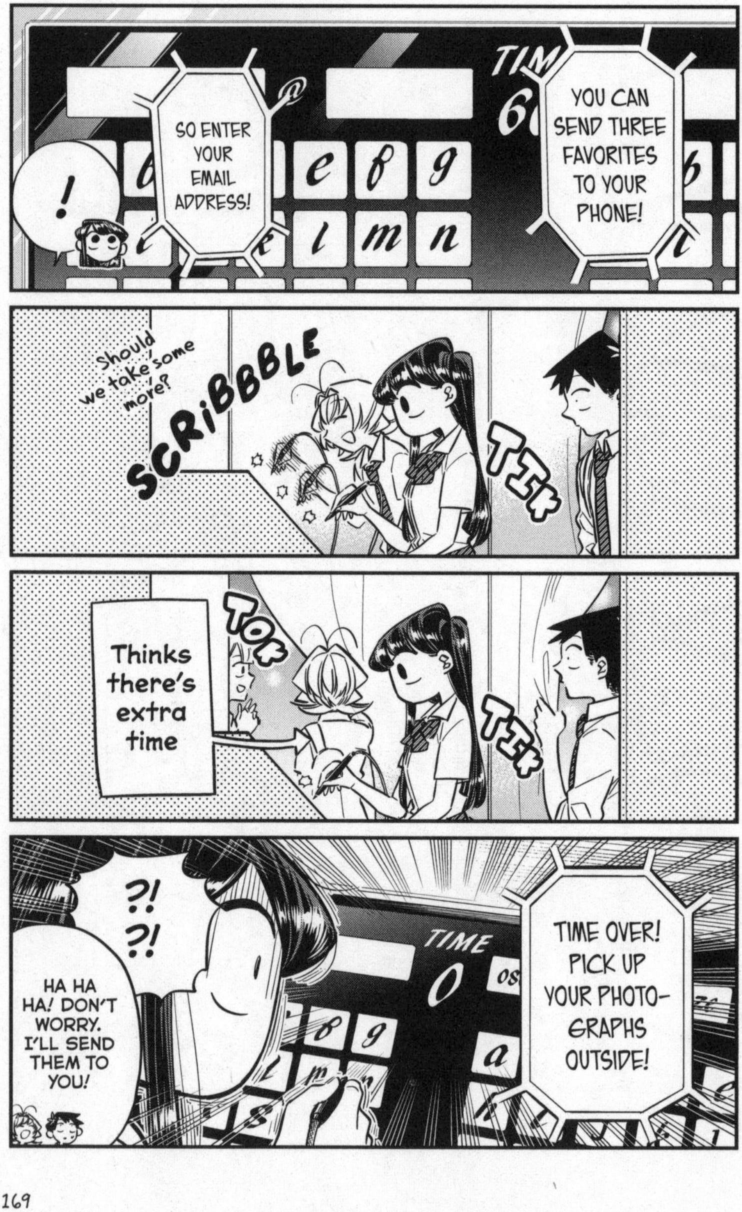
YOU CAN SEND THREE FAVORITES TO YOUR PHONE!
SO ENTER YOUR EMAIL ADDRESS!
!
TIK
SCRIBBBLE
Should we take some more?
TIK
TOK
Thinks there's extra time
TIME OVER! PICK UP YOUR PHOTO-GRAPHS OUTSIDE!
?! ?!
HA HA HA! DON'T WORRY. I'LL SEND THEM TO YOU!

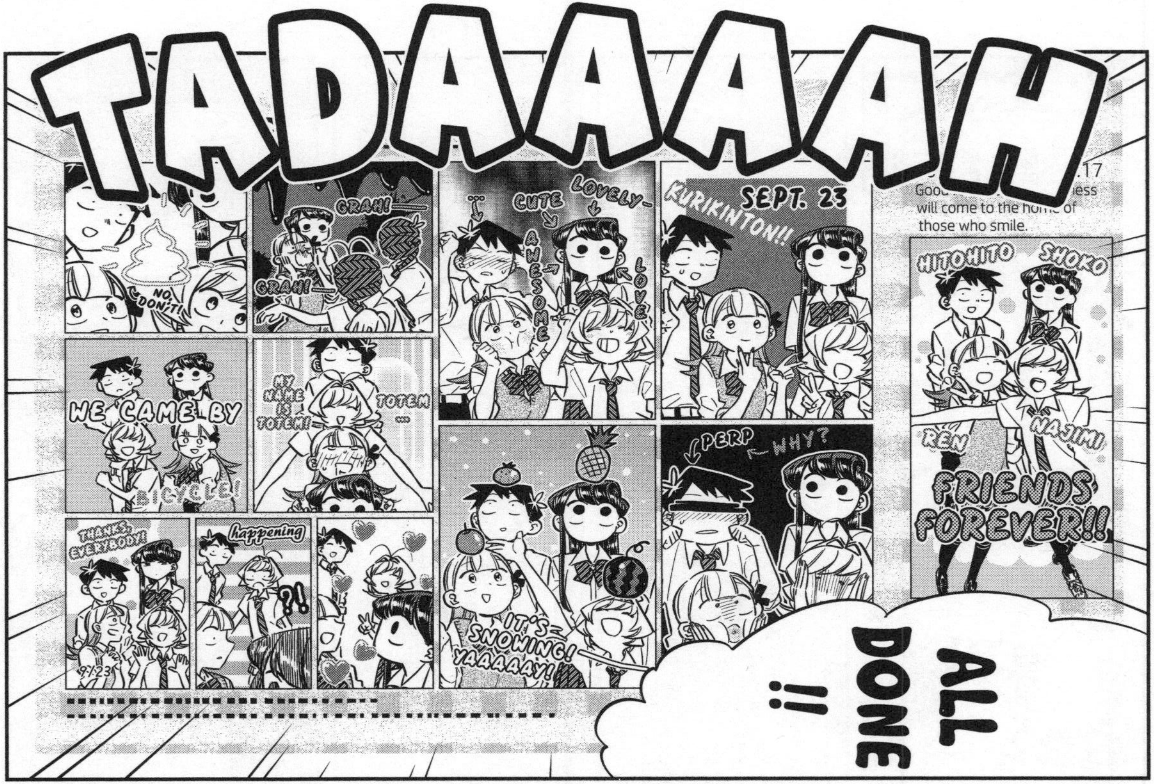
TADAAAH
...17
Good ... ness will come to the home of those who smile.
HITOHITO
SHOKO
REN
NAJIMI
FRIENDS FOREVER!!
SEPT. 23
KURIKINTON!!
PERP
WHY?
LOVELY~
CUTE
I
AWESOME
LOVE
IT'S SNOWING! YAAAAAY!
GRAH!
GRAH!
NO, DON'T!
TOTEM ...
MY NAME IS TOTEM!
WE CAME BY BICYCLE!
happening
?!
THANKS, EVERYBODY!
9/23
ALL DONE !!

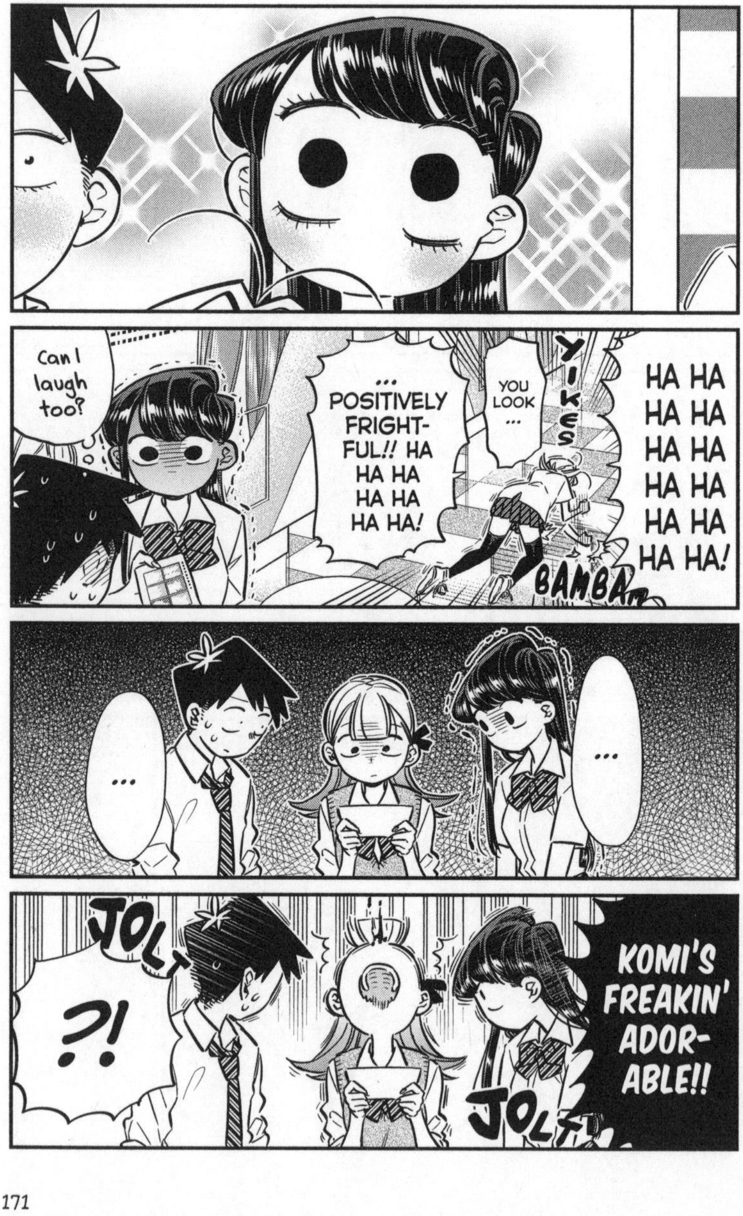
HA HA HA HA HA HA HA HA HA HA HA HA!
YIKES
YOU LOOK ...
... POSITIVELY FRIGHT-FUL!! HA HA HA HA HA HA HA!
BAMBAM
Can I laugh too?
...
...
KOMI'S FREAKIN' ADOR-ABLE!!
JOLT
JOLT
?!

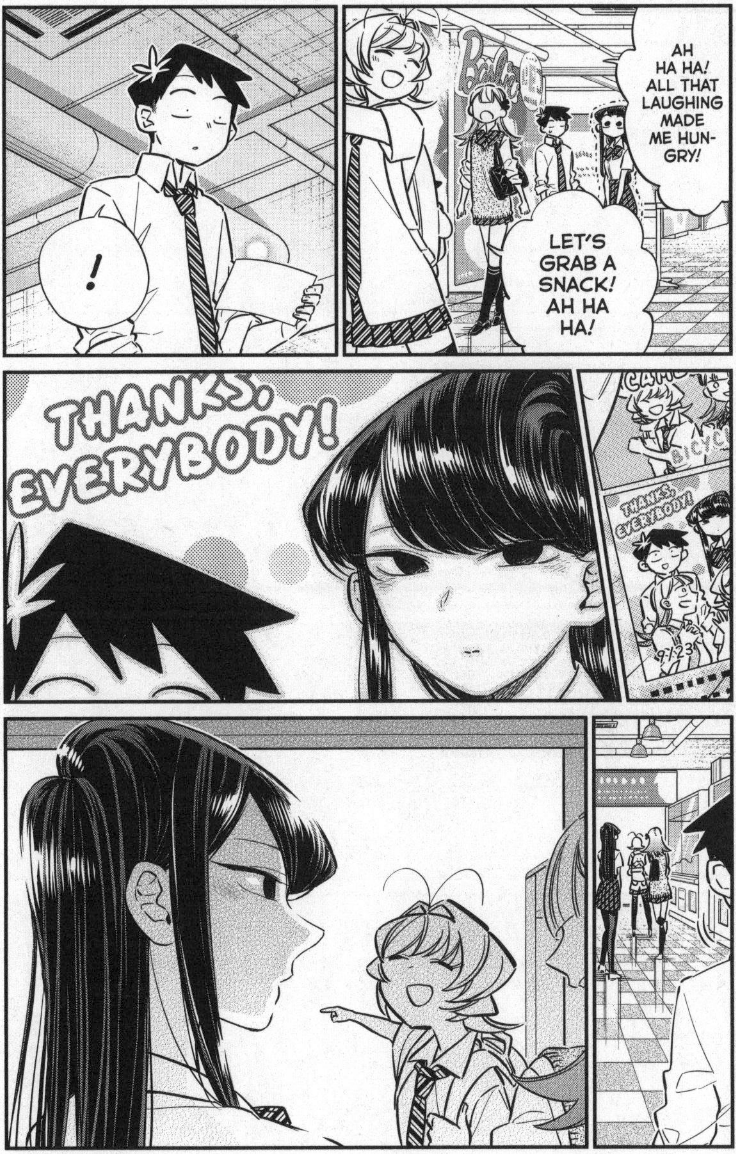
AH HA HA! ALL THAT LAUGHING MADE ME HUN-GRY!
LET'S GRAB A SNACK! AH HA HA!
!
THANKS, EVERYBODY!
9/23
THANKS, EVERYBODY!

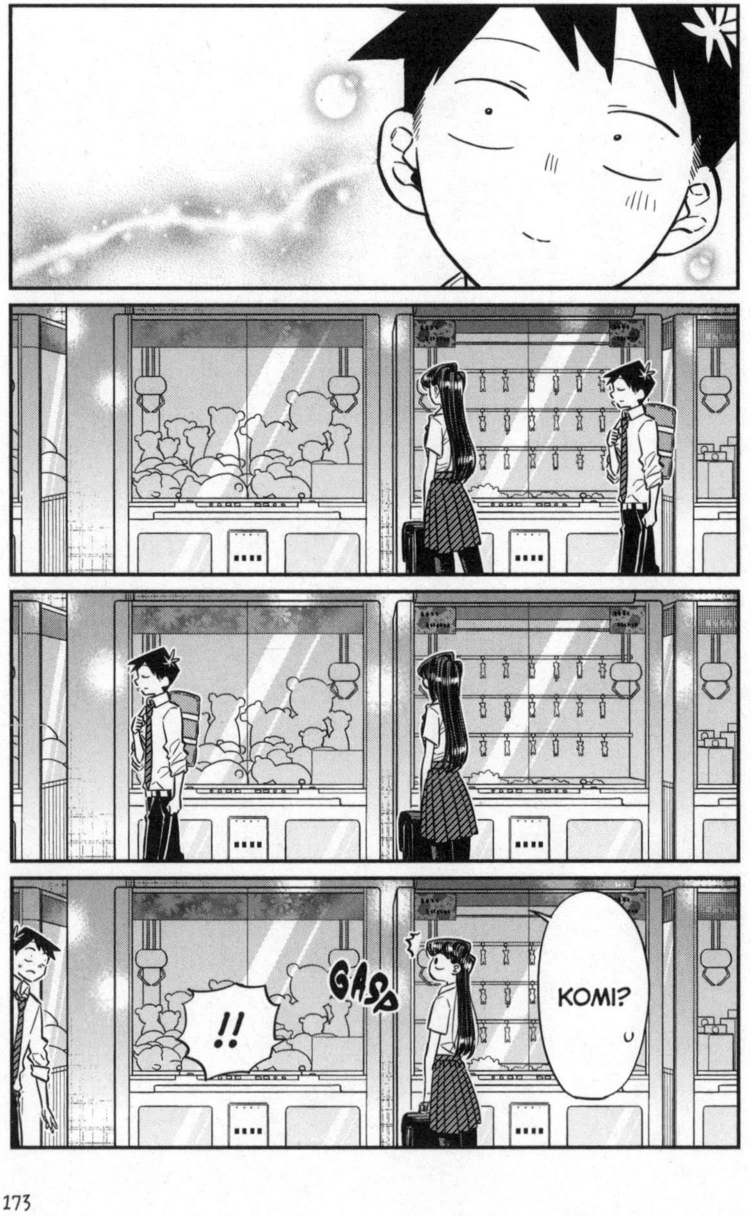
GASP
!!
KOMI?

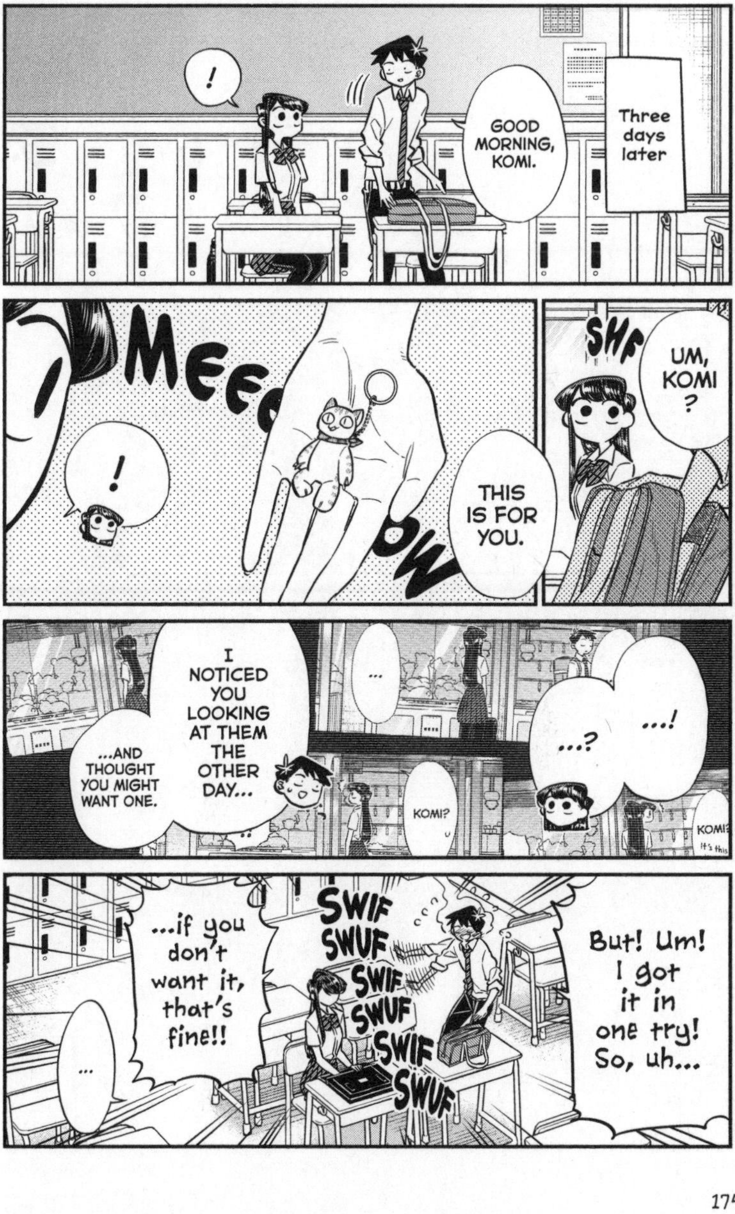
Three days later
GOOD MORNING, KOMI.
!
SHF
UM, KOMI?
THIS IS FOR YOU.
MEEOW
!
...!
...?
KOMI? It's this
KOMI?
...
I NOTICED YOU LOOKING AT THEM THE OTHER DAY...
...AND THOUGHT YOU MIGHT WANT ONE.
But! Um! I got it in one try! So, uh...
SWIF SWUF SWIF SWUF SWIF SWUF
...if you don't want it, that's fine!!
...

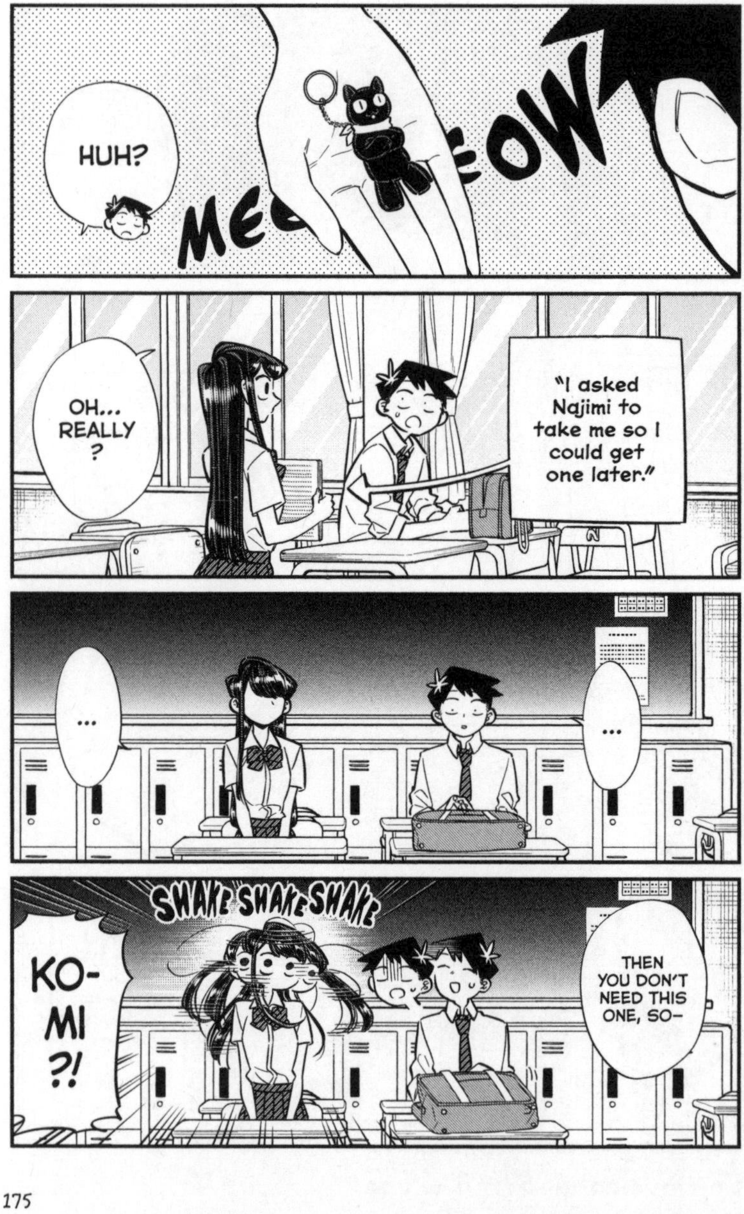
MEE OW
HUH?
"I asked Najimi to take me so I could get one later."
OH... REALLY?
...
...
THEN YOU DON'T NEED THIS ONE, SO–
SHAKE SHAKE SHAKE
KO-MI?!

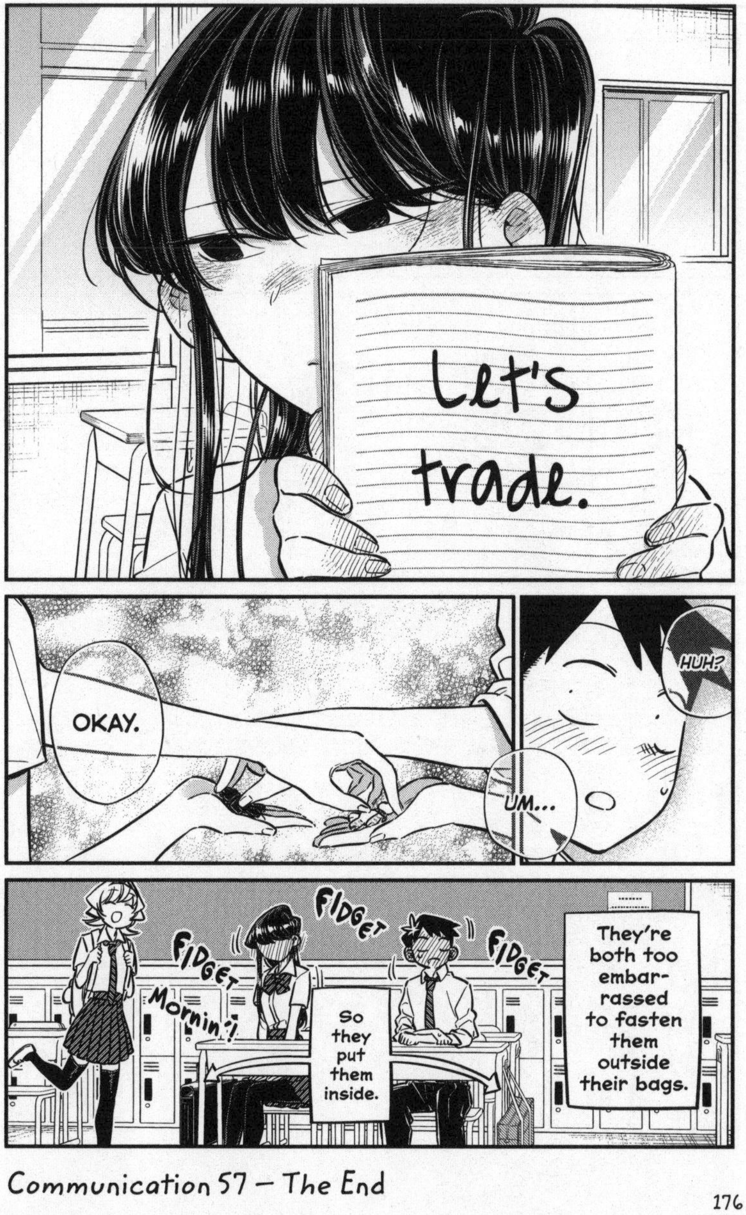
Let's trade.
HUH?
UM...
OKAY.
They're both too embarrassed to fasten them outside their bags.
FIDGET
So they put them inside.
FIDGET
FIDGET
Mornin'!

Communication 57 – The End

Komi Can't
Communicate

Komi Can't Communicate

Can Komi Make 100 Friends? Pressure from Najimi

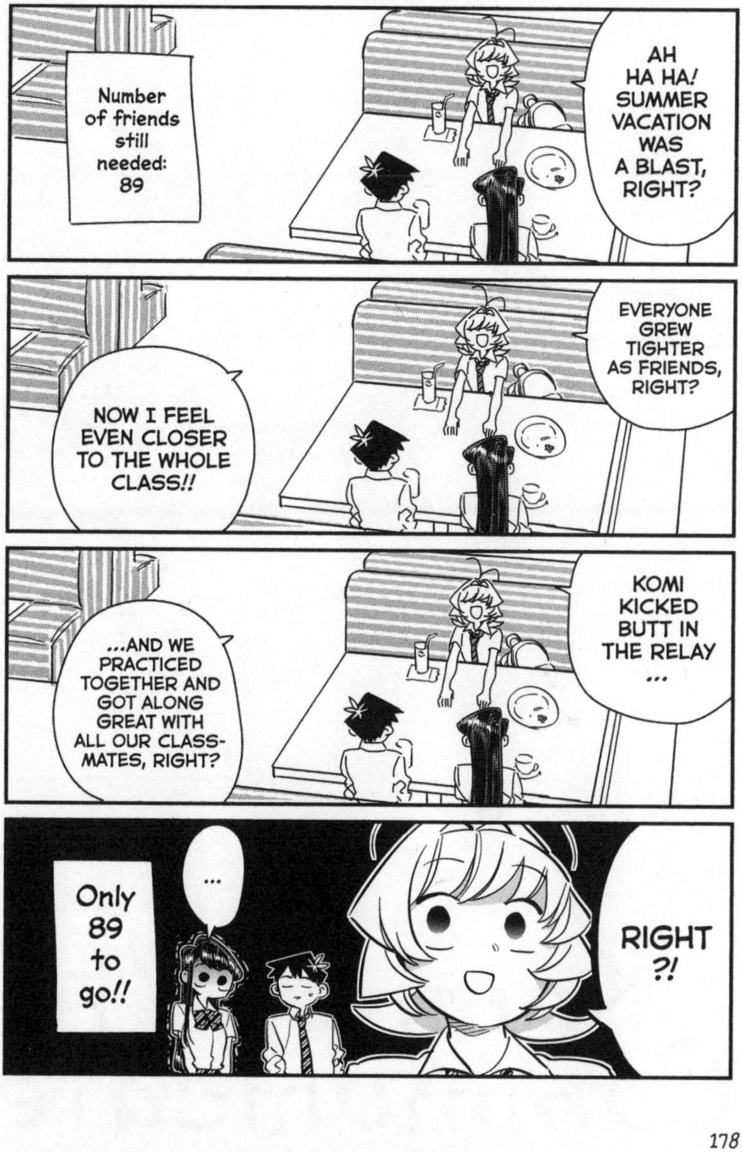
AH HA HA! SUMMER VACATION WAS A BLAST, RIGHT?
Number of friends still needed: 89
EVERYONE GREW TIGHTER AS FRIENDS, RIGHT?
NOW I FEEL EVEN CLOSER TO THE WHOLE CLASS!!
KOMI KICKED BUTT IN THE RELAY ...
...AND WE PRACTICED TOGETHER AND GOT ALONG GREAT WITH ALL OUR CLASS-MATES, RIGHT?
RIGHT ?!
...
Only 89 to go!!

Komi Can't Communicate

Can Komi Make 100 Friends? Komi Can't Help but Smile

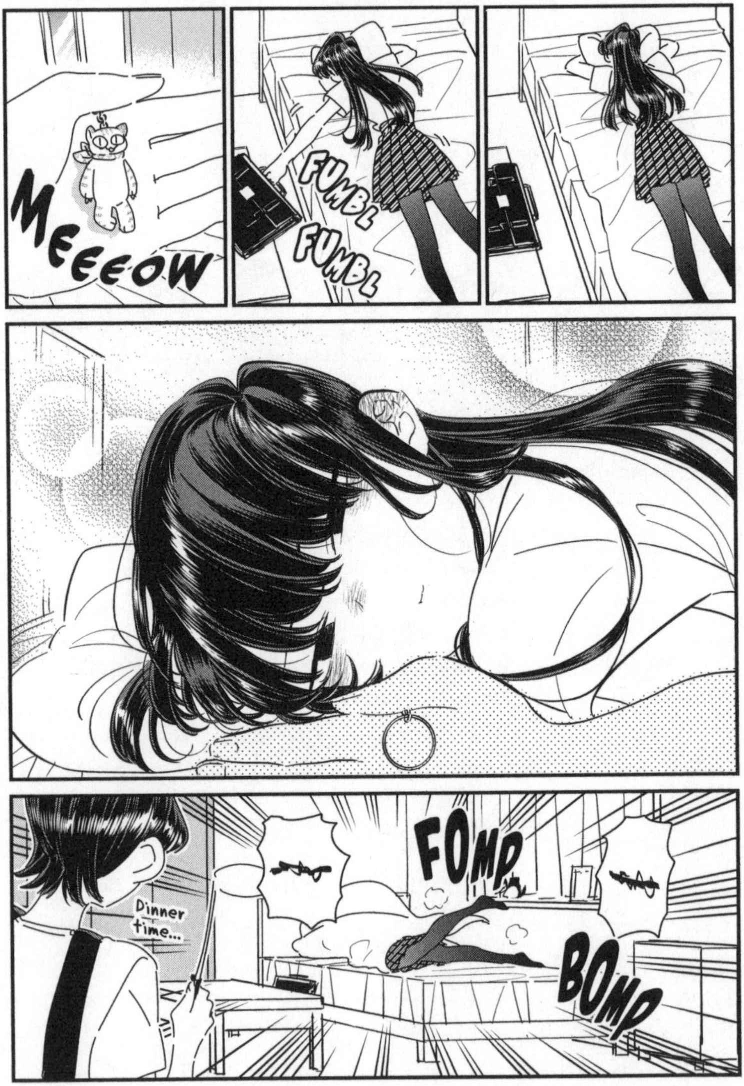
FUMBL
FUMBL
MEEEOW
FOMP
BOMP
Dinner time...

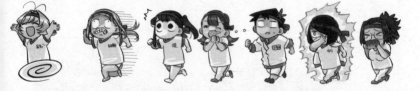

Tomohito Oda won the grand prize for *World Worst One* in the 70th Shogakukan New Comic Artist Awards in 2012. Oda's series *Digicon*, about a tough high school girl who finds herself in control of an alien with plans for world domination, ran from 2014 to 2015. In 2015, *Komi Can't Communicate* debuted as a one-shot in *Weekly Shonen Sunday* and was picked up as a full series by the same magazine in 2016.

Komi Can't Communicate

VOL. 4
Shonen Sunday Edition

Story and Art by Tomohito Oda

English Translation & Adaptation/John Werry
Touch-Up Art & Lettering/Eve Grandt
Design/Julian [JR] Robinson
Editor/Pancha Diaz

COMI-SAN WA, COMYUSHO DESU. Vol. 4
by Tomohito ODA
© 2016 Tomohito ODA
All rights reserved.
Original Japanese edition published by SHOGAKUKAN.
English translation rights in the United States of America, Canada, the United
Kingdom, Ireland, Australia and New Zealand arranged with SHOGAKUKAN.

Original Cover Design/Masato ISHIZAWA + Bay Bridge Studio

Printed in the U.S.A.

Published by VIZ Media, LLC
P.O. Box 77010
San Francisco, CA 94107

10 9 8 7 6 5
First printing, December 2019
Fifth printing, April 2022

viz.com

shonensunday.com

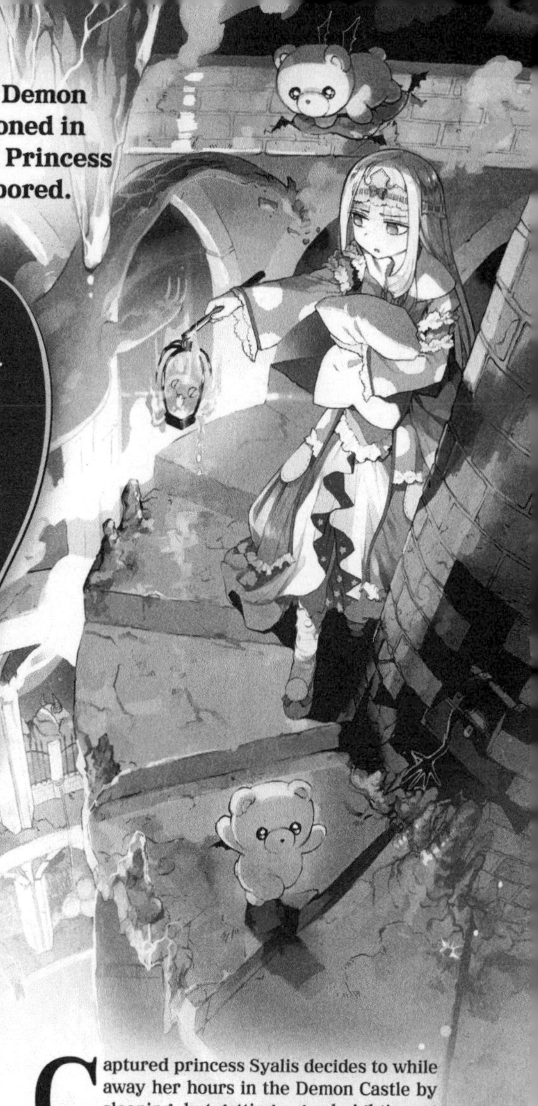

Kidnapped by the Demon King and imprisoned in his castle, Princess Syalis is...bored.

Sleepy Princess in the Demon Castle

Story & Art by
KAGIJI KUMANOMATA

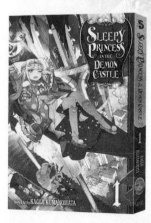

Captured princess Syalis decides to while away her hours in the Demon Castle by sleeping, but getting a good night's rest turns out to be a lot of work! She begins by fashioning a DIY pillow out of the fur of her Teddy Demon guards and an "air mattress" from the magical Shield of the Wind. Things go from bad to worse—for her captors—when some of Princess Syalis's schemes end in her untimely— if temporary—demise and she chooses the Forbidden Grimoire for her bedtime reading...

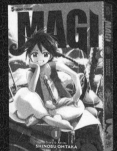

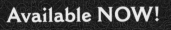

This is the last page!

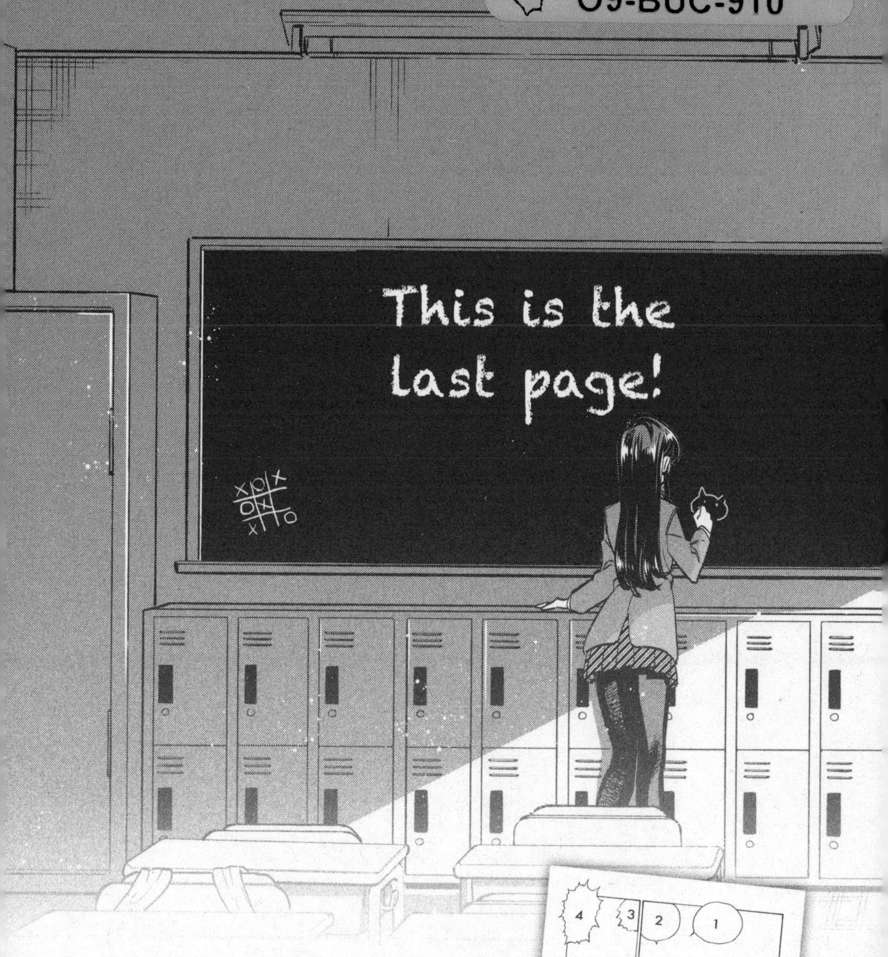

Komi Can't Communicate has been printed in the original Japanese format to preserve the orientation of the artwork.

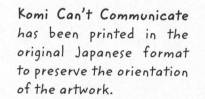

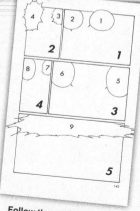

Follow the action this way.